CW00499828

Advance Re\

"Carol can't say a sentence—she can't write a sentence—without making you laugh."

Henry Winkler, Emmy-award winning actor, director, producer and bestselling author

"I'm sitting at my kitchen counter having lunch and I just opened your book to where you first meet Clint and then I just couldn't stop. I'm up to chapter five. You are such a good writer, Carol. And I've laughed out loud a bunch. Reading about Clint makes me feel horny and jealous."

Jane Fonda, actor and activist

"I wish I could write as elegantly as Carol Schlanger. I wish I was as brilliantly funny as Carol Schlanger. I wish I had joined her commune in the 70s and lived her outrageous, back-to-the-land life. But since I wasn't and didn't, reading her riveting, gut-busting and brave work is the next best thing. Strip down, light-up and catch her as fast as you can!"

Arlene Sarner, award-winning screenwriter (PEGGY SUE GOT MARRIED, BLUE SKY), playwright and author

"A miracle! Both a poignant confessional and darkly comic Roman à clef, about a life led on such different planes that it is astounding there was ever any intersection. The story of how a young, deeply urban woman learns to live off the grid in the Pacific Northwest, gutting fish, chopping wood, and making love like an accidental, Jewish she-wolf is sensational. I couldn't put it down."

Carl Gottlieb, award-winning screenwriter (JAWS), director and author

"Carol Schlanger's wild ride of a memoir gallops hilariously through the early seventies commune experience that all of us old hippies meant to have. She has the perfect voice of her generation. Honest, rebellious, sensual, politically astute, she's invited us into history to live and love through her. We dare not pass up the opportunity because being Carol is in itself an adventure."

Barbara Bottner, *New York Times* bestselling author

Hippie Woman Wild

Hippie Woman Wild

a memoir of Life & Love on an Oregon Commune

CAROL SCHLANGER

Wyatt-MacKenzie Publishing
DEADWOOD, OREGON

Hippie Woman Wild

A Memoir of Life & Love on an Oregon Commune

Carol Schlanger

ISBN: 978-1-948018-46-3

Library of Congress Control Number: 2019941102

Wyatt-MacKenzie Publishing
DEADWOOD, OREGON

www.WyattMacKenzie.com

Requests for permission or further information should be addressed to:
Wyatt-MacKenzie Publishing
15115 Highway 36, Deadwood, Oregon 97430

Printed in the United States of America.

Dedication

For Ezra

&

Grandma Schneiderman

Table of Contents

PART ONE

PART TWO

Foreword

by Henry Winkler

I first met Carol in the early 70s, when we were in our twenties, during our freshman year at the Yale School of Drama. Before you think there was anything romantic between us, let me stop you right there—there wasn't. We were friends; a little like oil and water, but we both loved to make people laugh. A lot of great talent was in that first year acting class, but Carol was different from the other women—more opinionated and rebellious, less circumspect and more New York Jewish. From the very beginning I could sense the polarity inside her. Underneath, she was as soft as a cotton puffball, yet she had a sophisticated, cutting sense of humor that was as sharp as a chef's best knife. It sliced you right down to the bone but underneath you could sense her extraordinary warmth. It made her multi-layered. And surprising.

Ms. Schlanger was no shy wallflower. No...she was an entire garden of every imaginable color and texture. That picture of her on the cover when she was twenty-three and lit up like a million watts, is exactly how I remember her...so lovely.

I always knew Carol had an incredible way with language. She approached a text and improvised with a riveting charm and intelligence that made you sit up and listen. In the summer of our second year, we were both cast in a political review at the *New York Public Theater* (the Joseph Papp). I remember that her American Housewife soliloquy, which she also wrote, always got a standing ovation. The audience loved her. She was so real and vulnerable.

I didn't know her as the hippie she describes in her memoir. In a few uproarious scenes she tells how she morphed into one after she met Clint, a big, gentle Texan she'd fallen in love with and for whom she left New York, abandoned acting and followed into the woods. That man was an artist, both steady and calm...while Carol, OMG she had this amazing energy that came through in her laugh. It was inescapable. You could hear it in a neighborhood in another city. As the great Mildred Dunnock (the original Linda Loman in *Death of a Salesman*) once said of Carol in her evaluation of Carol's acting: "Carol loved life more than she loved the theater." However, it was that zest for living that launched her on her great adventure into the back-to-the land alternative life style that's the basis for her compelling story.

We lost touch for a few years—while Carol was running around half-naked, hunting and gathering, I was working in television—fully clothed. Until I read her Chapter 33, "On Heaven's Door," I wasn't aware that my TV and film work had been a touchstone for her to reconnect with her love of acting. As she tells it, the first time she saw me as Fonzie in *Happy Days* (on a tiny television that operated off a truck battery because her hand-built house had no electricity) what was buried inside her resurfaced. Watching my character with his swagger and upside-down charm ignite the live audience, brought the thrill of performance back to her. For an actor, there's nothing like that human-to-human charge. I'm so very glad my work inspired her to move forward with her life and reestablish her career. Who knew?

Now, Carol and I talk about three times a year about our family, our kids and our grandkids. With the publication of *Hippie Woman Wild* our connection has been heightened and has reminded me that our forty-year friendship is a rare treasure. Her book transported me to a time and place that was pivotal for my baby-boomer generation. Because I am dyslexic I am a slow, and not exactly avid reader, but I was fascinated to discover through Carol, what it was like being a hippie in the woods back then and what that meant for a young, idealistic and formally urban woman. Carol presents her natural world in a way that put me right there with her—I could hear the wind, inhale the fresh air and see the stars at night.

If Carol asked me, and she has, I would characterize her writing as sometimes shocking but consistently multi-leveled and hysterical. Her authentic voice is a little twisted with an undercurrent of laugh-out-loud humor. She can't say a sentence—she can't write a sentence—without making you laugh. And there is always truth in what she says and writes because it is built on the foundation of the human condition and is never without it. She is so real about who she is and what her struggles are in different and conflicting worlds.

Carol marches to the beat of a different drummer that not everyone can hear. It is her gift but also can get her into big trouble. It did at Yale. But I'll let her tell you about that herself.

I've left the best thing I can say to you about *Hippie Woman Wild* to the last: The sexy parts are just that—sexy, bawdy and outrageous. What a woman!

I'm proud of Carol. I love her book and I hope you will, too.

Preface

It was the best of times, it was the worst of times...
CHARLES DICKENS, *A Tale of Two Cities*

I'm lying naked in a hammock that's strung between two ancient alders while listening to the rat-tat-tat of a giant woodpecker. He's the size of a cat with a feathered red head. A breeze blows off the Pacific through a mountain draw and lands in my hair with its fragrance of cedar and sea. Sunlight warms my body. Does it count toward nirvana that when you are happy and content you realize how happy and contented you are? Probably.

I promised myself I would remember that breeze, the bird, and the trees for the rest of my life—and I have.

Fifty years later, I've gone back to the Oregon coastal mountain range and to Flores Creek: to the glow of our lantern-lit dinners, the fierce winter winds, the Foxglove in spring, the woodstove-baked bread, the friendship, being young and free and at peace.

It didn't last long, those best of times. The detested Vietnam war ended along with our communal fire and dedication. President Johnson was gone, Nixon was on his way out, taking with him our youthful exuberance. Soon, we'd boomerang back into the world we'd escaped, to either change it or to once again, change ourselves.

During the Trump era, as it did in the 60s and 70s, everything has gone haywire. Completely nuts. Dickens' description of the 1789 French Revolution feels as real as it did fifty years ago when we decided we could trust no one over thirty. Now, no one can trust anyone or anything. For the counter-culture, during those heady 20th century good ole, bad ole days, hope ran neck and neck with despair. Dropping out and giving the finger to all that kept us from a more meaningful life was real and possible. Now, with cyber technology, there's nowhere to run and nowhere to hide. But for old hippies, even as the icecaps melt and bees disappear, we see our dearly held beliefs go mainstream, commercial, and viral.

Forgive me if I boast but we were right about everything and the list is endless. I'm hoping to stop myself from filling up this page. I can't promise, but I'll try: Organic and free range everything, not only chicken but children. Toxic chemicals kill and mutate. Plastic sucks. Goodbye gasoline dependency. Yes, to all clean energy: wind, hydro, and solar. Recycle. We are all one on Spaceship Earth. Give peace a chance. The earth is our mother, the sky our father, and all animals our brothers. What goes around comes around. Don't care too much for money, it won't buy you a life or love. Pure food is our medicine. Doctors and hospitals don't know everything. The military industrial complex kills everything except the military industrial complex. Good sex is great. Age naturally, live simply, beauty comes from within. All sexes and races are equal. There are no borders for the human heart. Clean water and fresh air are a human right...okay. I'll stop.

All this is where my book lives, but not what it's about. It's about entering an unexpected new world; where an off-center, spoiled, idealistic and talented young actress from Manhattan's tony Sutton Place, learns to chop wood, carry water, and transforms from girl to woman. It's about loving an imperfect man, imperfectly. And about having to choose between art and life. For those middle-class Baby Boomers like me, who had never before experienced want or real poverty, the ride was hard and bumpy but always bolstered by the delight of living in nature and the comfort and protection that came from a tribal community; there for each other because our lives depended on it.

Hippie Woman Wild has been a long time in coming. Hungry Ghosts got in my way. But I plowed through because I had to share my youthful joy in living skin to skin, with the earth between my toes, of making endless love under a blanket of stars, of feeding twenty from next to nothing, and learning to read bear scat. Being a hippie was a privilege and a pleasure and I can't thank myself enough for the experience.

Oh yes. There were bad times, but even the most painful were part of a hyper-reality, a moment-to-moment existence that was so unknown and unknowable that, it felt cinematic, as if I were both watching and steeped in an unworldly adventure—becoming my own avatar.

We were stardust. Astronomers now inform us that humans and their galaxy have 97% the same atoms. How did we know this half a century before empirical science proved our hippie intuition? It's inexplicable and part of our magic. We were golden and did get ourselves back to the garden. And some have stayed.

I have changed names, combined characters and events, and although I have fact checked, I cannot promise perfection. Some scenes have been embellished, but the emotional truth and essential time line remain exact.

CAROL SCHLANGER

For those dear, old friends who lived through the experience with me, I thank you. I have not done so formally, using your real names but I know you will recognize yourselves and hope you will enjoy the work and forgive my trespasses.

May your life be long, your country sane, and your tomatoes fat and juicy.

Wonderful, Wonderful Day

He came out of nowhere
Walkin' through the door.
Lookin' straight my way.
Can't wait till I'm with him
In our cabin just for two,
Sheltered and secluded
Only trees near us
No one hearin' us
And so you'll forgive me
If I simply throw out my chest and say:
Wonderful, wonderful day!"

Millie, *Seven Brides for Seven Brothers*
LYRICS BY **JOHNNY MERCER**

PART ONE

Run from what's comfortable.
Forget safety.
Live where you fear to live.
Destroy your reputation.
Be notorious.

RUMI

CHAPTER 1

Any Day Now

Manhattan, May 1971

The shoe shot through my open window, torpedoed the baby avocado plant onto my Greek *Flacati* rug and changed my life forever. It was a man's loafer—scuffed with tassels. Not big, maybe a size ten. I picked it up and turned it over. The sole was worn so thin a hole was spreading through the middle. A dead man lay face down on the third floor balcony of my artist-subsidized studio apartment. A smashed Hasselblad camera was wrapped around his neck. On his right foot, only a sock. The sad flying shoe that had covered it now sat on top of wool and potting soil. I guessed the man hadn't fallen; he'd jumped. It was just a guess, but one formed by experience. Suicide had infiltrated my building. Misery was in the halls. Six months earlier, before I'd moved in, the lead viola of Uncle Abie's Neo-Klezmer Band had jumped off the southern edge of the roof and crash-landed onto West Street. Now someone was screaming with such a piercing sound it made my ears ring. God, she was loud. My throat was raw and tight—it was me.

Wearing thigh-high boots and a tiny skirt, I was poised to audition in fifty minutes for the role of hot Honey Harlow, the great Lenny Bruce's stripper lover in *Lenny*, a new play slated for Broadway. I'd practiced being Honey all the day before and that morning, seven hours of Honey. A woman debased: swiveling hips, wet parted lips, lower-chakra-ed. Honey was from Manila, Arkansas. I'd called a pharmacy, a gas station, and a post office in Manila and kept them all on the phone for as long as I could to hear their accent and make it my own:

"Say, you carry children's Bayer?"

"Sure nuff," they'd answer. "Ya'll want me to set aside a bottle for ya?"

In Manila, Arkansas there were some real considerate folk.

I liked being Honey. She had red hair and I had red hair. Even when she was wacked-out on heroin, Honey had a quick intelligence and a warm heart. She was a simple country girl who worshipped Lenny's genius. All Honey wanted was his baby and an occasional threesome with her best friend Sugar. I made Honey's needs my own by using Stanislavsky's substitution method—to feel what she felt. All I wanted was phenomenal artistic success and unconditional love. A threesome was out, but I'd have loved to get a puppy.

There it was—that rush that came before every audition. I had almost an hour to go before I could become someone else—to be me but lose the murky, indecisive quality of my life for the clarity and focus of my art. There had been a price to pay and I'd paid it. For this insane adrenaline high and its possible reward, I'd let him go without me—the only man I had ever loved who loved me back. He was off on his great Northwestern adventure to Oregon, an esoteric state with a name I wasn't even sure how to pronounce. Ore–gin, Ore–gone? I missed that man like a forest fire misses rain.

"New York City is bullshit—you know that don't you, Carol?" he asked while filling his dented canteen with tap water.

"But I love it here," I answered. "It's my home and I'm an actress."

"Yeah, I know," he said gloomily and was too soon gone, and now... now I couldn't find my luminescent pearl lipstick. It added a slutty touch to my mouth that my character had to have. As I excavated the sandy bottom of my purse to find it, the shoe hit the rug and all my method-acting prep vanished. In a flash, I became a terrified twenty-three-year-old middleclass girl watching blood puddle around the head of a man whose skull had just cracked open. Still shaking, I stopped screaming, came to my senses and realized that lying in front of me was both a human tragedy and a career emergency. I couldn't leave and I couldn't be late, not for a Broadway audition. *And where the hell was that lipstick?*

Squeezing into a tee shirt, I dialed my agent: "Marty! Help! There's a dead man outside my window."

He barely let me finish the last syllable. "Just in case, sweetheart, can you sing a cappella?"

"He's dead, Marty! What do I do?"

"Calm down, Carol. Call emergency. Take a cab and you'll make the audition on time. Dead is dead."

I dialed the emergency operator (no 911 in 1971) and in minutes, my small space filled with highly competent male energy, police officers, and great big firemen. I focused on their shiny red hats, their yellow slickers, and oxygen tanks. Sticking with real objects kept me from panicking. In forty minutes, I had a Broadway audition...for Broadway.

Heavy boots beat against my parquet floors and muscular bodies hid my serving island. The island was five feet long, three feet wide and thick, natural wood. Clint, my live-in boyfriend, had built and designed it—whatever he touched, he made beautiful with his hands. It had soothed me to watch his flat thumb, twice the size of my own, hold down a two-by-six as he guided his big skill saw across it. He'd perfumed my apartment with the fragrance of cedar and man sweat. I'd never known this kind of man before—a man in sync with nature—a gentle, quiet, man's man. He was handsome beyond anything my New York Jewish, "Hey, did you go to Bronx Science?" mind could have possibly conceived.

As he looked over my rumpled, unmade bed, a policeman with a sweet Irish face asked me if I was acquainted with the deceased. I told him I didn't know the dead man or how he'd fallen, but was freaked-out. Could he please let me leave? I had an important appointment and was late. "No problem," he said. His skin was the color of peaches and he thanked me for my cooperation. How kind, I thought—he wasn't a "pig," not a racist bully, but a good man doing a good job—and so adorable.

Leaving, I bumped into the stretcher carrying the corpse. His arms jiggled with the impact and I saw he was wearing a wedding ring. The firemen moving the body continued on. "Dead male Caucasian," one of them relayed into his hand-held radio. *Whoever the dead guy had been, he no longer had a name*. Life was a gift, but for some so was death. Mr. Hasselblad was gone forever. His vision lost. I wondered if fame or at least acknowledgement would have mattered to him. The answer came as I walked through the dimly lit lobby—Yes. It would have mattered a lot.

Westbeth, the artist-subsidized building complex where I lived, was a converted Bell telephone laboratory. The apartments were bright and stylishly architectural, but the windowless hallways were oppressive. As I watched the numbers above the elevator slowly illuminate—one, two, and finally three, I prayed in character to arrive at my audition on time: "Lord Jesus, git me there licketty-split..." When the heavy metal doors clanged open, I stepped inside and pounded on the red button marked "down." Soon I was moving away from darkness and death towards bright lights and Broadway.

Out on West Street, near the Hudson River docks and meatpacking district, a black sedan slowed down and a man shouted through his window, "How much, babe?" Keeping my eyes on the sidewalk, I hurried on. He followed me for a half block, screamed, "Fuck you! Fuckin' tease!" and sped towards 9th Avenue.

I'd passed for the real thing. "Good job," I told myself as I hailed a cab that would take me uptown and into my brilliant future.

"This land is your land; this land is my land, from California, to the New York Island," I sang while naughtily caressing my breasts and thighs. They felt like old friends who were there when I needed them. The audition space disappeared and I was transported to a seedy nightclub somewhere in Chicago, or Detroit. Glasses clinked in the smoke-filled room. Men whistled and cheered as I jiggled my money maker. "This land was made for you and me!" I didn't have to work it, Honey did it for me; I was where every actress longs to be—in the zone, my every pore exuding Honey's raunchy heat.

Shaking like a lascivious Jell-O mold, I pulled my tee-shirt over my head. Shit! The tight neck wouldn't go above my nose. I tugged harder, but no luck. The shirt hung from my face like a towel and I looked like the Elephant Man. Wait—big guffaws. Tom O'Horgan and Galt MacDermot, the director-producers of the Broadway megahit *Hair*, were laughing their heads off.

Just as my fingers unhooked my bra, they stopped me:

"That was fantastic, Carol. We loved it. Didn't we Galt?"

"We're so happy to have met you, sweetie," Galt agreed. "You'll hear from us soon."

Both shook my hand. Surely, Honey was mine.

☾

Nothing had been touched in my apartment. The avocado plant still lay on the rug. I was looking for the dustpan when the doorbell rang. A sad-eyed woman stood in front of me. She had frizzy brown hair with split ends. Her mascara ran under her eyes and down her cheeks. The two floppy ponytails that framed her face were tied with purple ribbon. "I'm Irma..." she squeaked.

"Irma?"

"His wife...Nate's wife."

The dead man had a name. Nate, Nathan—like a kosher hotdog, like my favorite uncle.

"They told me where downstairs," she whimpered. "I didn't know. Nobody called me at work."

Irma pushed me aside with her Gristedes grocery bag, walked toward the open window and looked out. A dark red blotch stained the balcony's cement floor.

"Today's his birthday," she said through tears as she noticed the telltale mark. "They all rejected him, the magazines, the galleries...his work was his life. That's all that mattered."

I wanted to reach over and say something generically comforting like, "I'm so sorry for your loss," but didn't because I knew that wasn't what Irma wanted. What Irma wanted was Nate back and alive to blow out his candles. A thin string of mucus hung from her nose as she croaked:

"He tried so hard! No one ever paid him what he deserved, no one cared. Except me."

While she rummaged through her purse, the mucus dropped onto her daisy-print blouse.

"Look," she said, handing me a frayed postcard. It was a photo of a poodle in a party hat dressed in little boy pajamas. "That's what he was reduced to, even worse...beagles!"

Nate, the photographer, had done his best but it hadn't been good enough. New York demanded success and he had none. In the wake of his artistic failure, his life meant nothing. I wished I could have known him, talked to him, and convinced him there was something beyond artistic acknowledgement—life. The beautiful part was when they were one and the same. He might not have listened but I could have at least tried. Poor Nate. He'd let the establishment, those who knew what was but not what was to come, dictate his self-worth—that was something I would never do—no way; if I did, then my art wouldn't be mine, it would be theirs. I could see what they couldn't see. Nate probably did, too. What most hurt was not sharing it. Life didn't support your art. It was the other way around. If I'd only have had the chance to remind him of how big the world was; that professional success was not worth giving up what made all the rest worth living. Love neutralized rejection. The hurt didn't stay, as long as the sky was clear and the wind off the Hudson blew warm. Instead, I reminded myself.

"I understand, Irma. I'm an artist, too, an actress."

"I'm not talking about you, lady!"

Irma put her groceries on the kitchen counter, turned and walked out the door. I watched her go for a beat, then grabbed her bag and followed her into the hallway. She stood hunched over at the elevator. "Excuse me..." I said as tenderly as I could and held her groceries out to her: "I'm so sorry, but you left this." She swatted at the air between us as if I was a huge gnat. "Go away!" she screamed and then turned her back to me as she continued to wait. I didn't move and said nothing more. When the elevator doors opened, Irma disappeared behind them.

Inside her grocery bag—a bottle of champagne, thin prosciutto wrapped in butcher paper and a loaf of fresh sourdough—their little birthday celebration. I pressed the bread to my cheek. Its yeasty warmth was comforting. Taking a bite, I felt better.

Back in my apartment, I rummaged through the kitchen drawers for a corkscrew to open the champagne but remembered the only one we had was attached to Clint's pocket knife. He'd taken it with him to Oregon. He and his knife were inseparable. He and I were not. I stabbed the cork with a cuticle scissors, punishing it for him not being there. "Why did Clint have to leave so soon?" I asked myself as I mindlessly scarfed down a dead man's meal. I needed my boyfriend and he was gone. To have a man and then not have him was worse than never having had him at all. The theatre wasn't enough. Westbeth wasn't enough. All of New York wasn't enough.

My mind kept bringing me back to him: to his voice, to his hands, to how rotten things had been for me before we met in New Haven—to Yale.

CHAPTER 2

Rag Mama Rag

A year earlier — New Haven, May 1970

Talent is nothing but faith in yourself, in your own powers.
MAXIM GORKY

A guillotine-like finality hung in the dean of the Yale Drama School's office. My head was on the chopping block and the blade was about to fall. Three months short of graduation, I'd been found guilty of "not having the talent to develop my talent." Or as I saw it, declared dead while still breathing.

"But Marvin," I pleaded, looking up at the dean from my sunken spot in a studded leather chair. His books, his desk top, his heart—all were leather bound.

"Excuse me, Carol!" he interrupted. I was accustomed to calling the dean by his first name—a familiarity he'd once encouraged. We'd been pals. He'd loved all my essays. Especially the one comparing dark and powerful Martha in *Who's Afraid of Virginia Woolf?* to dark and powerful Lady Macbeth.

"I'm sorry, SIR," I said, finding myself unexpectedly close to tears. Capitulation was easy. Expulsion was hard. "If you withhold my degree, I won't be able to teach."

"Come now, Carol," he said, removing his pipe from between his thin lips, "I thought you wanted to be a professional actress."

"Oh, I do, more than anything. But I need a fallback position."

He was lightning-quick on the uptake: "I speak for the entire faculty when I promise you, Carol, that teaching is our passion, not an afterthought."

"I understand, sir. But when you were young, surely you wanted to do something bigger, something more worthwhile than just being a teach..."

His eyes clouded over. I had insulted and minimized him. Oh God, I thought to myself, why didn't I think before I spoke? All my classmates knew how to shut up when it was expedient. They were actors, they could kiss ass like the professionals they were about to become...but not me. Perhaps I could plead temporary insanity brought on by political overstimulation...or get a letter from my therapist: "Dear Yale Drama Faculty, please be advised that my patient Carol Schlanger has impulse control issues, and whatever she says should be discounted as the outpourings of a young woman with a strong social conscience who doesn't know what the fuck comes out of her mouth." I did not want to be kicked out of Yale. It would not look good on my resume.

I was a Jewish New York liberal turned radical—a subset emerging from Queens, Brooklyn, the Bronx, and the Upper West Side. I'd marched on Washington to protest the war in Vietnam, was horrified by the Mai Lai Massacre and the inhumane napalming of civilian South Vietnamese. I knew the United States government was lying to us all. We weren't winning the war as President Nixon assured us; we were losing it because there was no win to be had. That awareness grew into a distrust of all institutions with unbridled power—medical and academic as well as economic. I loved Jane Fonda. I'd read Herbert Marcuse and R.D. Laing for Christsake! The young men of my generation were being drafted and dying for Wall Street, big banks, and Exxon Mobile—losing their lives and limbs in Vietnam, not for freedom but for money. What did he The Dean expect? I had both passion and commitment. Wasn't that what art was all about?

During my first year at Yale, I'd worked with a far-left student director to create the role of the *American Housewife*, as part of the radical *American Pig* review. We were a standing-room-only smash hit at the New York Public Theatre. My piece was a television commercial turned comic nightmare. A housewife is so obsessed with her laundry detergent it becomes her friend, her child, and her lover. The critics loved us and loved me the most, as did Columbia University's SDS. We sang along with Country Joe and the Fish's famed recording asking what we're fighting for. Our cast included the politically committed as well as those like Henry Winkler (later to become the iconic Fonzie on *Happy Days)* who just loved to act.

So what if I'd grown up with a maid and a doorman and attended an Ivy League University? I saw the light. It was shining from the West down to the East.

Both student directors of the *Pig* had been influenced by *The Living Theatre*, a controversial performance collective. The Dean of the Drama

School had invited their radical company to show us a revolutionary use of theatrical muscle. And what a muscle it was. With sweat streaming down their ripped, half-naked bodies, they screamed their message from the stage and into the audience:

I am not allowed to smoke marijuana!

I am not allowed to travel without a passport!

Right on! No false boundaries! The Living Theater understood the world could be transformed through trust and love into a paradise—now. How? They didn't say. But amazing sex had something to do with it.

When founders Judith Malina and Julian Beck's lithe troupe emerged from their body pile and ran naked and unafraid onto York Street, half the audience, myself included, followed—enchanted. *Paradise Now,* still ringing in our ears:

The body itself; that of which we are made, is taboo.

We are ashamed of what is most beautiful.

The Living Theatre was brave. The Living Theatre was naked. The Living Theatre was under arrest. The New Haven police dragged them away for public indecency. Their headfirst dives of faith into the crowd below had broken the fourth wall and achieved what theater was meant to do: cut through the boundaries that separated us as humans. And they were fucking gorgeous.

With God as my witness, I promised myself, I'll never wear a bra again—ever!

Yes, I, too, would abandon a system that sent my generation off to die in a useless war, poisoned our food with hidden chemicals, and valued success over kindness, money over love, and white over black. Yes, I, too, would become an instrument of change, an artist of and for the Revolution.

Avanti Popolo!

"Carol, are you listening?" the dean interrupted. "It's hard to tell. You drift away. It's right here in your progress report: 'Carol drifts away. She seems bored and uninvolved.'"

"Yes sir, I'm listening," I said as the smoke from his pipe snaked toward me.

"You come from a financially secure background and as an attractive, if not beautiful, young woman," his false smile exposed his gray teeth, "you will, in all probability, never have to support yourself."

I realized I might be pleading my case to an alien life form. Short, bald, but totally self-assured, The Dean honestly believed a woman didn't have to earn a living. Or most likely it wasn't "a woman"—it was—

this woman. In a personal letter, I'd called him a "Jewish Nazi." That just might have pissed him off. And he was right. While I had no trust fund (inherited fortunes were the territory of old money at Yale—those Skull and Crossbones guys), I knew if I jumped into the unknown, my parents' financial safety net would soften my landing.

"And you seem to be unable to accept our prescribed curriculum," he continued. "True, you have improvisational ability and write very well, but we are an acting conservatory, not a messy hodgepodge."

My mind spun. I felt certain The Dean's actions were not about my talent—they were about my strong personality and what he perceived as my politics. I supported draft dodgers and liked the Black Panthers, loved gays and thought little of his liberal authority. In place of locution and sword play, I'd begged, but not been allowed, to take classes in playwriting and film history. And even though Paul Sills, guru of the Story Theater technique and co-founder of *Second City*, had given me a summer job in Chicago to help him develop his Broadway-bound Ovid's *Metamorphosis*, the dean still found me wanting. The acting program, the dean insisted, was dedicated to a classical form of intense training: There had to be boundaries. Acting was a discipline, a learned craft. If I mastered it, I could study other forms like directing and screenwriting on my own time or not at all.

What was the matter with these people? I asked myself as my head lowered onto the chopping block. Didn't they know that artistic talent was infinite? A writer could act and direct, an actor could direct and write. Didn't they see I was a messenger of the truth and that the truth would set them free? No, I decided. They preferred tenure.

"Sir," I asked, "what about Woody Allen? He acts, writes, and directs."

"You call that acting?" the Dean said.

I had no answer.

In tears, I rushed out of the dean's office, down York Street to Chapel and on to the vibrating Yale Campus. Protests were everywhere. The cool and conservative Connecticut air had been seeded with revolutionary rhetoric and soon it was gonna rain. Counterculture luminaries Abbie Hoffman, Jerry Rubin, Timothy Leary, Benjamin Spock, and Jean Genet were crashing in Yale dorms and giving incendiary speeches to an agitated student body. Bobby Seale, the chairman of the Black Panther party, was about to go on trial for murder. Filled with an angry black population and draft-eligible young men who did not want to fight in Vietnam, New Haven was ready to explode. The vibe was thrilling and scary.

I was…hungry.

Yale's school of Art and Architecture, had, unlike the drama school, a great cafeteria loaded with high levels of testosterone and crisp head lettuce.

Every day for lunch, I strolled over to the A&A building and ordered a Cobb salad. An animator named Moe and I had developed a trade relationship. He gave me his bacon bits for my hardboiled egg. On this day, despite the pending riots, Moe was sitting at "our" table. We ate together but said little. During the mayhem, all my classes had been suspended as had most others throughout the school. Because I was free for the day, Moe offered to take me to a graduate architecture student seminar that was still in session: "Structural Alternatives." I had little use for structure but was always interested in alternatives.

We entered a large light-filled studio. At the far end of the room, a big bearded man sat above the others on a high wooden stool. One long look at him and the chairs, the drawing tables—the students—everything else in the room disappeared. Only He remained, blazing like a burning bush. The electricity in my brain shorted out. He was gorgeous—more Norse God than human.

In my teens, I devoured *True Romances* comics. Inside their pages, the swooning heroine always fell madly in love, accompanied by a zigzagging blast of energy. *Sigh! Bang! Pop!* As my eyes met his, a flash of lightening zipped across the ceiling and connected our bodies. It was insanely real. Having been hit by a cosmic love bolt, I watched, stunned and immobile, as the magnificent man removed a pen from his shirt pocket and scribbled something on a piece of paper. Time flew away and when it returned he was walking across the classroom toward me. Watching him put one big sneakered foot in front of the other, I lost my ability to breathe.

He silently handed me the note and with a glance that shut out the rest of the world, crossed back to his seat. My stomach roller-coastered to my knees and I felt so sexually charged that it was all I could do to prevent myself from bending over and presenting. Embarrassed by my own heat, I nervously scanned the room but none of the other students seemed to have noticed my arousal. My legs wobbled ahead of me. As I stumbled out the door, I left Moe of my salad days behind. Nothing mattered except the note in my hand.

On the graph paper in clean, architectural print, a Dwight Street address and the message: "Magic Lady, please stop by soon—Clint Helvey." He used the word "magic" just like Santana did in *Black Magic Woman*. Obviously, the guy had soul.

Two hours later, I found myself at his door. I didn't need to knock because it was wide open. A tall, blond, and bedazzling man so not Clint Helvey stood in front of me. "Jesus," I thought to myself, "I've finally hit the hot-guy mother lode." The man gave me a quick once over, immediately lost interest and gestured toward the bare living room floor; a gallon jar filled with what looked like M&Ms but turned out to be Window Pane acid sat in the middle. "Grab a handful, it's on the house," he said and walked off. Another blond guy slept next to the jar. His long hair fanned out across his back. A beautiful blond woman was curled up next to him. They were rolled together in a ratty, green army blanket.

"Is Clint here?" I called after Mr. Shiny, but he'd disappeared. The sleeping couple didn't move.

Clint, I was about to learn, shared this big clapboard house with Southcoast, a Texas-based architecture collective filled with lanky, smooth-talkers sporting waist-length hair and silver belt buckles. Day and night, folks wandered in and out of their bare living room and left with fistfuls of face-melting, time-altering, fifth dimension consciousness.

As I stood there, uncertain of what to do next and wondering if I was about to make a fool of myself, Clint walked toward me. He moved like a lion, his back straight, his legs bending and unfolding with grace. He'd heard my trombone voice.

"Thanks for coming," he said.

"Your place was on my way to the gym," I lied.

Women were not (yet) allowed to use the Yale gym but he didn't seem like the type who would know—or care.

"I'm Carol Schlanger," I muttered. I felt like an idiot but extended my hand. Instead of shaking it, he held it gently. His palm was deep and calloused. A hot jolt traveled down my back and into my pelvis. The walls of my vagina throbbed like a heart.

"Hi, Carol Schlillinger," he said.

I was used to having my name mispronounced; a lot of people mangled it. Those who knew German or Yiddish laughed when introduced; Schlanger sounded like Schlong—the Yiddish slang for penis—Carol Penis.

"No—Schlanger. It's Sch—lan—ger."

"Cool."

He wore a faded tee-shirt that said, "Plunk Your Magic Twanger, Froggy."

"*The Buster Brown Show*! Remember Midnight the Cat?" I asked, eager to engage in the knowledge of 50s TV trivia we so obviously shared.

"Huh?"

"Your shirt, it says..."

"It's not mine."

He smelled like a baked potato and I was about to become an easy lay. God, I prayed, please help me. Save me. He's so gorgeous but he's so not my type. I like smart, fast-talking Jewish guys who wear rimless glasses, study the law and quote James Joyce: "Stately, plump Buck Mulligan came from the stairhead..."

"This is a nice place," I whispered, my mind wiping away *Ulysses.*

The house walls were draped with Confederate and American flags.

"Thanks," Clint said and, taking my hand again, led me toward the light of another room—the kitchen. The sink was piled high with dirty dishes and the burners on the stove were encrusted with what looked like volcanic ash. "Hungry?" he asked. "We've got some leftover pizza."

"That sounds good."

He opened the refrigerator door and a brown paper grocery bag stuffed with marijuana spilled out. Bending at the waist, but keeping his legs dancer straight, he picked up the bag and sat it on a three-legged wooden table. The table's fourth leg was a black lawn-jockey statuette—a little plaster man dressed in a red and white striped riding suit and red cap—so not Huey Newton. With his index finger and thumb, Clint sprinkled marijuana onto a little white sheet of paper and deftly rolled it into a joint. Then in a move that was totally Paul Newman in *Hud,* he lit it on the stove's burner and handed it over.

"Thanks, but I don't smoke," I said.

"This is dynamite shit, you gotta try it."

I took it into my mouth and sucked deeply. The pungent smoke burned my nostrils, I couldn't breathe, and a painful cough exploded in my chest. Clint patted me on the back and handed me a glass of water. I gulped it down.

"Let's do something else," he said. "You just inhale; I'll do the rest."

He took a long toke, placed his lips over my mouth and exhaled. The man-filtered smoke went down my gullet smooth as cream. Our lips remained together. When we stopped, I felt like a plug pulled out of her socket. Again, he steered me towards another room—his bedroom, but not before he dipped his hand into the jar of acid candy.

I liked being led. The pizza was forgotten.

"What a dump." Those were Martha's first words to her husband

George in Edward Albee's *Who's Afraid of Virginia Woolf?* Unlike Martha, I looked down at the yellowing foam rubber mattress on Clint's bedroom floor, the rumpled sheet, the smudged silk parachute hanging from his ceiling and kept my mouth shut. The parachute made the room almost acceptable. It was as if I was entering the lair of a sloppy Bedouin—transported to another continent where all that I'd ever known was useless and untranslatable. Clint pulled me down next to him and swept a pile of dirty clothes off the bed onto the floor. We had hardly spoken; I didn't even know what films he liked or what God he believed in. A woman's blue polka-dotted sunhat languished on top of the pile.

"Whose hat is that?" I asked.

He picked it up and threw it across the room.

"It's Nancy's."

I waited for more details but all I got was silence. Maybe, I told myself, it wasn't my business anyway...yes, it was.

"Oh?"

"She's my old girlfriend. We just broke up."

"When was that?"

"Tomorrow."

I had to laugh because I knew he meant it. At least I thought I knew he meant it and that was good enough. Sheepishly contrite, he chuckled along with me. We could laugh together—that was a good sign. So what if he was a slob; straight men never made their beds. This guy was from the land of the free and the home of the brave and was sucking my left nipple and then my right. My legs spread open by themselves and my knees bent up to my ears. I was as open and quivering as a freshly-shucked oyster.

The bedroom floor shook and trembled along with me. A stack of books fell off a milk crate and landed with a thunderous clap. A gooseneck floor lamp tumbled toward the foam bed but was thankfully caught in the folds of the parachute. Rising panic edged out my arousal.

Then I heard the sound—a deep rumble that grew louder and louder as it came relentlessly toward us. Clint unplugged himself and in one quick motion rolled onto the floor. He grabbed my arm and yanked me to my bare feet. *Hell,* I thought, my mind moving nowhere near as fast as his body, *it must be an earthquake...but this is Connecticut—Connecticut does not have earthquakes...then again, maybe some ancient Tectonic Plate is sliding past...*

Clint tossed me my blouse and hurried into his jeans. Even in the confusion, I had to take a moment and watch him zip up his fly; the way he leaned back and drew in his stomach. Half-dressed, we ran to the front door. It was wide open. Rolling down the empty street was a parade of armored tanks. The National Guard had arrived. I'd heard rumors they were coming but I hadn't believed it. This was the United States of America, we did not attack our own with tanks and machine guns. This was Yale, the Goddam Ivy League. No one here had achieved a four-point grade average, scored a 1600 on their SATs, become a virtuoso on the tuba, or used family connections to be shot through the gut with an M1. The cannon atop the lead tank turned and aimed at us. I was about to frantically wave a dirty white pillow case to surrender when Clint encircled me in his arms and held me close. Instead, I surrendered to him, rested my head on his broad shoulder and burrowed my way into his body. Now I was Ingrid Bergman catching a few moments of stolen bliss before the Blitzkrieg hit. My once-serenely-beautiful Swedish face filled with trepidation—danger and the unknown were close and moving closer.

By Yale Drama standards, I was a card-carrying member of the radical fringe. But by my own reckoning, I was just a middle-class New Yorker who saw the light, someone who would never willingly put her body in harm's way. Wrapped in the arms of this sweet big man, I felt totally safe.

Death was on its way but not on that day, not for us and not for the Yale students on the ground. The tank cannon withdrew and moved on. Four days later, thirteen unarmed protesting students at Kent State in Ohio were not so lucky. The Ohio National guard killed four and wounded nine.

The next morning, I lay naked on top of Clint's bed tripping on Sunshine acid. It was a mind-blowing high, during which I learned all the secrets of the universe and then forgot them. We made love all night. I came so hard and so often that his foam mattress turned squishy in spots and smelled like the hallway of a walkup in the East Village. Floating above the floor, looking down at my body, I heard only the soft coo of voices outside the bedroom door. The tanks were long gone and the parachute above Clint's bed floated over my head like a summer cloud. A big man's hand, bent at the wrist, drooped over my breast, its fingers lightly skimming the surface of my satisfied skin. This feeling...I told myself, this must be the reason I am alive.

I forgot my own little apartment and moved in.

Making love two or three times a day, every day, my brain, previously my most developed organ, quickly retreated, both hemispheres grateful for the sabbatical. Sex on acid had catapulted me into another galaxy and nothing could bring me down. In whatever direction I turned, some Lone Star male named Sky, Pepper, Pete, or Roy, with a pungent leather pouch swaying from his belt loop, passed me a joint. Time and worry were filtered out by the sweet gauzy haze of THC.

☾

A few days later, during my third quarter acting evaluation, my acting teacher, Mildred Dunnock (the original Linda Loman *in Death of a Salesman*), who knew of my pending dismissal, told me my REAL problem was that I loved life more than I did acting.

"So," I asked her, "what's wrong with that?"

"Nothing really," she answered. "I recognize your type. You can't help yourself. You'll choose the next man who gives you what you think you need or an adventure on the high seas, anything that takes you away from the long, hard haul of your craft. You, my dear, may have the talent but don't care enough to be great."

"But I do, Miss Dunnock, I do care," I protested. "I want to be great. I have to be." She nodded her head knowingly and grinned—it wasn't a smile, but something that pulled her thin cheeks toward her tiny ears and exposed her feral little teeth. In that moment, her face scared the shit out of me. In it I saw a death mask that could see beyond the present. Mildred was an acting icon, revered as one of the best. She knew what I didn't know I didn't know. "Time will tell, Carol," she said, as if she and my future were in cahoots, "Time will tell."

A day later, I received official notice that I could no longer attend classes or graduation. They might have loved me once, but they didn't anymore.

I fought back. I had to. I saw myself as collateral damage that also ejected a beautiful black actress suspected of being a Black Panther, two gay male students and far-left leaning professors of directing and playwriting. CR Lawn, the reporter who interviewed me for the *The Yale Law Advocate* quoted me as saying: "They kicked me out because I indicated that I thought the Yale School of Drama was oppressive, now I think that the acting department has made it deadly." William Henry the III, the *Yalie Daily's* theatre critic who championed my case, had his article censored before it went to press and was immediately fired. When I wrote a letter to Kingman Brewster Jr., the president of Yale, pleading my case, he wrote back saying although he was sympathetic, it was not his policy to interfere in individual graduate school issues.

A week later, William Henry, who had wept at his dismissal, got his job back. (Later in life, William Henry III received a Pulitzer Prize for Television Criticism)

As the months dragged on, I grew weary of the battle. I wanted to act, not litigate. So, unable to further my career and banned from performing, I packed my bags, told Clint I loved him and left, hard hit by my first lesson in how real power, academic or otherwise, worked: Speaking your truth could lead to losing your head or graduate degree and arriving at Grand Central Station, dragging an oversized suitcase behind you—out on your little chutzpah-filled, radicalized ass.

CHAPTER 3

Manhattan Again

August 1970 - May 1971

If you live in New York or any other big city, you are Jewish. It doesn't matter even if you are Catholic; if you live in New York, you're Jewish. If you live in Butte Montana, to me you will be goyish even if you are Jewish."

LENNY BRUCE

It was with much relief that I moved from New Haven back to New York and had the good fortune to be allotted a new studio apartment in Westbeth, a rent complex, subsidized by the city for lower-income working artists. The Montmartre of the meat-packing district—every floor of Westbeth was filled with composers, musicians, writers, actors, directors, dancers, choreographers, photographers, sculptors, and painters. It was a heaven on earth.

After graduating Yale in Environmental Design, Clint left Connecticut and joined me. As soon as he arrived, before he could even unpack his big, mismatched tube socks, he had a job. As a still out-of-work actress, I looked at his immediate gainful employment as something of a miracle. Agung, Clint's well-connected buddy from Yale, a mover and shaker whose father was an appointee to the U.N., used his influence to secure Clint work remodeling a section of the Indonesian Embassy. When inside the Ivy League, you don't realize how well it connects you, until you leave it—then the big world can become harder—but not always.

Clint's connection with Agung, a Muslim prince among many Indonesian princes, was strong. For two months after my expulsion, he and I had lived in Agung's spacious New Haven apartment with both Agung and Louise, Agung's soon-to-be Jewish wife. The four of us became close friends. At their slapdash Connecticut wedding, Clint had been Agung's best man and I was Louise's maid of honor. Even though it rained and the homemade wedding cake was so soft in the middle that the little plastic bride and groom sank into the icing, the couple was happy. When, dressed in slickers and rain hats, they took off in Agung's van to launch their utopian life style in rural Oregon, I could see the longing in Clint's face. He wanted to be there with them—headed for the Great Northwest Back-To-The-Land Adventure. An adventure rooted in the massive Earth Day demonstrations of April 22, 1970, where hoards of the young and prescient made their furious demands for the end of land rape.

Instead, this man, who'd never in his life eaten an onion bagel with a schmeer, moved to lower Manhattan to be with me—and make money to bankroll his own dream. He would leave eventually, but not, he promised, for a long time and not without me beside him.

While Clint worked at the embassy, I did what all out-of-work actresses do: took singing lessons, Afro-Cuban dance classes, and auditioned. At night Clint and I ate dinner together, watched TV, made love, and fell asleep. I thought we were having a great time...for my Texan, not so much. He didn't fit—he enjoyed his job but couldn't take on New York. If someone pushed him aside and took the cab that he'd hailed, he'd stood in bewildered silence and lost the ride. The subway system also had him beat. Even with maps, the rush and the crowds confused and upset him. Often, I waited for him to meet me for dinner or a movie for what seemed like an eternity, only to finally give up and go home. Then I'd get his call:

"Jesus, honey," I'd say into the phone, having just walked into the apartment, "where are you? I waited and waited."

"I'm in a place called Bay Ridge, Carol. There's no bay here and no ridge."

"Clint, you're in Brooklyn. You were supposed to meet me on Canal Street...it's in lower Manhattan."

" What's the difference?"

"They are two different boroughs," I'd answer, struggling to believe that anyone on planet earth didn't know that fact. "You must have stayed too long on the BMT after you missed the stop."

"Maybe I got the letters mixed up. I do that a lot."

"Dear God."

"What?"

"Nothing."

But it was something.

On March 6th, 1970, the Weathermen, a radical underground organization dedicated to overthrowing the U.S. government, accidentally blew up the West 11th Street Greenwich Village brownstone belonging to the wealthy parents of Cathlyn Wilkerson—a Weatherwoman. With their "bring the war home" fury and a lot of hallucinogens, they felt that only acts of violence could bring down capitalism, materialism, and the war in Vietnam. Three Weathermen, all in their twenties, were assembling a bomb, when one of them accidently put two wrong copper wires together and—bang! Nothing remained of them except bones, teeth, and a fingertip. Two women, Kathy Boudin and Cathlyn Wilkerson, were also involved but escaped; badly singed, but alive.

Six months after that home-grown explosion and a month after Clint joined me in Manhattan, as I was grabbing a hotdog at Gray's Papaya on West 72nd, David Gilbert, a driving Weatherman force, recognized me from my American Pig performance at an old Columbia University SNCC (Student Non-Violent Coordinating Committee) rally. David, now a high ranking SDS leader, had loved our show and dubbed my performance "out of sight." Hell. The guy was a fan. I was amazed that he still knew who I was because instead of army fatigues and wild Janis Joplin hair, I was now wearing a neat ponytail and a sleeveless sheath for a commercial audition. I wanted the job badly because, even though I had revolutionary consciousness, I still needed cab fare. As soon as I saw David, I plastered my arms to my sides so he couldn't tell that I'd shaved my armpits—it was bad enough I was wearing nylons.

David looked haggard, disoriented and frail; a seedy phantom of his former self. I'd been impressed—no, mesmerized—by the passion of his rhetoric. But now, his Rasputin eyes were red-rimmed and puffy, his clothes were dirty and torn. He smelled of cigarettes and stale sweat and he lightly grazed my shoulder with tobacco-stained fingers.

"David," I asked in idiot mode, "can I help you in some small way?"

"Sure thing. Give me whatever cash you have on you."

I reached into my purse and quickly handed him two twenties.

"Thanks comrade," he said, stuffing the money into his sleeve. "The New World Order won't forget you."

That was a major relief. Recognition always appealed to me.

His face lost its dark edge. As he asked for my phone number and address, he drew so close I could see the moth holes that covered his shirt and smell his sour breath. Without hesitation, I wrote the information down for him. He then disappeared into Gray's. Through the store window, I saw him pick a half-eaten leftover frankfurter bun off someone else's plate and stuff it into his mouth.

That next morning, as Clint ran his soapy hands down my leg, the doorbell rang. I stood farthest away from the shower spray.

"Someone's at the door."

He didn't hear me.

"Mind doing my back?" he said as he handed me a loofa.

The bell rang more insistently.

"I'll get it," I said and pushed open the shower curtains and hurried, dripping wet, into my robe. I was expecting my next-door neighbor, another photographer, with contact sheets for my new headshots. Instead, it was David Gilbert, accompanied by a stunning dark-haired woman I recognized from her recent photo in *The East Village Other*. It was the legendary Bernadine Dohrn, a law school graduate turned political street fighter. She was the most powerful Weatherwoman of all. Compared to Ms. Dohrn, I was a bourgeois puffball.

"Hello," I whispered.

"Carol, this is Bernadine," David said as he gestured toward Ms. Dohrn. It wasn't really an introduction; it was a statement. Bernadine raised eyebrows as if to say, yes, that was who she was; but the information was more than I deserved. David spoke with his back turned away from me. He was tapping the walls to judge their thickness.

"We need your place for meetings. It's small, but it'll do."

"What do you mean?" I asked.

"A safe house, that's what—you into it or not?"

Fear blew acid into my belly.

"Oh...I guess. Sure..."

"Beautiful," Bernadine said and put her hand on my shoulder. She was shorter than I was.

"Told ya Carol would be cool," David said.

I couldn't catch my breath. I was a people pleaser and so wanted everyone to like me. If friends asked me to call my theatrical agent to recommend them, I did—even if they sucked. If someone needed to crash at my apartment for a week or two with their over-heated tom cat—I let them. But this man...this man was not in his right mind.

"Um...guys...it might not work out...you see....my mother wouldn't like..."

I was beating away the nasty domestic terrorists with the threat of a sixty-eight-year-old woman who had just undergone hip replacement surgery—and paid half my rent.

"There'll be eight of us," Bernadine informed me. "We'll use the stairs instead of the elevator so as not to attract attention."

"Eight's okay," I said.

Oh sure, eight was just fine. Then I remembered—Clint. The shower was still going. "You can't stay while we're here," David added. "All Weather Underground meetings are strictly closed. We don't want you to know who we are."

"If I never see another Weatherman again, it won't be too soon."

There, I'd said it.

David continued without missing a beat.

"We'll be here early and leave at dark. Have an extra key made and stock the fridge. No junk food, just the basics."

Great, I was going to feed them, too. It was a wonder I didn't ask what kind of dressing they wanted on their salad. I was a deer caught in their headlights, paralyzed by bourgeois guilt and hatred of violence. No one would make bombs or craft violent strategy in my kitchen. But I couldn't bring myself to tell them to leave. I shivered, thinking they might have their way with me.

Steam from the bathroom floated toward me and brought with it the smell of Zest soap. Clint had finished his shower. An oversized bath towel, imprinted with a Zuni pottery design that I'd bought at Bloomingdale's annual White Sale, was secured around his waist. Water dripped from his long chestnut hair and down onto his shoulders. Westbeth's bathroom door was porous—he'd overheard.

"You're not meeting here, so just go," he told David calmly.

"No way brother, we were just promised we could..."

Before David could say another word, Clint lifted him by the back of his shirt and dragged him to the door—

"Go now...buddy, jes git!"

While in the Naval Air Force, Clint had learned to both give and take orders and he'd almost seen active combat. In snapshots he was a clean-cut uniformed young man, with a square chin and broad shoulders. With one hand, he opened my front door and with the other pushed David into the hallway. Clint then turned his attention toward Bernadine.

"Don't you dare touch me," she growled and stomped out of my apartment to join David.

"Fuck you co-opted Yalie Pigs!" David screamed back as they both walked away.

The Weathermen were gone! The wind took them in another direction.

Clint and I stood together in the door jam. He wasn't even breathing hard.

"Thank you," I whispered.

"What jerks," he said, reducing the Weather Underground vibe to its simplest form. "In Texas, babe, we don't invite the rattler into the barn."

I kissed his eyelids, one by one, paying homage to his decisive manliness.

"Tell me again why you left Texas," I whispered.

"Didn't care for it much so I quit football and joined up with the Navy."

"But you love football," I said, nibbling across the chewy rim of his ear.

"Love to watch it, that's all. It's a blood sport—they make you into a gladiator."

I could just see him in his sandals and little toga, so brave and so strong. The crowd roaring his name. Clint! Clint!

"Couldn't you have gotten hurt in the Navy just as easily?"

His beard scratched my skin—in a good way.

"Yeah, but the Navy was real," he said as he drew away from me. "If I was gonna git all busted up, it had to be for somethin' more than a game."

Even if he hadn't been there, he assured me, I could have handled the situation myself—I was that strong. Clint might have been certain, but I wasn't. To not be swayed by others, to hold my ground when I could so easily trip. The Weathermen were a nightmare, their fury cannibalizing itself. They didn't care if I lived or died. To them, I wasn't really a human; I was a thing to be used. That brain zap, the kind that lets you see what's really happening went big and wide: Hardline politics were not for me and never had been. Protest—yes. Murder—no. I wasn't furious, just a young woman who no longer felt at home in her own country.

"Clint," I said as I followed him back into the bathroom where he was clipping off the uneven bits of his beard, "like Gandhi says, we change the world when we become the change: dropping out and living off the grid." In my mind and heart I saw a remote cottage, where we could live entwined forever, surrounded by song birds and trees. We would be so crafty and industrious that we'd never again have to depend on the outside world.

"Right on!" Clint said as he checked out his hairy chin in the mirror.

"Someplace," I continued, "where we can grow our own food with clean water and live like Helen and Scott Nearing*, on almost nothing but having everything."

"The sooner the better, Carol."

"Land is the real thing, the substantial thing, isn't it Clint?"

"Got any idea when we can leave?" he asked, turning slowly toward me. "Just name a date." It was a challenge rather than a request. Silence. My only response was to tell him that his shave was uneven. Hope left his face. I was stalling and he knew it.

"I'm hangin' in there, Carol," he said, his eyes clouding over as he ran the razer under the tap, "but I can't stay here forever."

Watching his brown suds circle the drain, I didn't allow myself to believe him.

☾

It was on one of those shining New York mornings, when the weather inexplicably turns warm that I awoke to the clank of metal on metal. Clint had finished the Indonesian embassy remodel and all his tools—hammers, screwdrivers, a skill saw, and nail gun lay in a mound on an old tarp. Blurry-eyed, I watched as he tied the ends of the thick canvas with rope.

"What are you doing?" I asked him.

"Making a square knot."

As Clint yanked the skeins to be sure that they were tight, he continued, "Coffee's ready if you want some."

The parquet floor chilled my feet as I glanced back at the indentation our night bodies had made across our sheets. I wanted so much more from him than coffee. "You're leaving?" I asked, dreading his answer.

"Yup. Figured I'd make it fast and quick, that way it won't hurt much."

Great. He sounded like a Band-Aid about to rip himself off an open sore. So he was having a hard time adjusting—so what, he could learn. Yet there he was, taking his clothes out of our closet and stretching a rubber band over the lid of the Chock-Full-of-Nuts coffee can that held his loose change.

"When are you coming back?" I asked, desperately trying not to sound desperate.

* Co-authors of *The Good Life*, A classic book in rural homesteading based on their life in Vermont where the Nearings hand-built their houses, grew their own food and followed their own enlightened interests.

He smiled his big open smile, exposing perfect white teeth whose sparkle he attributed to Nacogdoches, Texas adding fluoride to their drinking water.

"In ten minutes," he answered. I turned toward him to give him a full-mouthed morning kiss, but he held me back.

"I'm loading up, babe. I'll be gone after breakfast."

"Why?! Why can't you wait for me?" I whimpered, suddenly turning into a cross between Marilyn Monroe before she downed her last Nembutal and a fury-mad Medea ready to flush our two baby goldfish down the toilet.

"Carol. I can't stay. Agung and Louise found a farm house to rent—real reasonable. Sky's already there and Pete and Froggie; everything's comin' together in Oregon."

That "everything" was all that Clint and I had discussed over the past year: How the Masters of War were immutable and to make change happen, we'd have to live without their drugs, their food, their institutions, their gas, their credit, their phones, and their electricity. How "the system," run by the greedy, rich and powerful, had obliterated all hope for a real democracy and because the U.S. government was beyond fucked, we needed to live outside its reach. The thought brought joyful expectation because it was so right. So right on.

Pete, Froggie, and Sky were members of Clint's beloved Texan architectural collective, Southcoast. But Clint wasn't going just to join his like-minded buddies, he was rushing to meet his future, and at thirty-two, nine years my senior, felt he was already late.

My stoner cowboy was about to gallop off, leaving me behind in a cloud of reefer dust. I sat on our bed and watched as Clint packed his duffle bag, neatly folding his few shirts, his old Pendleton blanket with a cigarette hole burned through the middle, his bundle of thick, white socks, and his faded, red, down jacket—the only jacket he owned, which, when he'd worn it to an opening night party at Sardis's, had embarrassed me horribly. There had been men in Armani and Clint with duck feathers sticking out of his shoulder seam. Now all I wanted to do was hug that jacket to my chest and never let it go.

"Come with me now, Carol." His soft voice was as smooth and irresistible as hot fudge. This was a fine man, a hard-to-find man, a man who came from a kind, cloth-coated Christian family. His father was an Episcopalian priest, his mother a concert pianist and white-gloved church lady who raised three rambunctious boys and drank too many Harvey Wallbangers. Clint had unclogged my kitchen sink, fixed the wiring in my reading lamp, and driven me in his beat-up old Ford Falcon to wherever I needed to go. He kept me in good operating condition, always there, always available, always kind. Clint never ate with his mouth open. His food never fell from his fork into his lap. During the Bay of Pigs crisis in Cuba when the world had been a hair's breadth away from nuclear holocaust, he'd flown a B2V over the Windward Passage in his underwear and was grateful that he didn't have to bomb Havana. After that, he shed all his clothes at Woodstock and never looked back, reborn after three days of incredible music, dope, acid, and mud. For him, hell was wearing a necktie. Never, he told me, would he again wear anything that constricted his neck.

"How can I come now?" I whimpered. "I have a lease, I have a bed and a television and a toaster oven. I'd have to store everything and sublet, and Westbeth doesn't let you sublet."

"Do it anyway."

Easy for him to say, he had no idea what it took to get a rent-controlled, artist-subsidized apartment in Manhattan. Moving back to the land and off the grid required the courage to discard all of my old life—courage I didn't yet have.

"I'll come soon," I said.

"I can't stay here, Carol. I can't be who I am in the city."

Clint could read the sky, know that low stratus clouds preceded a cold front, but not how or when to tip a doorman.

"But I want you with me, baby…always," he continued.

On any other day, I would have become uptight at being called "baby." It was sexist, it was demeaning, but in that moment, it was right.

"Clint, I love acting. I won't be able to act in Wherever, Oregon. They don't even have a repertory company."

"You can act anywhere. You're always acting. Besides, it's just showing off."

"No, it's not—it's nothing like that…plus, I'm afraid of the dark."

"That's okay."

Okay for him. When alone, he didn't have to sleep with a night light and the television blaring.

"And I can't drive," I said.

"You can learn."

My refrigerator buzzed in the background like an angry wasp.

"I hate cars, Clint. I'm big on public transportation. Does Oregon have a reliable bus system?"

"Not if you wanna get anywhere quick."

We'd been down this route to nowhere before. It was a dead end.

The light in his eyes dimmed, and something gray and frozen took its place. He pulled a large purple bundle out from under our bed.

"Here, this is for you. When you come, bring it."

It was a sleeping bag. The tags were still on: "100% Canadian goose down, good for temperatures to 20 below zero. Dry clean only." I knew it had set him back more than he could afford; I liked that. The bag meant reclining in dark, earthy places, on the ground and under the stars. It meant a life together, transient, uncharted, and free. I pulled it out of its casing and undid the ties, but couldn't figure out how to unzip it. I tugged hard–nothing happened. "Gimme," he said and in one quick motion, took it from me and laid it out flat on our bed.

"Thank you. It's beautiful," I whispered. "I love it."

And I did. It was my engagement bag, my promise of things to come. We kissed for a long time. Clint looked at his watch. It was nearly ten in the morning. He was well past getting an early start and Clint always wanted to start early. He hoisted his heavy sack across his back. The weight pulled back his shoulders. The man looked taller and straighter than ever.

"Carol, in Oregon there are big waterfalls we can swim under naked. The water's so clear you can see to the bottom and no one's gonna be around but us. The only thing I want to do fast is to go slow and...I love you."

The wrong words bolted off my tongue and kicked their way through my lips: "If you really loved me, you'd stay."

"If I stayed," he said, "I'd never be enough for you. But I'll wait for you, Carol. As long as you need." His beard brushed my cheek as he gave me a fuzzy whisper of a kiss. I watched, uncharacteristically mute, while he opened the front door, stepped into the hallway, and quickly escaped down the stair emergency exit instead of using the elevator. He didn't turn to look back at me.

He was moving on.

I picked up his empty coffee cup. It had a dark ring at the bottom. I rinsed it off but the ring remained and I was glad. It was a residue of the man–all I had left.

A week later, on my way to Afro-Cuban dance class, as I held onto the hand strap on the Express to Times Square, I read an overhead advertisement that suggested I "Meet Miss Subway," a heavily made-up Bronx stenographer from Cabrini Boulevard who enjoyed flower arrangement and figure skating. I looked across the aisle at the other passengers, their flesh pasty, their faces nowhere near as pretty as Miss Subway's, but just as deadened. They no longer reflected life's infinite variety, only its downside. The zombie air smelled of dejection. The subway was a clanking crypt on wheels. I never wanted to ride it again. What I wanted was to live where a woman didn't have to wear makeup to feel beautiful. What I wanted was to be part of the longhaired, barefooted stampede West—to make Woodstock Nation last forever.

"Come with me, Carol."

How could I leave? I was attached to New York by an umbilical cord that pumped theater, dance, art, music, and film into my bloodstream. I loved the tinny whiff of wind that blew up from sidewalk grates; the sudden, winter snows that softened a concrete world and crippled busses; the severely palsied man whose wet lips hawked "Only a dime" pencils at the 59th and Lexington entrance to Bloomingdale's.

Exiting the subway station, I walked past an old Puerto Rican street vender selling giant pretzels. I loved him, too.

"We'll live the way a man and woman were meant to live. The way nature intended."

The mouton coat I found in a secondhand fur warehouse on Delancey Street, with its torn inner pockets that caused my gloves to drift into the lining—that, too, was New York. If I ever left Manhattan behind, I could kiss my family, my fabulous woman's support group—and my dream of working with Robert Altman, Paul Mazursky, Woody Allan, and Mike Nichols forever goodbye. New York was who I was and all I'd ever wanted. Until now.

CHAPTER 4

Ladies of the Lowlands

A woman without a man is like a fish without a bicycle.
GLORIA STEINEM

June 1971

"If you have to go with him—then go, Carol. I understand what's stopping you, but it's not enough to keep you here."

"Why, Stockard, why isn't it enough?"

There were five of us seated in my small Westbeth combination living room-kitchen-bedroom. Not tiny and cramped, I'd told myself, but minimalist and sleek. Stockard, the most famous of this very smart, very accomplished monthly woman's support group, was speaking. I was only half listening because I was mesmerized by her blouse. It floated around her. For someone who rejected materialism, I loved material. Stockard was sitting on my best chair, actually my only chair. The rest, all four, were seated on the couch. All their families were richer than mine, all their apartments bigger. Claudia had an academy award nomination for a documentary, Stockard was a known film actress and Broadway star, and Ellen, my favorite, had won a prestigious architectural prize. These women intimidated me but it seemed they liked me too, and I sure liked them. Desperate to impress, I'd gone all out. They eagerly gobbled down the olive tapenade, baba ghanoush, gruyere-stuffed figs, cashews, and grapes: a major hors d'oeuvre success which cost me nearly a month's phone bill.

"Look at me," Stockard continued. "At present, and I can't emphasize the 'at present' enough, I have no one. So what if I'm a working actress? So what if I'm living my dream? I come home every night after the show to nothing, zip, nada...except my dog. I'm a star but my dog has macular degeneration. He's always bumping into things. *Pauvre petite bebe.*"

"But Stockard, I love acting. Maybe I'm not as good as you, but... but..."

"Enough 'buts,' Carol," she said as she brought her face closer to mine and I could see her eyeliner was smudged and slightly crooked.

"No more buts, darling. Bottom line—love trounces all. Believe me, I know. I've had two husbands. Gay or not gay, I adored them both. Your couch thing is positively inspired. What do you call it?"

"Foam on plywood."

"Oh," she said, repositioning her lovely behind.

She hadn't said, "Carol, you are a brilliant actress. The theater would be bereft without you." No, nothing of the kind. It broke my heart a little but I was glad she liked my couch.

Stockard was the most illustrious, but not the prettiest of the group; Ellen was. A great friend and Summa Cum Laude from Radcliffe, the only thing not understated about Ellen was her mind. She knew everything:

"You love Clint, Carol?" she asked. "Really? Love? And what makes you so sure of that?"

Her tone was derisive. I didn't like it. She was making fun of me, this woman I so respected.

"He feels like home to me, Ellen," I answered.

Instead of placating her, my response spurred her on. "Carol, he does everything for you," she said. "It's a wonder he doesn't blow your nose."

I turned away from Ellen and looked out my window at the row of flowerpots I'd put out on my terrace to hide the dark bloodstains and grow Japanese basil. Maybe, it occurred to me, my allegiance to a man over our friendship hurt her, but before I could digest her blunt warning, another voice rang out:

"I don't agree with Ellen, not at all! Having things done for you gives you the time to do what you need to do for yourself."

That was Faith speaking. Her mainline, old Protestant family owned everything on the Eastern seaboard: homes in Hyannis Port and Riverside Drive, factories in New Jersey and Puerto Rico. Her support for the Black Panthers was legendary. She'd furnished all their leather jackets and natty felt berets.

"Thank you, Faith, I really appreciate..." I stopped in mid-sentence because my tooth hit something hard: an olive pit. I heard a crack, felt a sharp twinge, and let out a suppressed yelp.

"Are you all right, Carol?" Claudia asked.

"Thanks, I'm fine," I said as I spit the pit into my best cloth napkin.

It was a lie. My tooth was throbbing.

"To be a liberated woman," Claudia continued, "you have to make choices that are empowering, to not make a man what you want in life, but to want the best for yourself."

"Right on, Claudia!" Ellen shouted. "You have to take responsibility for your choices, Carol. You have to consider the consequences of your actions and grow up."

My tongue stuck inside my mouth. I just wanted to be with Clint, my body ached for him. That was a woman thing, too.

As if hearing my thoughts, Ellen continued, "Going away with Clint is antithetical to everything we've achieved as women. Following him is running from yourself. You're negating every woman who ever tried to stand on her own two feet."

"Ellen," I finally managed to get out, "I'm not just following Clint. I'm going back to the land. To something I believe in. To a place where I won't be eating tomatoes out of a can, but to where I'll be plucking them fresh off the vine, to where I won't be buying clothes at Bloomingdales, Bonwit's, Macy's, and Klein's but recycling and making my own."

"Making your own clothes, Carol? You know you can't sew. You've never been able to follow a pattern—any pattern."

Oh God, Ellen sounded just like my mother, and sadly, she was right. I once tried mending the hem of a skirt but accidentally attached it to my own pants—my needle going through both fabrics. When I stood up, the skirt dragged behind me.

"And what, Carol," Ellen continued, "is wrong with Bonwit's and Bloomies?"

"Absolutely nothing," Faith answered for me. "Bonwit's return policy is fantastic. I bought a winter coat there and returned it, God knows when, months later, and they took it back—no questions asked."

"Guys," I got in, "I'm not talking about department store return policies. I'm talking about not paying a doctor what workers in Guatemala make in a year, about using herbs and proven folk remedies instead of pharmaceuticals, about living in nature."

"Carol," Ellen said, "I don't believe your back to nature bit. For your own good, think like an adult."

"For Christsake Ellen, she's in love," Stockard said in my defense.

Stockard's front tooth had a little dab of red lipstick running across its edge, or it might have been a smidgeon of fig. It was hard to tell, she was always elegantly lopsided and always understood unanswerable needs. She was, after all, an actress. Ellen, however, was a feminist to the core, implying I'd sold out all of womankind in front of the women I'd done my best to impress.

Me (voice low, quivering slightly): "Ellen, I do so think like an adult."

Ellen's straight blond hair was beautifully cut and landed just at her chin line. "If you go with him," she continued, "it's a passive choice, a baby choice, a Daddy-take-care-of-me choice. I'm sorry; I'm only saying this because I'm your friend."

And she was my friend—my closest. Ellen was everything I never thought I could be: organized, responsible, and law-abiding. But as much as I hated to admit it, she had a point. Cradled in Clint's warmth and protection felt so good—maybe too good. To be cuddled by life differed from being nurtured by it. I loved my work and my art; it was what I was—to have it support me, the goal. And I was so close.

But without Clint...well, there couldn't be a without Clint.

CHAPTER 5

Across the Great Divide

July 1971

Any path is only a path. Look at every path closely and deliberately. Then ask yourself and yourself alone one question. Does this path have a heart? If it does, the path is good; if it doesn't it is of no use.

CARLOS CASTANEDA

My big, sweet lover had been gone for a month and I had no way to reach him. He called once from his friend Pete's parents' house in Eugene and sent a postcard with a picture of an enormous, hooked salmon flying across it: "Hi sweetheart. Love, Clint." This was too cryptic for me. All I could understand was that he couldn't write—yes, he was word-challenged, but I could accept it. I had enough words for us both.

The only way I could fall asleep at night was to conjure up the feel of his strong, warm legs and his scratchy heels. In acting this is called "sense memory," in life—longing. I'd doze off while watching the *Dick Cavett Show*, having stuffed myself with anything I could find in my refrigerator. Old Camembert rinds, frozen string beans and nearly penicillin pumpernickel. While I was lost in chewing, my thoughts drifted... the United States had lost its mind. It didn't know up from down. Right from wrong. Richard Nixon and Lyndon Johnson were total nut jobs—their war in Vietnam insane and unwinnable. Tricky Dick's "peace with Honor," was a cruel joke. He'd dropped half a million bombs on Cambodia and sprayed 11 million gallons of lethal Agent Orange on South Vietnam. Vietnamese civilians, women and children, were being burned alive with a horrible jelly called Napalm and even though Congress had passed the Mansfield amendment urging a withdrawal of American troops, the bill was overturned and the fight with the fierce Viet Cong continued. Because induction meant dying for what they abhorred, words like patriotism and love-of-country lost their meaning for the resistant in my deeply urban New York. All the draft-eligible guys I'd known as an undergraduate at CCNY had gone to great lengths to fail their physical exams. Isaiah Millstein had stayed awake for a week on Black Beauties (a three-hundred-milligram amphetamine), swallowed his own urine and poured Chile pepper into his eyes. Henry Bloom had dressed in drag and infected his arms by stabbing himself repeatedly with dirty needles, and Larry Lubin had starved himself down to ninety pounds and had lived on windowpane acid to realistically hallucinate and appear mad.

Others rejected our country's direction in more symbolic ways: Abby Hoffman, the great clown king of the Chicago Seven (a radical group that disrupted the Democratic National Convention in 1968), had stood on the balcony of the New York Stock Exchange and showered fistfuls of dollars down on the frenzied traders. He'd redefined the word "freak," giving it a new, positive connotation. Like Abby, those of us who'd been freaks all our lives, disaffected and unlike the rest, realized we were becoming avatars in a world that conservative Americans couldn't even visit.

Being a freak was the best thing ever: cutting-edge, beautiful, and wise.

I was a freak and proud of it.

Then *SWISH*—the loafer, like a karma-seeking missile, shot though my open window and my freaky world tilted on its axis.

Three days after that, the phone finally rang.

Marty, my agent Marty, always made the phone calls he didn't want to make at the very end of his work day. It was 7 PM. He broke it to me quick and fast: I didn't get the job. Although they loved me, Valerie Perrine, a fine actress, had been given the role of Honey in *Lenny*. Valerie had been a stripper in Las Vegas and like Honey, she was a real southern girl whose hair was Tennessee, not Jewish-red. I knew she was more seasoned, better built, and a more dedicated actress than I ever wanted to be. The rejection hurt but moved me forward. Yes, I loved the theater and was a very good at what I did, but perhaps not great. Over the coming years if I were lucky, I might hit it big or just grow old trying. Nate the dead photographer came to mind. Never would I wind up like him, my life cut short by a paucity of vision. My route to soul satisfaction could come from any direction. I just had to find it. There was something I did amazingly well. Something that the world might need and I could give. It had no name...but I knew it was there, patiently waiting for me to claim it.

It was time to act and not on the stage. Leaving my career and New

York wasn't giving up, it was giving in: submitting to a higher calling. The universe was giving me travel directions and I had to listen. I didn't know why, I didn't know how, but I wanted growing land and it was on that land I wanted to live—a place where an open heart and a free mind could escape the toxic and enslaving. Dropping out would drop me into a kinder, softer America, a place where the corporate, military-industrial fist had no hold. No, I wasn't compensating for losing the role because losing it told me that I wanted more than acting could give. My acting teacher—the great and annoyingly perceptive Mildred Dunnock, had skewered me correctly, but luckily my Texan Tinkerbell had sprinkled me with fairy dust and assured me I could fly. So, even though my only real skill was pretending to be someone else, I made up my mind.

I was going to Oregon.

It was...somewhere north of California.

As I gave away everything I owned to travel light into the next dimension, I wondered what I would do with the thing inside of me that always had to been seen and heard. Who would take that off my hands? My work had been my highest form of play. I loved the reality in make-believe and even if I'd wanted to, I couldn't leave that behind.

Days before leaving Manhattan, I called my parents to say goodbye. It was a courtesy call; we were barely speaking. Minnie and Mike were in their brand new 15th floor Hallandale, Florida, apartment overlooking a yacht-infested canal leading to the Atlantic. Just retired, they'd owned and operated *Kubies,* one of the first Health Food stores in Manhattan. Working ten-hour days, six days a week for thirty-five years, they'd given me every advantage they could afford. I was their beloved only child, their future, and they felt I owed them a good one. Now, every afternoon my big-boned mother, a former fierce business-woman and lawyer, darkened her tan while diving, with toes pointed, off the Golden Isles condominium's high diving board. After putting herself through Fordham Law, she'd practiced for just four years before joining business forces with my dreamer of a father. "It's a man's world," she'd warned me again and again because of how hard she'd had to fight it. Just starting out, she'd been propositioned by a judge and when she denied him, found herself almost disbarred and eventually left the law. Less of a jock than my mother, my father, red-headed and blue-eyed, avoided burning bright pink as he played gin rummy in the rec room with his new "cronies." Even more than playing the game straight, he loved to bluff, loved to fool others into thinking what he wanted them to think. Both were close to forty pounds overweight—

too much unsulfured dried fruit, whole wheat pasta, yogurt, almonds, cashews, and raw honey.

"Carol," my mother said after I told them I was leaving for Oregon, "ever since Daddy dropped you on your head, you haven't been exactly right."

"Not the drop on head thing again, Mom, please," I said, thinking for the hundredth time that if she'd been so concerned about brain trauma, why, when I was two, hadn't she stopped my father from throwing me up in the air and catching me like a beach ball?

"I didn't drop her, Minnie. She wiggled her way out," my father insisted on the extension. "She was a very frisky kid."

"No one said it was your fault, Mike," my mother told him. "What happened, happened." They really thought something was wrong with me. That I was damaged goods.

"Mom. Dad. I hate to interrupt, but you could say goodbye and wish me luck. That would be nice."

"You're going with a dirt-poor goy into the wilderness," my father said. "Living with who knows who, doing who knows what, so you'll need all the luck you can get. Just don't get eaten by a mountain lion. You are breaking our hearts but we can't stop you."

"Thanks, Dad."

"You're a mashuggah kid, but we love you," he continued and then his voice cracked. "Goodbye and good luck."

They'd met Clint only once and just didn't get him.

"Go ahead, ruin your life," my mother said on her end, "but for Godssake don't give away grandma's lamp, it's a Tiffany."

I couldn't tell her—it was already gone.

By 1971, the 1967 Summer of Love had soured and ended. On the streets of San Francisco, horse and coke had replaced weed as the street drug of choice; the gentle and open-hearted "flower children" had morphed into the forlorn and addicted. From those dead ashes a movement took shape and spread. Back-to-the-land hippies everywhere were becoming part of a new anthropological drift. Instead of crossing from Russia to Alaska across the Bering Strait, they were jumping onto the iconic bus that Ken Kesey warned we were either on or off, and migrating to remote rural America: Northern California, New Mexico, Oregon, Idaho, Washington State, Vermont, Tennessee—self -sustaining places where the land was cheap, the air clean, and the water clear. I was about to become one of them. Then, while I was trying to decide whether to stuff my best pair of high heels into my duffle bag, disaster hit. It was unexpected and ill-timed. It was my cousin Freddy.

I hadn't seen him in months and when I opened the door, I almost didn't recognize him. His clothes were rumpled and his always sad face was sadder than ever. The skin around his gray eyes sagged and their rims were a festering red. At nineteen, Freddy looked thirty. A recent dropout from Williams College, he had been sleeping in the hallway outside his parents' tony Sutton Place apartment because his father wouldn't let him inside until Freddy stopped using and Freddy couldn't stop. Anything he could score—weed, acid, coke, even heroin; it didn't matter to Freddy. When he came in and saw my studio was bare, Freddy sat down cross-legged on the floor and asked for a glass of water.

"Take me with you, Carol," he called out to me as I ran the tap.

I didn't think I'd heard him correctly. "What Freddy?" I asked, handing him the glass.

"Take me to Oregon, Carol," he pleaded. "You have to take me! I don't belong on this planet. I'm all wrong here. My mother told me you were leaving; she wants me to go with you."

It was my guess that, as soon as she'd hung up with me, my own mother had called my uncle and told him about my plans. Brother and sister, they had always been highly competitive. He was a doctor, she'd been a lawyer, and she now had proof positive that her daughter was just as crazy as his son, maybe even more so. Either that or she didn't know who else to confide in. My aunt Lillian must have overheard their conversation. She was nearing a nervous breakdown over Freddy's behavior.

"What about Uncle Nate?" I asked.

Freddy's face contorted.

"My father wants to cut me open, take the real me out, and put someone he likes better back inside, someone like him!"

My uncle was a powerful, self-made man: a successful heart surgeon who loved his son but had driven him hard—too hard. Freddy grabbed my hand and held it to his concave chest. It was a gesture meant to connect us, but it had the opposite effect. I drew away.

"Freddy," I said as firmly as I could. "I'm so sorry. I can't take you anywhere. I can barely take myself."

"You have to!" he screamed, standing up and pulling at his long hair. "You have to! I'll do whatever you want. I'll be your slave!"

A year ago, this slender and ethereal boy had been playing classical piano and majoring in medieval history. That boy had disappeared. Something in his mind had snapped and he was trying to fix it the only way he knew how. I did my best to explain that if he wanted to come, he must come on his own. I couldn't be responsible for him.

My heart broke for my sweet cousin, but my compassion was limited. The burden of his illness would ruin everything. Freddy needed more help than Clint or I could give. Then my mind went into reverse. How could I turn down a close relative so terribly in need? Where was all the love in my heart? The answer came as quickly as the question: love was out there, protecting and telling me what to do. Before saving Freddy, I had to save myself. I couldn't take him and didn't have to. The responsibility was too much. I was twenty-three years old and wanted to be alone with my boyfriend. "Look Freddy," I said, knowing I wasn't being straight with him, "just as soon as we get settled, say in a month or two, you can join us. I promise. Okay?"

"Really?" he asked, his eyes begging for the truth.

"Yes," I said, so plagued with guilt that I momentarily meant it.

In a mercurial turnaround that seemed to be a family trait, he immediately calmed down. "Oakey dokey," he agreed, his head moving slowly up and down on his slender neck as if he were one of those little perpetual nodding toys. Without another word, he handed me his empty glass, kissed both my cheeks and was out the door. "Goodbye Freddy," I called after him, "take care and when you come, don't forget your sleeping bag."

☾

From the air, New York looked like an impenetrable miniature kingdom. I tried to find Sutton Place and the building I'd grown up in but couldn't. Watching the city's spidery bridges and skyscrapers shrink in the distance, I grew nostalgic even though I'd just left. The year before, a review in the *Village Voice* had called my American Housewife solo in *The American Pig* a "virtuoso" performance. Fans had recognized me on the street and the hot dog vender on 8th and Broadway had reverently tipped his cap and covered my bun with extra sauerkraut. Along with the city I loved, I was saying goodbye to my future and identity as an actress.

The morning sun shining through the 707's oval window grew blinding, so I pulled down the shade and Manhattan disappeared. In its place I imagined Clint and me in our little rose-covered cottage—a fire crackling in the fireplace, a golden retriever dozing off at our feet. That sweet dreamscape lulled me into a deep sleep.

Six hours later, we landed.

The city of Eugene was a checkerboard of green, its tarmac near empty. My first glimpse of Clint as he waited for me at the gate was a shock. His hair was longer, his clothes dirtier, and his beard so scraggly and thick he looked like a werewolf. As we drew close his body odor was overwhelming and I had to pause before diving into our kiss. But when we came together, everything felt right. Holding him rearranged me toward bliss. At baggage claim, while he grabbed my duffle bag and backpack, I marveled at Mahlon Sweet Field's serene glass-enclosed garden and near empty ramps. The Oregonians in their bright outdoorsy clothes and unfashionable shoes all seemed to smile at us. The frenetic pace of New York slid off my shoulders like an old army-navy surplus jacket.

The driver's door of Clint's totaled 1963 red Ford Falcon was forever glued shut with polyurethane foam. It was a testament to his powers of improvisational repair, but not helpful if he needed to get out in a hurry or get out at all. The passenger door, however, did what it was supposed to do: open and close. I slid inside beside him. We could not stop touching each other. As we drove away, in spite of a steel coil making its way through his torn upholstery and up my butt, I was awestruck by what I saw.

The lush beauty of the Willamette Valley was everything Clint had promised and more: green pastures dotted with grazing cows and horses, orchards filled with rows of apple, pear, and plum trees, cabbages as big as Audrey, the giant man-eating plant in *The Little Shop of Horrors*, and squash plants the size of a Volvo. The air had a fresh-cut perfume. We were on our way to Greenleaf, Clint told me, to a small farm nestled in a cultivated valley, bordered by a creek brimming with fish. There we would grow our own vegetables, grind our own wheat, bake our own bread and bid all that was chemical and over-processed a forever goodbye. We'd recycle, compost, and live gently on Spaceship Earth. Or in Clint's own words: "Drop the useless and live simple." Oh yes. I was going to have a righteous and fulfilling life. Great sex and bud included.

Over a rickety bridge and down a winding dirt road, bordered by thick blackberry bushes, we drove past an open pasture and toward a rundown farmhouse. Junker cars and trucks sat parked everywhere. A few actually had wheels. Broken lawn chairs, their shredded plastic weave hanging like tongues from their frames, encircled a fire pit. There was no cozy cottage, no climbing roses, just a yellow patch of grass that passed for a front yard. Beyond a bale of wire, I saw the Indonesian prince—Agung. He was sitting picking cherries in the lap of a tree. Others I didn't recognize were doing the same. Sounds of hammering and the buzz of a chainsaw came at me. Maybe we were visiting with friends before we got to our REAL home.

"Clint," I asked, "who are all these people?"

"Good folks. All of 'em really nice guys. Course you know Agung and Louise."

He put his arm around me but I shook him off.

"We're all sharing one house? Don't tell me that, Clint. Please don't tell me that!"

"Okay."

A long silence.

"How many of them are there, Clint?"

"Fifteen or so, some are just visiting but...."

"Fifteen are fourteen too many!"

In college, I'd been the only one in a dorm of hundreds to be given a private room. When at first denied, I'd protested by sprinkling talcum powder all over the halls. At summer camp, I always took the cot closest to the far wall. A bunk bed was my idea of a nightmare. I loved people but they distracted me; I couldn't block them out. What they said invaded my thoughts and stayed there. I could focus with laser intensity, but the slightest disturbance sent me jumping out of my skin and off point. In the 70s, ADD stood only for the opposite of subtract (forty years would pass before I was diagnosed).

A small ragged group, including Agung, walked toward us. They wanted to suck out my brain and turn me into one of them.

"Roll up your window Clint," I shouted, "I don't want to talk to anyone!"

"But Carol," Clint said, trying to keep the anger out of his voice, "they're excited you're here, you could at least...."

I leaned over his body and grabbed the handle to close the driver's window. It refused to budge. Incensed, I turned toward him and hissed:

"You were afraid to tell me we wouldn't be living alone. You knew I'd hate it. You think I'm spoiled and self-centered. You're right, I am. So, fuck you!"

"I never tried to hide anything from you, Carol."

Tears ran down my cheeks. I could have held them back but I wanted him to know how miserable he'd made me so he could reverse the damage. As I began to sob, Agung appeared at the car window, grinning from ear to ear. His straight black hair reached below his shoulders and his honey-colored skin had darkened to bronze. To hide my misery, I bent over and pretended I was looking for my sandal under my seat. All Agung could see was my lower back.

"Shit woman!" he shouted to my L5 vertebrae. "We're all stoked you're here!"

To my amazement, Clint covered for me:

"Hey Aggie," he said, "Carol's got a bad headache or something. We're gonna go rest up and catch ya'll later."

With that Clint gunned the engine, leaving everyone behind and coming to an abrupt stop in front of a tiny outbuilding. After I wiped my tears with the tail end of his shirt, he put his arm around my waist and said:

"Here's our place, Carol. Everyone else wanted it, but I got it."

"Our place" had a wooden door held shut by twine looped around a large nail. "It used to be an old tool shed, but I fixed it up," Clint continued. He might as well have been presenting me with a penthouse overlooking Central Park, he looked so proud. I stopped crying—being equally adept at stopping as starting. It sunk in: Clint and I would have our own space. He'd done his best to make me happy and that was good enough—for the present.

"Why didn't you tell me?" I asked, placing my bare foot on his dashboard.

"You didn't give me a chance," he explained. "Figured you'd like it."

There it was again; I had been too quick in the knowing, Clint too slow in the telling. I more than liked our new shed-room, I loved it. All ninety square feet of it was ours and ours alone. The interior had its charms: a recycled window, a platform bed, shelves, and a smooth plywood floor. It was like the inside of a ship's cabin; tight and functional. I couldn't resist flopping down on the foam mattress.

"I'm so sorry, sweetheart," I said. "It's been a long morning. This place is beautiful and I so appreciate what you've done." And I meant it. He'd gone all out for me.

Clint dropped my duffle bag to the floor and lay down beside me. This time his body odor turned me on. It smelled like a man—my man. I nuzzled his armpit and inhaled deeply. In that funky darkness, I flashed on my girlfriends in Manhattan, still shopping for the perfect purse, still lingering in cafés longing for the intangible while I had a big, calloused hand down my pants, its fingers slowly spreading apart the damp walls of my pudendum.

Some men are born to know how to find the g-spot; others still doubt its existence. Clint was a believer; and an explorer. As my need rose, I spread my legs, begging for penetration. It had been too long. Just as I was about experience the sweet satisfaction of having what I desperately wanted inside me, there was a loud knock on the door. "Don't answer it!" I whispered. Above our heavy breathing, I heard a man's voice that reeked of Brooklyn, Bensonhurst probably, calling from outside:

"Hey Clint, youse in there?"

Clint threw me an apologetic look; the kind you might throw a lame horse before putting it down.

"Yeah Joey, we're here. What's up?"

"Everybody's leavin' for Slippery Rock," Joey, whoever he was, called back, "and Agung's van is full. Can I catch a ride with youse guys?"

"Tell him no!" I whispered.

"Sure thing, Joey," Clint said. "We're kinda busy right now but we'll finish up soon."

"No worries, I'll wait." Joey answered.

Finish up soon!?

Clint's response was an instant lesson in what I was facing and I didn't like it. This group I'd landed in had an unspoken ethic. I felt it inside Clint's quick and easy generosity. In my old life, I had willingly shared my time, space, and energy—by choice. Here, I felt, there was no choice. Everything and everyone were equal all the time and always. The thought hit hard. At Greenleaf, sharing was the rule, not enforced, just understood. As a result, I realized that I'd have to let go of a lot I never expected to let go of and was about to live in a new way with people not of my own choosing. For now, all I could do was to accept it. Go with the flow. Adjust. Not easy. No fuckin' way.

So, while Joey waited, we didn't.

☾

Driving down Route 36 from Greenleaf to Slippery Rock, we were the lone car on the road. The Coastal mountain range ahead was brimming with fir trees and scarred with bare patches of clear cut. Joey stretched in the backseat like a contented family pup.

"Don't rememba me, do ya Carol?"

"No," I said, not interested enough to turn around to face him, "I don't."

"I met youse and Clint atta big party in the Village," he said. "I had this cool act with a snake."

The word "snake" jarred my memory. The party had been in an artist's loft on Bleecker Street. She was famous for her portrayal of giant naked Amazons straddling replicas of the Empire State Building.

"Oh God ," I said, now turning to look directly at him, "that snake!"

"Pinky!" Joey shouted. "Pinky was the only mutha fuckin' albino python in the whole mutha fuckin' Village. Me and him, we had our game down. Me playing bongos. Him wrapped 'round my neck and freakin' everyone out—like we was dancin'."

I hated all snakes, but Pinky was especially hideous.

"We was doin' great," Joey continued, "but then I ran out of mice. That's all he ate."

"What did you do? "I asked, annoyed with myself for actually being curious.

"Had to give him up," he said, his voice cracking. "Bronx Zoo took him, but he couldn't adjust, he was totally Greenwich Village, totally downtown...The Pinkster died of a broke heart."

The only consolation I had in having to live with this guy was that it would be without Pinky.

☾

The roar told me it was there. The sound was thrilling. Clint had parked at the Slippery Rock way station, named for the enormous flat rocks that laddered down Lake Creek. Joey ran ahead while Clint and I walked along an overgrown path. My bare leg stung and began to grow bumps. I'd stepped into a nettle patch—a nasty little weed that grew everywhere. As I hopped around in response to the fiery itch, Clint plucked a different plant and rubbed its oily leaves into my skin. "Sorry" he said, "I shouldda warned you, but this Dock will fix you right up. It's a natural antidote." I thought about how kind nature was to provide its own remedies and how knowledgeable Clint was in knowing how to use them. He could fix anything—maybe even me. He'd once concluded that "If you put the two of us together, we make one normal person who can do it all, handle whatever comes our way." How right he was. The itch was gone in seconds. I'd had my moments of uncertainty but now I knew for sure: we were meant to be.

The roar grew louder, but I still didn't see its source. Agung, Joey, and a very pregnant woman were lying on the baked sandstone bank, sunning themselves like pale seals. Below them a turquoise pool flowed downstream onto an enormous, natural waterslide. I could hear others laughing and talking in the distance, but saw no one, including my good friend Louise, Agung's wife. She and I were close and I was looking forward to reconnecting with her. Fast, funny, and industrious, Louise, who'd studied city planning at Yale, was, unlike me, organized and cautious, but just like me, she'd been swept off her feet by a man who'd changed the trajectory of her life.

Agung and Clint were opposites in looks and religion: short and tall, Episcopalian and Muslim—one a cogent master of words, the other eloquent only with his hands. But their effect on Louise and me had been the same. They had knocked us off our chosen paths and blown us into the unknown. And complicit, we'd let them.

As soon as he saw us, Agung jumped to his feet. The top of his head reached my chin, but his hug nearly cut off my air supply. When Louise first introduced me to him in New Haven, I'd been aware of his race; now all I saw was my friend. Compared to the last time I'd seen him, he looked fantastic. His body was at fighting weight, his arms rippled with muscles and his eyebrows were back. At Yale, he'd picked at them until there was nothing left above his lids except an angry strip of flesh.

"Agung," I said, "you look like a new man."

"I'm cleansing," he explained. "I'm on a total fruit fast: blackberries, cherries, apples, melon, and grapes. Everything is brighter, more clearly-defined and I can see energy fields. Sometimes I slip and have a Hershey bar, but hey," he giggled, "I'm only human."

Even in hippie rags, Agung had an air of easy elegance. This man was a shape shifter, but no matter how hard he ran from the destiny his well-connected family had carved out for him, something always held him above the blood and guts. I'd seen it in New Haven and was certain it would occur in Oregon. The deeper he involved himself in poverty and simplicity the more powerful he became, and like most politicos, Agung could make what was real seem like it wasn't—and visa-versa.

"Welcome home, Sista," he said. "Welcome home."

Home? The word struck me hard. It was what I'd always wanted. As an only child, I'd been left alone with nannies and maids and then just alone. Home was supposed to be a place of ease and comfort, encircled by love and familiarity. But for me, it was lonely place where my only relief came from books and television. Always free to do as I wished, I had no schedule or direction. One reason I loved the theater was that when the lights went up, I knew what was expected and where to go. But when the curtain fell, I was lost. Great blocks of my foundation were shaky and so was I.

"Thanks, Agung. It feels good to be here," I lied, but almost wished it were true. "But where's Louise?"

"Hey, don't worry, she's here," he answered. "She had to go into Alvadore for u-pick peaches. They're only four cents a pound. Can you fucking believe it? She was afraid they'd be all gone by the time she got there. You know Louise."

Yes, I knew Louise. She was always on time and always there first.

A truck inner tube lay heating in the sun next to Joey. He stood up, took hold of it and signaled to Agung to join him. Both scooted inside the rubber ring and with their muscular arms, pushed themselves off to fly down the ladder.

No one had introduced the blond pregnant woman. Sitting on a faded bedspread, she picked up a wooden flute and played. Her music flowed with the water. It was Celtic sounding, magical and filled with fairies and heather. I looked toward Clint. He was now lying flat on his back with his eyes shut, drinking in the sun's heat. I sat down beside him. When the pregnant woman stopped playing, I took the initiative.

"Hello," I said to her, "I'm Carol. I just got here."

"Far out," she said with a soft Southwestern accent. "I'm Moonlove... I'm here, too."

Our eyes locked—hers were weary with dark pockets. Her nails were bitten down to the quick and she wore only a pair of baggy men's shorts. Her enormous belly stuck out and her giant, blue-veined breasts rested on her stomach. My mind immediately gave her an imagined history, a dramatic back-story: Moonlove was from some stultifying, small Texas town where in high school she hadn't been the prettiest girl or the smartest, just the one with the biggest tits. There were few on the football team who had not had their way with her, but Moonlove didn't mind. It was her way, too. I had a hard time with the hippie name she'd chosen for herself. It fell into the same irksome category as Sunshine or Rainbow. Without thinking, I asked her what her real name was. Guardedly, as if embarrassed by the very sound of it, she told me it was Betty. I could tell by Betty's crooked teeth and spent looks that she'd had none of my easy advantages, yet here we both were, in the same place watching Lake Creek flow into the Siuslaw toward the Pacific.

"Hey Carol," Clint called out, interrupting my vision of a teenage Betty, an empty football field and a line of buckaroos waiting their turn, "when the guys get back, let's go next."

"What about Moonlove?" I asked, suddenly egalitarian. "She was here before us, shouldn't she go first?"

"No way," Moonlove said as she patted her swollen tummy. "It's way too dangerous."

I looked down the laddered run. A person could fall along the way, break a leg, hit their head on a rock, get a concussion, and die. I saw myself like a well-fed Ophelia, my long red tresses floating in the current as my lifeless body bumped up against the shore.

"Clint, I can't."

"I'll be right there with you, Carol. You're gonna love it, trust me."

It was the assurance of his deep voice that turned me around. Yes, I'd go with him—trust him with my life because I already had. In minutes, Agung and Joey returned—elated. Agung silently dropped the truck inner tube next to Clint, signaling that our turn had come. Still in his cut-off jeans, which would protect him from any rough surface, Clint returned the tube to the water and held it steady for me to climb in.

We lay facing each other across the black, hot rubber. It burned our exposed limbs while the cold water chilled our covered rumps. With one hard push against the bank, we were off! The speed was incredible. Tiny white flies flew into our faces. A horned stag drinking at the water's edge, lifted his head to stare but remained frozen in time as we zoomed past him. Diamond light flashed off the water. My heart pounded. Nothing mattered except that ride. The trees that hugged the shore became one continuous green streak. Adrenaline soared through my body. I hadn't had such a rush since I was eleven, riding the Cyclone rollercoaster at Coney Island. At the bottom of the run we slowed to a stop. All I wanted was to go again. And again.

When Clint and I returned to the sunning rocks, only Agung remained. Joey, Moonlove, and the others had piled into Agung's van and returned to Greenleaf to unload cow manure destined for the garden. Taking a cigar-sized spliff from inside his headband, Agung lit it and handed it to me. The spliff's mouth was wide and inviting, the tip, tightly closed.

Like the seasoned smoker that I'd become, I held it between my thumb and my forefinger and took a long, hard draw.

"The guys from Tree Frog in Taos left us their stash," Agung told me as the smoke burned its way down my throat, "They didn't want to risk taking it across the state line."

In moments I was stoned. As can happen with certain strains of Indica, underneath the downy peace it gave, Tree Frog's weed carried a snippet of anxiety. Questions with no answers came and went. Would Joey, the former street urchin, Moonlove, the spaced-out mother-to-be, and the well-educated hippie cowboys be people with whom I could actually share a life? Could I be satisfied living on a broken-down farm that had only a few chickens and no discernible direction? Agung, like all guys from Harvard, had the answers to impossible questions. That's how they'd gotten into Harvard in the first place. I'd ask him:

"Agung, I was wondering how I can live a life ..."

"Salmon," he said, staring into space, "are guided on their journey to the waters in which they've been hatched by their sense of smell which lets them detect and differentiate their birth spot from all others. It is here, along this ladder that they end their old life and a new life begins."

"That's amazing Aggie, I mean, about the salmon and their smelling stuff and all...but what I need to know is...."

"Be like the fish, Carol."

"No way, I'm a Capricorn—a goat. But Agung...."

"Don Juan says...."

"Aggie, I don't care what Don Juan says."

Agung, his mind swirling in its own chemistry, ignored me and continued:

"Don Juan tells us that we must pay 'Second Attention.' At 'First Attention' we see the everyday world as it is, with the 'Second,' we see beyond it. Here is where your old life ends and you begin anew. That, Carol, is the answer to your question."

I was hoping Agung would tell me why he believed we overachievers could be happy living moment-to-moment with no plan or goal in mind, but the thought flew out of my head and into the cool water. Suddenly soporific, I let my arm dangle back into the creek and watched as tiny minnows snapped at my fingers, tickling my flesh.

"Carol," Agung said, "you have been led, like a salmon, to these waters, to your spirit home."

Spirit Home...and I'd always thought it was Central Park West.

Another toke and I was paying THC-enhanced second attention—below the water's crystal-clear surface were fantastic multicolored stones and pebbles. Agung's voice came at me like the narrator of a film, crystallizing reality and advancing the story:

"If your path has a heart, it is good. If it doesn't, it is of no use." That sounded right. It was something I'd try to remember, to help me make decisions, but would probably forget. Unzipping my soaked cut-offs, I slid into the deeper water. It was colder than the thin wet sheet of the shallow, slick slide. My skin contracted, the icy chill becoming my new reality. Clint came in right after me and together we swam upstream, toward the roar of the falls. The cold, dense, brackish water felt hard to kick through. It grew even deeper and colder as I swam ahead. The chill caused my body to stroke harder and I grew short of breath. I was about to let myself be carried back downstream when I saw it—the falls—twelve feet high and flowing like a transparent drape. The current grew stronger and impossible to get through. Now way ahead, Clint called for me to follow him and then disappeared into the falls. Pressing my belly against the exposed flat rocks that led to the falls' entrance, I was able to hoist myself up and out of the water. A few feet away, from the inside of the translucent curtain, Clint's arm reached out and guided me to the dry pocket where he sat on a black boulder. Thunder surrounded as we huddled together behind the tumbling waters. As the spray misted my body, all uncertainty vanished and I felt reborn, baptized by beauty and sensation. Nothing else mattered: not career, not art, not people—only the thrill of being so very alive.

My question was answered.

CHAPTER 6

Jingle Jangle Morning

July 1971

The determining factor of the mental health of a population is the condition of its natural love life.
WILHELM REICH, *The Function of the Orgasm*

The next morning, after a long, dead sleep, a rooster's crow woke us. No alarm clocks, just a big red, green, and black cock announcing sunrise. "Errrrr! Errrr! Errrr! Errrrrrrr!" Clint's eyes stayed closed and his hands lay crossed over his chest. I'd seen such men pictured on ancient Celtic coffins, men with powerful jaws and chiseled cheeks. And I, with a Bubby and Zadie from a shtetl in Bessarabia, had attached myself to one of their kind. The Great Somebody had opened the pages of a romance novel and pasted me inside, chubby-girl belly and all.

Outside the broken window, the shards held with duct tape, I could see a soft green meadow. Mist rose from the ground and drifted toward the coastal mountains. Stands of 100-year-old Douglas fir blanketed the hills. A small squadron of squirrels stampeded across the roof of our shed.

A platform bed took up most of the room inside. Beneath that bed Clint had stored his tent and tools, our duffle bags, and the heavy crates of books I'd shipped to Oregon before leaving New York. I never wanted to get out of that bed and I didn't have to. I didn't have to do anything: no expectations, no responsibilities, and nothing to succeed at. From the kitchen, a few hundred feet away, I could hear the murmur of voices, the banging of pots and pans, and the gravely whirr of the wheat grinder. On this, my first full day at Greenleaf, communal life was moving along without me.

Unexpectedly brushing my forehead with his soft lips, Clint bounded out of bed and hopped into his jeans. "Where are you going?"

I asked him, my voice heavy with sleep.

"Breakfast," he answered as he tied a double knot with the frayed laces of his old sneakers.

"Come back to bed."

"Can't, I'm the pancake man and it's time for pancakes."

I watched as he combed his long, chestnut hair, secured it with a thick rubber band, and walked out the door. The man truly enjoyed making others comfortable, I truly enjoyed comfort.

Above my head, in the corner between the window and the wood ceiling, a big black spider was sitting in her perfect web. I got out of bed, intent on destroying her world with a broom handle, but was afraid to get close. What if she were a jumping wolf spider and could land on my neck or face? The thought sent a shiver through my body and I decided to ask Clint to deal with her later. Besides, I'd crashed as soon as we'd come back from the falls, slept through dinner and was starving.

As I walked toward the farmhouse, a cluster of swallows descended from the eaves of an old barn. Watching their low-flying formation, I almost missed seeing a naked leg attached to a naked thigh. "Fuck me, fuck me, baby," it whispered from the tall grass. The rest of the body belonged to a naked woman making love to a naked man. Anyone walking along the road could not miss seeing them. The man's apple-tight buttocks slid up and down over the woman like a laconic yo-yo. Blood rushed through my body and I held my breath. How could they not know I was there? I was so close. If they didn't see or hear me, surely they could sense my presence. Then I realized—they knew I was watching. Maybe it turned them on, because it sure did me.

My conservative father, Michael R. Schlanger, always wore a tie and cufflinks. He was a proper man. At this moment, a vestige of his spirit turned my thinking around. This was wrong—spying on lovers during their most intimate moments. So, using the silent toe-to-heel First Nation's foot placement that I'd read about in *Mother Earth News*, I moved slowly and carefully toward the kitchen and breakfast. "Are you there yet, baby?" the male voice asked. It had the same lovely soft Texan twang I knew so well, much like Clint's, but not. I stopped in my Arapaho or Iroquois tracks as the woman let out a barrage of mousy yelps and thrust her tanned hairy legs into the air. The soles of her feet were gray with dust. This movement caused the man to bend forward onto his knees, up his rhythm, and savagely pound her into the ground. Grass shavings and dandelion wisps flew up around them. As the heat inside me rose, I understood this couple was "doing it in the road," a liberating activity first postulated by Ringo, John, Paul, and George, and perfected in the delicious wet mud at Max Yasgur's six-hundred-acre dairy farm. What I had in front of me were two acolytes, two newly committed followers to the Church of the All Natural. They wanted to be seen. Perhaps not interrupted, but definitely viewed.

The man suddenly flipped the woman over and faced me. I recognized him. "Hi," I said. He looked at me as if I had just peed on his shoe. This was Sky, a charter member of Southcoast, Clint's architectural collective. Aside from his pre-orgasmic open mouth, he was very cute—long, tan, and muscular. His face was chiseled and strong—not striking enough to be a lead in a Western or Space movie, but more like the knowledgeable second in command who everyone relies on. The devil in me, that uncontrollable little goblin of a girl, had to see how far these two would let me go:

"Hi. I'm Carol. I think we've met before in New Haven, but I'm not sure."

No response. I forged ahead:

"I was just wondering. Do you think there's poison oak around here? I'm hyper-allergic. When I was a kid I once got it so bad, it covered half my body and I couldn't stop scratching."

Sky lifted himself off the woman as if he were doing a slow push-up. His biceps bulged with male power. I hesitated. Should I continue? Tell them how I had to wear woolen mittens to prevent the pustules from breaking and spreading their poison...

"I was only about seven and to stop the itch my grandmother..."

"Hold the grandma story," Sky snarled, the furious look in his eyes edging out his Southern gentility. But there was no stopping me.

"...used her old home remedy: turpentine and brown soap."

"That's nice darlin', now fuck off," he finally snapped.

"All blessings...may the longtime sunshine and the clear light within you guide your way home," the woman added, sweetly maintaining her commitment to spirit.

"That too," Sky said.

I smiled and waved goodbye. They did not wave back.

As I walked toward the farmhouse my mind turned to the theatre... to acting—to how much I loved having an audience. Being on stage demanded attention just as much as fucking in the road. More even. Besides, exhibitionism was easy; showing your naked truth was hard. And suddenly, I missed all of it: the auditions, the applause, the lights, and even Marty, my agent. Marty believed in my talent. I hadn't had the heart to tell him I was leaving acting and New York indefinitely because I hadn't had the heart to tell myself. I'd be vacationing on a dude ranch—that's what I told him But Marty deserved the truth. He'd worked hard for me.

Inside the farmhouse, searching for a phone, I found Joey talking into a baby blue princess, the kind I'd begged for and received for my 14th birthday. Someone had drawn a peace sign on the inside disk. As soon as he saw me, Joey's faced paled. "Gotta go pal," he said into the receiver. "Someone's waiting," then hung up and whispered, " Please, Carol , don't tell anyone."

I didn't understand.

"Don't tell anyone what, Joey?"

"That I was on the phone. It's only for emergencies. Agung didn't want it put in because it connects us to the 'man.' But Louise said we had to, on account of Moonlove bein' pregnant."

"I won't tell, Joey," I said as I picked up the receiver and put it to my ear. "I promise."

It would be lunchtime in N.Y. and knowing Marty, he'd be at his big desk, eating his pastrami on rye with no mayo but lots of mustard.

"Hi Cynthia," I said in my best professional voice. "This is Carol Schlanger, is Marty in?" Cynthia was Marty's secretary. If Marty worked through lunch, so did she.

"Oh, hi Carol. It's so good to hear from you, Sweetie," she cooed. "Marty's been trying to reach you all day but he just stepped out for a smoke. I'll be sure to let him know you called."

"Thanks," I said and give her the farm number. I liked Cynthia. She had a little plastic hula girl on her desk that wiggled. It always put me at ease.

When I hung up, my stomach rumbled. I was hungrier than ever.

The kitchen was a flurry of activity and Clint was in flapjack mode. He was flipping the toasty golden orbs onto a big chipped platter emblazoned with the logo "U of O, Home of the Ducks." Like all the cups and plates at Greenleaf, it was made of what looked like either glass or clay. Wasteful paper or non-biodegradable plastic was taboo. Clink, clank, clink, clank—Louise was washing a mound of dishes at the big porcelain farm sink. The dishes hit the drying rack with record speed. Louise was a dishwashing sprinter. Wiping her hands on a faded American flag that hung from a towel rack, she greeted me with a hug, but her words held a slight censure. "So, Carol, you're finally here. I'm so glad!"

The straightest of all hippies, not only did Louise not smoke or drink but she had a waistline. Wearing a skimpy halter top, jean cut-offs and lace-up shit-kickers, her wavy dark blond hair fanned out below her shoulders. She looked sexy and powerful—a girl commando, a pioneering sabra—forging a new life in the land of food stamps and honey. After my expulsion, while the four of us still lived in New Haven, Clint and I had crashed for weeks at the large, comfortable apartment she shared with Agung. Both had been the most generous of hosts. At Greenleaf, it seemed they were carrying on that tradition but with a lot more people.

"Try a dollop of this," Louise said, handing me a quart-sized ball jar filled with a thick homemade yogurt. "We cooked it in the sun from scratch. It goes great with this," she added, feeding me a spoonful of her still-warm peach jam. "Oh, my God, Louise," I squealed, "it's amazing—tart, sweet, and creamy." Louise beamed. You had only to appreciate her cooking and she was yours. Louise was also the master planner of the garden, creating her own vegetable city. I knew this because taped to the farmhouse's ancient avocado green refrigerator was a layout of the garden, proudly signed "designed by Louise."

At Yale, she'd been a student of city planning, but had never planned on dropping acid and being swept off her feet by her brilliant, persuasive stoner husband. A community organizer and political activist on "The Hill," Agung identified with and was respected by New Haven's black and brown community. Too bad for Louise he came without a blueprint. She was a forthright but naïve Jewish girl from Cleveland who, although identifying as a radical feminist, still shaved her legs. She had married Agung because he'd told her that he'd be deported once he left grad school, and she'd believed him. She also believed that Agung's charisma was steeped in honesty and self-sacrifice. It had always been obvious to me, a woman who recognized great acting, that what Agung loved more than the truth was control: to run the show. He was a little bit Hugh Hefner, a little bit Chairman Mao.

"Have a seat," Clint said and pointed me toward the huge oak slab table adjacent to the kitchen. The massive table was roughhewn, flanked by long wooden benches. Right next to my plate, I found a week-old copy of the Eugene *Register Guard.* Before I had a chance to look at the front page, he poured me a cup of his strong cowboy coffee—boiling water and grinds filtered through thin towels. I followed the assured movement of his wrist as he raised the blue-flecked enamel pot. His gesture was so elegant that it made feel like a princess. One sip and I had a buzz, but the heat of it caused a throbbing in my damaged tooth. When that sensation died down, I tried again and jumpstarted my brain.

In the news: *Apollo 15* had safely returned to earth after landing on the moon, the ERA had still not passed, and George Shade, a former Eagle Scout from Veneta, had been run over by his own tractor. A celebration of his life was being held at the local Lions Club. I turned to my primary interest: the real estate section. In Oregon, paradise was for sale. Working farms, river frontage acreage, ocean views, orchards, and timber were all up for grabs and by New York standards, at astonishingly cheap prices. I felt like the lone customer at a *Klein's* bargain basement blowout and was ready to grab whatever I could get my hands on. What I craved was a beautiful, life-giving plot with rich loamy soil and clear water on which Clint and I could stake our lives. It was the American pioneering dream, and now, a hundred and fifty years later, it was mine. Just having that dream and the ability to fulfill it put me in a class so privileged that I was blind to the fact I was there.

"Good morning, Carol," Agung called out to me. He sat at the far end of the table stuffing a half-full Dewar's bottle with bud, creating a whiskey-infused cannabis blend to be added to the group storehouse of mint, ginger, and Cointreau-flavored choices. Well, I thought, you can take the boy out of the Ivy League but you can't take the Ivy League out of the boy. I remembered a night in New Haven, when he treated both Clint and me to a steak dinner at Mory's, Yale's iconic restaurant. There, between his Slivovitz neat, Clint's Heinekens, and my Shirley Temple, Agung revealed a deep dark secret of his privileged past, something he'd never want his Black Panther colleagues to know: He'd been chauffeured to his exclusive Jakarta prep school in the family limo. The Black Power movement was into Revolution, not servitude disguised as service.

The month before, while Agung, Louise, and Clint and I were protesting at an anti-war demonstration in Washington D.C, Agung noticed his old girlfriend and pointed her out to me. He'd been in love with her before Louise. Crowned with a monster Afro, his Ex was a tall ebony beauty in army fatigues with a strong, warrior stance. Catching sight of Agung, she thrust her fist in the air. He returned the Black Panther, 'Power to the People' gesture as if it were a kiss. Louise saw the interchange and smiled—but not happily.

In New Haven, in restaurants, on the street, at the movies, Agung was continually approached by persons of color and thanked for his community efforts. They knew of him by name and shouted it like a drumbeat: "Hey, man! Hey, Agung! Hey, brotha!" He ate it up. At Greenleaf, Agung infused the communal vibe the way he infused his weed, with something stronger. Like on "The Hill" in New Haven, where he organized and led, what Agung suggested, went. At Yale, he and Louise were just good friends to hang with, but on this commune, they were the muscle couple. It suited them, but not me. Status-wise, I no longer felt their equal and instead felt more child than adult.

Not yet seated at the breakfast table, a slender man was strumming a guitar in the adjacent living-room and gyrating along with *Honky Tonkin'*, an old Hank Williams tune. Froggie had a shiny rope of black hair that reached his waist. His pegged pants legs hit just above his ankles, making his look a cross between hippie and Appalachian hillbilly. At Yale, as an undergrad on scholarship, he'd dropped out and was now, at 20, prime draft material. His steel guitar had no strings.

As I considered Froggie's moderately insane behavior, a girlish giggle blew across the kitchen. The laughter, I decided, could not have come from Louise; it was too soft and saccharine. It had to come from the kind of woman I couldn't stand—the kind that dotted each "i" with a heart and had never read Kafka.

Cassy Jane, a pretty, pug-nosed blond who had grown up on her parents' bean and corn farm just outside of Eugene, was frying slabs of bacon over the electric stove. Apple-tinged smoke filled the room. When not turning the bacon, Cassy Jane cuddled up with her boyfriend, Pete, who I knew from Clint's beloved Southcoast Collective—a Texas offshoot of the famous Ant Farm. Pete stood behind CassyJane, his arms around her waist, looking both amused and satisfied.

"Hey, howdy Carol," Pete said, momentarily switching his focus in my direction until Cassy Jane slapped him playfully and whispered something in his ear. Their little adolescent duet annoyed me. Maybe it was because she wore a flowery 1940s style apron and nothing else. Her tight little butt peeked from the folds of the cotton material like a performer waiting for her entrance. Cassy Jane pranced toward me. Her big blue eyes were unfocused, her stare a little left of center.

"You wanna try some?" she asked, holding the dripping slice directly under my nose. It was thicker than any bacon I'd ever seen. "Comes offa my uncle's hog farm in Medford," she continued. "We got plenty to go round."

It was crispy fantastic. Everything pork had to offer.

I sat down at the massive dining table, which overflowed with a medley of Louise's jams and jellies: sour apple and quince, fig, blueberry, blackberry, strawberry, peach, and pear. All were set in ball jars accompanied by dark bread fresh out of the oven, sweet butter, eggs, and Clint's perfect flapjacks. An insanely opulent meal was being handed to me on a platter. No rushing to the 8th Avenue Deli because all I could find in the fridge was a crusty can of sardines; no waiting in line at the EZ coffee shop for my hit of java, dry toast, and dirty egg.

That morning, which I was told happened most mornings, visitors sat with stupefied faces at the breakfast table. They were friends of friends or passing hitchhikers who could not believe their luck. At Greenleaf, no guest was ever turned away. All were welcomed to stay and to share. Louise placed herself at the end of the bench, nearest the sink and stove so she could easily jump up and serve. Cassy Jane and Lila flanked me on either side. Along with her partner Sky, Lila, whom I'd last seen butt-naked in the dirt, was wearing softly flowing Yogic white. Leading a discussion on astrological birth control, she held her back ramrod straight and spoke in a voice so calm it agitated me. "It makes beautiful sense," Lila cooed. "Our moon cycles are attached to the sea and the stars, the waxing and the waning of the celestial."

Understandable: The sea was feminine; the moon affected her tides. They were girly linked.

Louise tore off a chunk of warm bread and slathered it with butter. "It's too woo-woo for me," she said. "I'm sticking with the pill."

"The pill causes cancer," Cassy Jane said.

"You don't know that," Louise responded.

"Yes, I do. The pill isn't natural."

"Just because it's not natural, CassyJane," Louise said, "doesn't mean it will give you cancer."

Cassy Jane scrunched up her pretty face and pouted, "Well, I think it does."

"Anyway," Lila added, staying on point, "you abstain from sex when the sun and the moon repeat the exact angle they made with each other at the moment of your birth."

"I don't know what time I was born," I said as I scratched a mosquito bite on my arm till it bled. "My mother told me that when it happened, she wasn't looking at her watch."

"Usually it's on your birth certificate, Carol," Louise told me.

"It's not."

"Then, astrologically speaking," she said, "you're fucked."

I was feeling a little cheated by the heavens when Sky and Joey, like knaves at a medieval banquet, entered carrying a gigantic salmon on a three-foot cedar shake. The table drew in a collective breath. Frogs trumpeted a fanfare and humming birds buzzed outside the open window. The fish, frozen from the last year's catch, had been part of Greenleaf's payback for helping a neighboring fish farmer line his pond. The Texans, Sky and Clint, genetically programmed for outdoor cooking, had smoked it over dry oak on a converted oil drum. I was stunned. This was only breakfast. What, I asked myself, could be in store for diner...a whole pig? Four and twenty blackbirds baked in a pie? I was envisioning oysters on the half shell when the phone rang.

No one moved and the ringing did not stop. Agung scowled and Louise looked as if she'd swallowed a whole lemon. Exhibiting a slight tick, Froggie pushed himself from the table and crossed into the adjacent living room. After a moment he called out, "Miss Schlanger, it's for you." Under his breath, but loud enough for everyone to hear, Agung said, "Louise, I told you, that thing doesn't belong here." For a split second, I thought he was talking about me.

Marty, my agent, was on the other end. I'd always been thrilled to hear his voice, a voice that held the promise of infinite possibilities—but not this time; this time I dreaded what I was I going to tell him, dreaded his response.

But before I could say a word, he cut me off: "Carol, you've got an audition on Thursday...for Broadway again." My stomach did a backflip. Broadway! Another shot.

"But Marty, I'm still in Oregon."

"Yeah. Sure you are sweetheart. It's for *Two Gentlemen of Verona,* John Guare's new musical. It's a great part, almost a lead. You have to sing, but not legit —just talk-sing—real natural, like Brecht. You'll knock 'em dead. I know you will."

"Thanks Marty. I can, I know I can!" I answered as my pulse pounded in my ears, "I'm great at talk-singing!"

"So, get on a plane as fast as you can."

"Oh God, Marty. I love John Guare!"

My throat tightened as my mind raced back to the concrete and taxi land of opportunity. I could stay on key if I had loud music behind me, preferably an entire orchestra. I had to go. Yes, I was going! If I didn't get the part, I'd come right back and if I did....

"I'm coming, Marty. I'll be there."

"Well, sweetheart, that's fantastic."

From the other room, CassyJane's kittenish giggle clawed its way toward me. Auditions were so stressful. They took total focus and preparation...

"Marty, how long do they think it will run?"

Anyone who knew anything about Broadway, knew a show could run for a day or ten years. There was no second-guessing a hit or a flop.

"Carol," he snapped, "just start packing. I've been putting them off."

"Marty, can you Express me the script?" (e-mail would take twenty more years to arrive)

"No can do. By the time it gets there, you'll have to be on your way."

His voice sounded weary. Marty never stopped working and smoked a pack a day.

"Marty, please, can I think about it and call you back?"

I was falling into an abyss, blanking out. A dirt-yellow strip of fly paper hung from the ceiling. It was covered with flies, too many to count. One...two...three...

"Sorry pet, I need an answer right now. You gonna get there or not?"

For weeks I'd sat in my apartment, waiting for the phone to ring, waiting for another chance. Now on my second day in Greenleaf, the call had come too soon and too late. Four flies...six...seven...eight...

"I can't Marty. I want to, but I can't."

"Well, sweetheart," he said, his voice becoming high-pitched, "you take care now."

"Marty, wait..."

"And you have fun in Hooterville riding those ponies." And Marty was gone. My heart pounded in my chest. I'd crossed my own Rubicon.

Back at the dining table, a line had formed in front of the salmon and everyone was politely serving themselves.

"Who was that on the phone?" Clint asked me.

Convinced I was starving, I cut in line behind him, edging out Froggie.

"My agent," I answered. Froggie tapped me on the shoulder and smiled. He said nothing but his eyes were murderously calm. Agung was his patron, supplying him with funds to build his get-away, escape-the-draft schooner to sail away to Indonesia. The boat, almost finished, sat in the garage.

"What did your agent want?" Clint continued, his voice rising. Clint did not like to raise his voice; it was an Episcopalian thing, ingrained in him by his father Orin, the Priest, and his mother, Earlene, the organist and white-gloved church lady.

"He wanted me to fly back to New York for an audition."

"What did you tell him?"

For the first time something in Clint's tone frightened me. It felt controlling. As if I were being interrogated for a misdemeanor. What, I asked myself, had I stepped into?

Men. Men. And more men.

"I said 'no,'" I reassured him, and allowing my New York reflex to take over, I elbowed Joey out of my way and moved further ahead. It felt good. Like the old me, the me who could get where she was going when she had to. Sky, the man who I'd interrupted mid-coitus, gave me a long, contemptuous stare. I got his message. He and Lila were Bodhisattvas of the earth, enlightened beings who purposely placed their serene, tantric selves behind everyone else—the last in the line. I, however, was a glutton, a lower life form, a troglodyte. And something even worse—a troglodyte without an agent.

"You eat like this all the time?" I asked Lila as I passed by her with my full plate. She looked at me with her swimming pool blue eyes and said, "Carol, stay in the now." In the now, I wanted to tell her to stick it where her astrological sun sign didn't shine.

Did I really care what these long-haired cowboys and their moderately annoying girlfriends thought of me? Yes. I did. As my cracked tooth throbbed, a sick feeling resurfaced: I was all wrong in this place, on this loosely bound commune in God -knows-where, Oregon. The feeling was familiar. It had hit me many times in my 23 years. The first, when I was just four and had been enrolled in Manhattan's exclusive *Lycee Francais* by my upwardly mobile but clueless mother. The only child in my kindergarten class from a non-French speaking home, the other children, most bilingual, understood what I could not. I tried to crack the code, but it was too hard and after a month, I was politely asked to leave ("*Au revoir mon petit bête!*") and never return. Not only did I not speak French, but I had caused a major boycott in the cafeteria by denouncing, in English, canned vegetables as poisonous: "They have chemicals inside that will kill you!" I'd also disrupted nap time by repeatedly refusing to lie down: "Don't you people understand English? I'm not sleepy!" Maybe I was a little bratty, but I was a brat who stood her ground.

Clint must have sensed I was having a hard time because he threw his arm around my neck and drew me into a headlock. Sweetly caveman-ish, that position spoke volumes. It said: "This woman is mine. She's a handful but I've got her under control." I wanted to kiss him and kick him at the same time. His protection was demeaning. Looking out from under his armpit, I saw Sky's, Pete's and Froggie's approving faces. Their macho indulgence, even though it made my skin crawl, gave me hope that we'd get along—but if that didn't happen, I'd live with it. I had just as much right to be at Greenleaf as they did. I was with the man I loved.

CHAPTER 7

Time Slips into the Future

August – Early September 1971

The 1960s (and early 70s) represented the last burst of the human being before he was extinguished.
ANDRE GREGORY, *My Dinner with Andre*

Days drifted into weeks into months and every day was Sunday. Relaxation replaced time. Basic felt good. Free felt right. The soles of my feet had hardened into flesh leather and had grown in size from a nine to a ten. Barefooted, I could walk on pebbles and even rocks without pain. The rest of my body had changed, too. My underarm flab had solidified into what was looking like muscle. Bras were a distant memory. Free at last, my large breasts jiggled when I ran—so much so that I had to cup them in my hands even though it cut down my speed.

The luxury of my new life was beyond seductive. Clint and I were on a hippie honeymoon: eat—swim—smoke—fuck—sleep—eat. All day, every day, I floated in an undreamed-of satisfied space and the farm no longer felt alien. The leaky toilet and the bare light bulbs were just there, ugly but useful. It was the beauty and sensuality of the outdoors that mattered: The great green forest, the soft, inviting pastures, and most of all Louise's lush garden pregnant with lettuces, kale, spinach, eggplants, zucchini, peppers, broccoli, cauliflower, and tomatoes. Seeing them in their well-tended artful rows sent peace and joy down into my belly and up my spine. If there was such a thing as cabbage and string bean nirvana, I'd found it.

Throughout September, while the inmates of Attica prison in Upstate New York rioted and met death by order of a wildly paranoid President Nixon and his lunatic, homophobic, FBI henchman, J. Edgar Hoover, I floated down Lake Creek, naked and stoned, having only to pluck fat blackberries from the banks. My molecules were realigning toward bliss. Unlike Kafka's *Gregor Samsa* who awoke to find he'd become a giant cockroach, I awoke in this golden time to find I'd become a giant orifice—always open, moist, and ready.

The counter-culture also flowered. George Harrison hosted the Concert for Bangladesh at Madison Square Garden; John Denver found the place he belonged via *Country Roads*, and Gloria Steinem addressed the first National Women's Political Caucus. I'd left behind the America I knew and was growing younger with no responsibilities, no television, and no mainstream newspapers or magazines. A cartoon poster published by satirist Gilbert Shelton called *Workers of the World Relax* resonated with my own thinking. Along with thousands of other formally middle-class overachievers with well-defined futures, I was sure that by doing "nothing" I was standing in the way of the Rat Race and changing its entire direction. As I grew accustomed to life with no constraints, endless marijuana and love making, my career ambitions dissolved into Lake Creek. I no longer needed to "make it," because I was already there.

On the other hand...

Louise, like Clint, was constantly busy and worked faster and more decisively than I did. When we picked blackberries, her bucket always filled twice as fast as mine. Her hands were capable whirlwinds. The woman even organized weekly trips to the laundromat. Because of Louise we were a counter-culture anomaly: hippies with clean sheets. But no actress, not even a former one, likes standing in the wings. At Greenleaf, like in the theatre, the whole was bigger than any one of its parts. Each person's role defined who they were. I floated, hoping to fit in somewhere, but landing nowhere. Louise, unlike me, planned and executed and I grew jealous of her consistent offerings. She was an innovator who did everything right, while I hardly did anything at all. My endless leisure time became both enjoyable and degrading.

Stop!

Hadn't I come to Oregon to revolutionize my life, to change and to grow? No. Not really. But in the now, in the moment, "being there" as Ram Dass suggested, I knew I had to develop a skill, something simple and necessary that said I was there and a part of the whole. But what?

Cassy Jane had used my hairbrush and misplaced it—again. I'd looked everywhere: under the sink, (cobwebs!) in her bedding, and on the pantry shelves. When I got to the front porch, instead of finding my hairbrush, I discovered Sky grinding wheat berries. His body rocked back and forth with the machine's cast iron handle. The wheat berries sliding down the metal spout sounded like falling rain. At the end of their run they were transformed into flour. The metamorphosis was magical: frogs into princes, straw into gold, berries into wheat. "Can I try it?" I asked Sky, thinking this might be the job for me, my new calling. Yes, I could see myself as a miller, a provider of the staff of life: Biblical just like Ruth, Sarah, and Rebecca—a bountiful woman of grace draped in simple and humble, raw cotton.

"You bet, Carol," Sky said, flashing his cute alligator smile. "Give it your best shot."

As he stepped away from the grinder, gratitude welled up in me. Sky was encouraging me. He wanted me to succeed, to bask in the beauty of a job well done. I grabbed the handle; it fit snugly in my palm—a sure sign.

"Ya know," Sky said as I strained to move the metal gears, "I never planned to live on a commune either."

During Sky's undergrad years at Rice he'd been a beer-guzzling Phi Lambda Pi frat boy. At CCNY in psychology 101, I had argued that Freud was a sexist and his theories were bogus. Now Sky was a spiritual seeker of exactitude and transcendence. Now I was a woman who wore no underwear.

"You didn't?" I said while exerting all the muscle power I possessed—nothing budged.

"No, I didn't, but when it happened," he continued, "it seemed like the most natural and logical way to live."

Sky had never meant to live on a commune. Well, who did? No one who took her SAT exams, believing that her life and future depended on achieving a high score. No guidance counselor ever suggesting that somewhere, somehow, cooperation might outdistance competition.

"Throw your whole weight into it," Sky instructed. Placing one foot in front of the other and leaning in, I did exactly as I was told. The handle moved for one rotation and then refused to budge. I tried harder—and harder. A shock wave jumped into my lower back, but I refused to give up. Then my coccyx turned to molten jelly and my back went into full spasm—I gave up.

To hell with Ruth and Rebecca. They were dead anyway.

Bent over like a coat hanger I was trying to straighten myself out when Louise zipped by. Louise never walked. She zipped. Dragging a black plastic garbage bag stuffed with dirty laundry, she forged ahead powered by her eight-cylinder metabolism. Joey followed. Reveling in middle-class martyrdom, I ignored my pain and called out to her, asking if she needed my help. Yes, she answered. She sure did.

Louise was driving. I'd swallowed two aspirin without water and because there was no ice in the freezer, I sat next to her in Clint's truck with a package of frozen liver stuck to my back. It was defrosting and dripping blood down my buttocks and onto someone's Bob Marley's "*Soul Rebel*" tee shirt. The thing smelled like, well, liver, but I didn't care, it was working. My pain was going away. As we drove along Route 36, passing rundown houses, their scrubby yards filled with junked cars and forever-docked boats, my excitement grew; I was taking a giant step into my communal future. I'd never done my own laundry before, much less for eleven. This was epic.

The *Soak and Suds* was a clammy place, filled with chipped benches and abandoned copies of *Good Housekeeping* and *Cosmo* magazines. A vending machine sold miniature boxes of *Tide* and *Duz*. On this autumn afternoon, the rumbling room was empty; but in winter, I had heard, it would fill to capacity with folks needing to stay warm.

While Joey and Louise unloaded, I checked out the laundromat's soul: the bulletin board. Covering half a wall it was filled with "For Sale" and "Want" ads. Most were hand-written on three by five cards and held by pushpins: "For Sale—Two Himalayan Alpaca Lamas, non-spitting and friendly"; "Wanted—doublewide trailer; will trade '69 Harley Davidson chopper and ten cords firewood"; "Start your own business with the magic weight loss worm from Mexico—results guaranteed." I'd been able to drop out into a hippie lifestyle because I had been born into so much. The people behind those notices hadn't dropped out of anything because they'd never been able to drop in. Reading their writing was like peeking into the darkened windows of their tumbledown houses, each illuminated by the blue light of relentless television.

"Carol!" Louise's voice honked. "Do you have quarters? We're short." As I filled the coin slot with change, my mind turned to the magic worm—probably a tapeworm. I had seen a picture of one in an old *National Enquirer*. A lady in Des Moines pulled a twenty-footer out of her butt. The thing had a head and eyes and the article said that if you didn't kill its head, the body would grow back bigger than ever.

The worm was still on my mind when Joey tapped me on the shoulder to help him fill the jumbo washer. It was elephantine: metallic gray and three times the size of the other machines. I'd just clicked open its latch when I saw the couple walk through the front door. Looking like they belonged on a billboard, they were both fiftyish, trim, with short graying hair and crisp, bright clothing. Through the *Soak and Suds* picture window I could see their parked Winnebago. It was as crisp and clean as they were. Our funky appearance obviously repulsed the woman and, never taking her protective eye off her giant box of *Cheer*, she crossed the room to unload her wash into the machine next to our jumbo—she had no other choice, it was the only one not in use. The man, who insanely enough wore a bright blue sports jacket, appeared nonplussed…as if he weren't doing wash at all, but instead golfing on some distant course.

In laundromat time, it was sixteen quarters and six dimes later.

Tribal family pride swept over me as I helped Louise and Joey fold and pack up our clean, dry laundry. Louise's speed hastened my own. When we folded the sheets, we each grabbed an end and then met in the middle. The sisterly action, sweet and effective, first drew us together and then pulled us apart. The sheets themselves came out smooth and symmetrical—exquisite in a clean-sheet kind of way.

I was trying to figure out how to fold the arms of a brown Gold Beach Forest Ranger shirt when the Winnebago Lady grabbed it out of my hands and screamed, "Hey there Missy, that's ours!"

"Sorry," I said, "I thought it was ours."

"Sure you did!" she said, her face so close to mine I could see the age spots on her cheeks and then she turned away to claw her way through our pile of folded laundry.

"This isn't yours either!"

She clutched a polyester blouse to her breast as if finding her long-lost kidnapped child.

"You hippies are all goddam thieves! I oughta call the Law!"

While gesturing with one hand for Winnebago woman to take it, with the other Joey dropped a ten-dollar bill on top of the dryer closest to her. "We're so sorry, Lady," he said softly, bowing his head like a penitent. "Please forgive us, we wuz so wrong." A kid from the streets, Joey knew how to beg for forgiveness. And he'd said "us," even though the mistake had been all mine. Joey wouldn't let me be the fall guy. He was bigger than that. But where, I had to ask myself, had that ten-dollar bill come from? Joey, I was certain, was penniless and his bribe was the kind of smooth move I might have expected from Agung, but not from a kid who'd lived his life scrambling for cash and never giving away what little he had.

The woman carefully hung a dry brown and white, polka-dotted blouse on a hanger covered in brown and white wool. The matchy-matchiness of it was, in my Manhattan 55th and Sutton Place mind, right up there with scrapbooking and coupon collection. Keeping her eye on the prize, the woman silently pocketed Joey's cash and continued folding her laundry as if we were no longer there. Looking straight ahead, Joey and Louise wheeled the rest of our newly folded and bagged laundry out the laundromat door and towards our truck. I followed close behind.

"Fuck 'em." I whispered to Louise.

"Right on, Carol. Fuck 'em!"

Now I remembered—I loved Louise. We were sister-hippies, not of the straight and narrow world and united in its prejudice against us. But Joey. Where'd he get that ten?

"Her husband slipped it to me," he explained when I asked, "and he gave me another five not to tell anyone where it came from."

So, this was their little ritual. Whatever mistake Winnebago Lady made, Winnebago man paid for. How deep their dysfunction went... only their steering wheel knew for sure. Marriage, I thought to myself, could drive anyone crazy, especially if the lone and isolated couple was stuck inside an RV, always on the move but going nowhere.

On our drive back to Greenleaf, the three of us were silent. The only sound was the THUMP of the old Chevy's wheels as it bounced along the old highway. Hearing it kept me from falling asleep. While my head rested uncomfortably on the closed passenger window, a distant memory came:

I am home from second grade—sick and not sick. The radiator in my bedroom is THUMPING. It is a freezing cold winter's day in Manhattan and my prewar building's boiler is overheating. My mother knocks on my door, but because I don't answer, she pushes her way through the chair barricade that I'd set up to keep her out and tells me if I want to stay home from school, I have to clean up my room. She works all day in Kubies, our family health food store, and has not had the time or energy to teach me how to clean anything.

My mother, father, and I live on the 15th floor of 360 East 55th Street. Our apartment overlooks the East River. In my bedroom, the floor, the bed, and the windowsills are carpeted with my clothes, comics, toys, and Mars Bars wrappers. I do not understand how to do as she asks. I've never hung anything up or put anything away—whatever I drop on the floor stays there for Beatrice, our maid, to pick up. When my mother leaves, I push open my bedroom window and toss out whatever I don't want. Things look clean and tidy. It seems like a wonderful solution.

That evening my mother comes home from work. She's sweaty underneath her long, black mink coat. In one hand she holds a bag of Chinese take-out and in the other a headless Ginny Doll she's picked up off 1st Avenue. Kenny, our doorman, she says, was grazed by my wooden-wheel Tonka Toy—it bounced off the awning and onto his epaulet. He has told her he was lucky it didn't put out his eye. When my mother tells me this, I feel guilty because I like Kenny; he always lets me into our apartment when I lose my key. However, I have no clue as to what else I could have done and tell her so. She slips out of her coat, tosses it on a chair, and feels my head. I'm not sick anymore she tells me and laughs. She thinks I'm funny.

Beatrice comes in the next morning. She is surprised to find that my room is so neat.

CHAPTER 8

Heaven's Door

Mid-September, 1971

Earth teach me quiet ~ as the grasses are still with new light.
A UTE PRAYER

Ineptitude haunted me like a ghost.

The only place my mind did not fragment and run off in different directions had been on stage. There, I knew where I was going. At Greenleaf, my self-worth stock plummeted and I felt more less-than and less more-than. Not so with Clint. It was as if we were on a see-saw. In New York, he'd been the weight and I'd risen to the top, but at Greenleaf his head was way above mine. The balance also changed with Agung. He had become the "say so." I first understood it when he insisted the telephone Louise had installed in case of emergency be removed. They argued. Agung called for a general meeting.

I didn't know Greenleaf had general meetings.

"Ladies," he said, pulling at his eyebrows, "there is no excuse for letting the oppressor into our lives—not now, not ever! They will have records, they will know who we talk to and what we say. Louise sweetie, you're not in Cleveland anymore." Louise's face caved in and her shoulders slumped as she folded into a smaller woman. The vote was eight to two. Everyone else, Clint included, sided with Agung. It made no sense. Our gas and electricity were both supplied by big corporate powers. The decision felt democratically oppressive. Besides, I loved telephones.

Another blow—whenever I did the dishes, Agung redid them. No matter how hard I tried to meet his standards, I left little bits attached—oatmeal or salad, chicken, or cauliflower. It was hard to tell. Watching his aristocratic, soapy hands redo what I'd done, was demoralizing. Even if I offered to do them a second a time, he refused me. There was no arguing with Agung. At Harvard, he'd been captain of the debate team. At CCNY, I'd played *Anfisa* in Chekov's *Three Sisters*; an 80-year-old Russian servant with arthritis.

Agung held up a piece of steel wool and said, "To clean a fork, Carol, you have to get between the prongs."

A prince was teaching me the finer points of dishwashing, so even though it went against my nature, I listened and followed his instructions.

"Excellent," he said on inspection. "Soon, who knows—you might even be able to tackle a plate." I wanted to hit him. But didn't.

Agung's assured, altruistic presence raised the whole Greenleaf vibe; but when he belittled me, I believed him.

☾

It was in mid-September when the tomato stalks had turned brown but the tomatoes themselves were still ripening that I heard Clint rev up his big BMW motorcycle. (He'd dragged it across country, hitched to his Falcon.) I loved that Rrrrrrr sound. It meant adventure. I was on the back seat, my feet on the rear pedals, my arms around his waist. We were on our way to Jack Monroe's, the local junk and car parts dealer in nearby Deadwood. Our mission: to buy a second-hand carburetor for Clint's truck and a used rearview mirror for Agung's VW van. We never bought anything new. New meant overpriced and too expensive. Feet from our destination, Clint stopped the bike, turned to me and said, "Hon, Jack's backcountry, and not used to dealing with women—hippie women especially. So best leave the talkin' up to me."

"Not used to dealing with women." The words infuriated me but I knew they were true, so I maintained my cool; but it was like wearing a hijab around my heart...and mouth.

Piled up against the dark beauty of a forest, Jack Monroe's mound of junk cars and parts was intrusive and surreal. A native Oregonian, Jack had lost both his right hand and his left eye in logging accidents. He wore no patch and his exposed socket was mottled—a skin crater. A steel hook was attached to his right wrist. Jack's two grown sons, Buck and Vern, stood behind him looking country mean and stupid. Neither acknowledged us and each was missing a finger: Buck his thumb and Vern his middle. I was to learn that their fingers had been severed while setting choker; a difficult job where a man wound a steel cable around a log and then hoisted it up into the air with a huge crane.

Jack's wife Lulu weighed over four hundred pounds and seldom, if ever, got up from the couch on the front porch of their trailer. The whole Monroe family lived on a diet of potato chips, Coke, beef jerky, and Budweiser.

Dismounting, I stepped onto the newly tarred Deadwood Creek Road and a chunk of it stuck to my sandal. Jack was rummaging through his metal pile and singing, *How Much Is that Doggie in the Window,*" in a falsetto. A breeze blew across his body and came toward me. His stench was so overwhelming I had to step away. So as not to appear rude, I removed the tar from the bottom of my Birkenstock with a twig. As I stood on one foot, he moved toward me. His breath...his breath... was so bad that I could not hold back, "Mr. Monroe, hope ya don't mind me sayin', but you smell like hell after a shit storm." *I'd made that one up on the spot and felt dern good about it.*

Buck and Vern ambled toward us—their faces somber. Jack said nothing but ran his one eye slowly up and down my body. I held my ground even though it felt as if I was being eye molested. Local men thought all our women easy and our men weak. Buck held a jackhammer at his side and Vern a giant pliers. Either tool, if used as a weapon, could inflict terrible harm.

"Funny you should bring that up, little lady," Jack said and broke his stare to bend down and lift a piece of machinery that lay on the ground. As he hoisted it up onto his shoulder, the thing dripped black gunk on his neck."My wife's bin buggin' me 'bout the same damn thing."

Buck spit a wad on the ground while Vern opened and closed the pliers. Clint gave me the stink eye.

"Well, Jack," I said cheerily, "that sure is coincidental."

Jack grinned, exposing brown teeth, and wiped the black goo from his neck with the tail end of his shirt. His sons, instead of applying torture, walked right past us toward the skeletal remains of a Willis jeep. Buck slammed its undercarriage with his jackhammer and Vern pried off the hood. Each then grabbed an end and heaved the big piece of metal into the junk pile. It flew through the air and landed with a metal-on-metal crash. Vern then gave Clint and me a thumbs-up (Vern still had both of his).

I'd been wrong—they didn't want to hurt us. They liked us. They liked me!

Jack, whose whole life was junk and grease, was tickled a young woman took an interest in him. And his scan of my body wasn't sexual; he just had a weak-muscled, wandering eye that that moved in its socket like a pinball. The smelly fellow was a lamb in skunk's clothing and surely deserved the best advice I could give: "Bet if you took a bath, Jack, you'd put a wag in her tail."

"Wag in her tail." I'd made that one up, too. When it came to improvisation, I had talent.

Clint kicked at the ground. He was far from happy.

"You think it'll help?" Jack asked me, his face as helpless as a dirty baby's.

"I sure do, Jack," I reassured him. "Us womenfolk are real sensitive."

I was about to launch into a folksy diatribe on how unchecked depression could lead to morbid obesity when Clint stopped me. "How much for the carburetor, Jack?"

"It's on the house," Jack said as he winked at me, the grease crinkling up in his cheeks. "And tell ya what else I'm gonna do," he continued. "Yer little yeller fella came 'round here t'other day askin' for a rearview. Didn't have one then—do now. Gonna throw that in free and clear."

"You sure, Jack?" Clint said in disbelief. Jack had a reputation for giving nothing away.

"Sure," Jack said, looking at me with what can only be described as admiration. "Glad to hear what a woman's got to say. Real helpful."

I'd done it—finally found my calling. With my ability to bridge cultural boundaries, I'd exchanged my perspective for much needed stuff worth big bucks—anywhere from fifty to a hundred. My skill as an empath, as an actress and as a woman who did not shy away from truth had actually worked. Like sunshine after a rain, Clint's disapproval turned to delight. If there was one thing he loved, it was a freebie. He wiped off his new carburetor and tied it and the "rear view" to the passenger seat. "Nice work, babe!" he shouted at me above the starting roar of his bike's engine. Zooming home, I couldn't have been happier if I'd been in a stretch limo on my way to the Academy Awards.

Five and a half miles later and back at Greenleaf, Clint was setting his kickstand when Agung ran toward us holding a pitchfork. He was flushed with excitement. Scores of salmon, he told us, were swimming upstream. All the other men were wading in the creek, feverishly spear fishing. Agung barely noticed the rear view mirror he'd asked for when Clint handed it to him, but when Clint told him that Jack had given it to us for free, Agung's eyebrows shot up to meet his forehead. He was beyond amazed.

"Carol got him to do it," Clint continued. "It was like she hypnotized him or somethin'."

Agung looked at me as if he'd never seen me before and handed over his pitchfork. "Here, Carol," he said. "You spear yourself one of those big Sockeye."

If there was one thing I never considered doing, aside from hunting Bengal tiger, it was spear fishing. I'd rather watch and told Agung so. Taking me at my word, both he and Clint waded into Lake Creek to join the rest of the men.

"Good luck guys!" I called out after them.

"Shhhhh!" Joey, who was close to the shoreline, whispered, "You'll scare them."

"Who?"

"The fish!"

I squatted on the bank not making a sound. The sun, blazing a blood orange, sank into the mountains. Watching Clint, Sky, Agung, Joey, Froggie, and Pete, their long hair flowing behind them, their tan, muscular bodies coiled, ready to skewer the migrating Chinook and Sockeye, I was thrown back in time. Surely, I thought, this was how it must have been when the Siuslaw tribe fished these waters, their copper skin glowing, their women close by, nursing papooses and beating their buckskins against the flat rocks. I'd read all about their native habitat on a placard at the state park.

My First Peoples reverie was cut short by Agung as he waded back toward me.

"Carol," he whispered, "did you hear that?"

"Hear what?" I whispered back. I'd heard nothing.

"Exactly," he said, switching his pitchfork from one hand to the other. "He has just passed."

"Who? I didn't see anyone, Aggie."

"A very old salmon, Carol. It made a high-pitched whistling sound as it went by. All the other bird and insect sounds suddenly stopped, as if in tribute to a dying warrior."

Aside from the flow of the creek, the silence was absolute—not a buzz, a whistle, nor a chirp. The men downstream were mute. Nature was saluting nature and Aggie had gone out of his way to share it with me—with me alone. I stared further out into the water and just below its surface, I saw them: some bright pink, some mottled, some gray with age—the salmon— all sluggishly swimming toward their end until a voice hastened their movement.

Then as suddenly as it began, the silence ended:

"I got one! I got one!" Clint shouted. A huge salmon thrashed on the end of his pitchfork, its eyes growing cloudy, its tail desperately jackknifing the air. Clint stood tall and let the fish stay skewered for all to see. Oh, yes. He was my fine, hand-eye coordinated man. Despite my former subscription to *Ms.* Magazine, my respect for the feminism of Bella Abzug, Germaine Greer, Gloria Steinem, and the dire warnings of my New York women's support group, my heart swelled with pride as I watched my brave provide.

The next big catch was Sky's. His salmon, a reddish-gray, evil-looking Chinook, was even larger than Clint's. On seeing Sky's Texan shit-eating grin, delight dropped from Clint's face. Men, I thought, they never let go of their "mine's-bigger-than-yours" competition. They were the Big Bang.

Our male population, without any female assistance, soon speared enough salmon to smoke and last us for months. But for me, the most important catch of that fall evening, when the last of the summer broccoli had balked, was mine. It wasn't a salmon. No, it was what Agung said as we gutted the fish, removing their innards for the chickens to gobble down: "Carol, you've got genius going for you; any woman who can charm a freebie off Jack—that's talent!" His words did not go undetected. Sky, Joey, Pete, and Froggie, also gutting and scaling, looked up at me with the kind of respect that felt like a standing ovation.

"Thanks Aggie," I said, while slitting a white fishy underbelly, "but you should have seen me as Marie in *Come Back Little Sheba*. I killed."

Of course, he had no idea what I was talking about.

CHAPTER 9

Ticket to Ride

October - November 1971

It's dangerous when people are willing to give up their privacy.
NOAM CHOMSKY

The sun disappeared and took my hippie honeymoon with it. With the Fall rains, what was once dry was now wet. In the limp days of early summer, before I'd landed at Greenleaf, Agung had put all his and Louise's cash into a teapot and declared it free for the taking. The expectation was that everyone else would be inspired to do the same. But, Louise told me, Agung had made the gesture without consulting her and had given away every penny she had. She'd freaked, but on thinking it over, decided combining everyone's cash promoted communal cohesiveness and her bitterness evaporated. Louise didn't always talk herself into things, but when she did, believed it entirely.

By the time I arrived, the kitty was stuffed—bills on the top, change on the bottom. With a chip at its lip the stout little pot sat on a kitchen shelf and gave the message we were conjoined—a family who cared for each other. But no one, even had they tried, could have matched Agung's relentless generosity. It was as if he couldn't wait to divest himself of anything that said he had more than the others. With a simple request or compliment, he'd give away whatever he owned as long as he didn't need it to survive.

A beautiful batik hung over his and Louise's bed. It depicted a peacock with its feathers fanned out in gold, green, and indigo. I made the mistake of admiring it and as soon as the words were out of my mouth, Agung took it down and gave it to me. Louise, close to tears, told me his mother had sent it to them from Bali as a wedding present. I tried to give it back but Agung wouldn't hear of it and promised Louise his mother would send another, even more magnificent. His family, he explained, had hundreds. Louise, I had a feeling, didn't believe him.

Folks delved into that teapot to buy anything from toothpaste to gasoline, no questions asked. Encouraged by Clint ("Come on Carol, it will come back to you twice over.") I contributed eighty dollars; all my ready cash. While waiting for my money to double, I held onto my own very private and secret stash. Not a soul knew about it and I kept it sewn up in the lining of my backpack so I would never be tempted to use it except for its designated purpose. It was a cashier's check for $3,500, everything I'd saved from my performance in a Draino commercial.

My mission in coming to Oregon, aside from cleaving to my hunky boyfriend, was to buy land, a beautiful piece that could sustain us. That hidden check was for a down payment. Because I would not and could not follow Agung's lead, I faced a vexing duality. I wanted to be a player in the new world of barter and love and still have some purchasing power. I didn't believe what the Weathermen believed, that "property was theft." No. Property was freedom. Property was independence. Fertile land, clean, clear water and fresh air was everything and what proper stewardship could bring. Having grown up between massive blocks of steel and concrete, just the sight of a patch of grass or a healthy tree promised something alive and not dead. But I'd been born of a hard-asset-loving woman and could not give up the liberty that having my own money allowed, and I didn't have to. We were anarchists. Our only law was that no one could tell anyone else what to do. I was living inside a paradox, my "I" becoming a '"we." It felt safe and warm to become pluralized, yet I held tight to being separate, to what belonged to me.

☾

It was when the cold fall nights forced wearing a jacket that Ed, an alcoholic friend of Joey's, took advantage of Greenleaf's open-door policy and came to stay. Too soon after his arrival, he dove into the teapot and helped himself to all our cash. No one tried to stop him.

That afternoon, Louise, always ahead of the curve, was wrapping jars of her fruit preserves to send back East for Christmas; Sky, Clint, Joey, Froggie, and Agung were embedding dime bags of their best weed into hollowed-out wax candles to be illegally mailed as gifts to friends and family; and Ed, capping off a week of drinking and smoking, dropped two huge kegs of beer onto the front porch and declared, "Party!"

Minutes later they roared in; a low-riding biker club from Illinois.

Ed had run into their number, about ten, in Eugene. One had been both his old high school buddy and former cellmate.

Alerted by their inescapable thunder, we gathered in the yard to watch them park their hogs. They looked like they'd jumped out of the pages of *The Fabulous Furry Freak Brothers* comics *(Spoing!)*. With their pot bellies, skinny legs, bulbous noses, and waterfall mustaches, they were repulsive in an appealing way. Ed threw his arms around his friend who wore a dirty bandana and big Carmen Miranda banana earrings. When the two men separated, Ed pointed to the back-porch shouting, "Knock yourselves out gents, it's on the house!" Agung gave Ed a hearty slap on the back and shook the skanky biker's hand. It was as if Agung and Ed were smiling for an invisible camera and running for office on the same ticket. Ed's low-riding biker pal was so skinny that his leather pants and chaps sunk well below his butt crack. His black leather jacket fell short of intimidating because the skull and crossbones on the back appeared to have been drawn by a seven-year-old. As Agung, Ed, Joey, and Ed's friend entered the farmhouse, the rest, with their my-crotch-is-my-life swagger, walked to our pasture for an actual pissing contest—golden showers of urine arched toward the garden.

Louise, Clint, Pete, Sky, and I leaned against Clint's truck, watching.

"We're gonna let them stay?" I asked Louise.

"You have a better suggestion?"

I didn't. But I demanded to know what right Ed had to invite these unappealing men who were not hippies to make themselves at home—at my...our home.

Carol," Louise explained, in a tone so brittle it reminded me of Weatherwoman Bernadine Dohrn, "Greenleaf is a free open space for the people—all people. Whoever wants to visit can if they don't cause trouble and they do their share."

I couldn't hold back. My heart was racing and I could feel anger rising from my belly:

"I call this trouble, Louise."

"They're not gonna be a problem," Clint assured me, "if we just treat 'em nice and let 'em be."

"Jesus Clint," I whispered, "they're peeing on the spinach!"

"Have some faith, Carol," Clint hissed under his breath.

"Faith?" I asked. "I have faith one of them might mistake me for a bag of pork rinds and rip me open with his teeth."

"You know," Clint said, "you really are a snob."

I was assuring myself that I was not a snob, but a woman with a few healthy boundaries, when a dwarfish biker walked up to us, held out a crumpled pack of *Lucky Strikes* and offered up a smoke.

"No thank you," Louise said, "but it was kind of you to offer."

Louise, I thought to myself, was a serious ass kisser. Or a diplomat. No matter, she pissed me off.

"Don't mind if I do," Clint said and took one.

"Clint," I reminded him, "you don't smoke cigarettes."

"Jes being polite," Clint said as he lit up. "Stay cool," he added, patting my shoulder. "It's all gonna be fine."

His optimism felt misplaced. His pat was irritating.

"Fine? Are you sure about that, Clint?" I asked as I watched Moonlove who sat in a lawn chair a few feet from where the bikes were parked. "You call that fine?"

Moonlove wore a stupid half smile. The pink tip of her tongue poked out between her lips. Her knees had flopped open underneath her granny skirt and her enormous breasts overflowed the dam of her half-zipped sweatshirt. At eight months and counting, Moonlove was throbbing for a little biker action. Being abused in her past had resulted in her being used in her present. I felt sorry and frightened for her; but also frightened for myself. If very pregnant Moonlove with her welcome-wagon thighs was so available, then she was giving these dirty bad-boys the message all our women were the same. The bikers, I was sure, saw us as holes with hindquarters—a warm, wet place to stick it. Their few women looked as mean and scruffy as hyenas—like overused bottom feeders.

Sky lit a monster joint and passed it on to a lowrider, who, when he nodded in acceptance, caught his handlebar mustache on the chain of his own crucifix. Watching him struggle to undo himself gave me the giggles, but I had to stuff them down. Then, as if the low riders were not ten feet away from us, tossing their empty beer cans into the helpless grass, Louise strolled to her garden to lay copper wiring around her carrots so slugs couldn't get to them. Even in the worst of times, the woman remained practical. And hers was discrimination in reverse, accepting of anyone. It was a wider net than I could handle and immediately begged Clint to take us away on his own bike—to escape; but he refused. He could not, he explained, leave his tools behind unprotected. His nail gun, his socket wrench, his lathe...they were his children.

"What about me?" I squeaked. "Who's going to protect me?"

"Don't worry, babe," he said. "They're harmless. Besides, nobody's gonna mess with you while I'm around. Just stick close."

He didn't have to do any more convincing. I trailed behind him like a duckling.

Agung exited the farmhouse and strutted our way. "They're just staying for the night," he gushed. "It's totally cool. They're brothers from Chi-town and good buds with Cha-Cha Jimenez."

"Chi-town Agung? Oh...you mean CHICAGO, Aggie." I said, put off by his phony street slang. I knew who Cha Cha was because I'd worked on *Story Theatre* in Chicago during the furious 1968 Democratic convention and Paul Sills, our brilliant director, had admired him.

"Who's this Cha Cha guy?" Clint asked.

"He's the leader of the Young Lords, Clint," Agung answered as if he were speaking to a kindergartener. It was the only time I'd ever heard him talk down to Clint. "They do for our Latino brothers what the Panthers do for Blacks."

"Cool."

"Soy un extranjero en mi propia tierra," Agung said in his excellent Spanish. "I am a stranger in my own land. That's the inequity Cha Cha is fighting against."

"Cool," Clint said again and for the first time in our two-year relationship, I felt embarrassed and sorry for him.

Evening descended with a chilling bite. The sky turned a steel gray, sucking the living color from the Douglas firs and meadows in the distance. Cassy Jane and Pete escaped and drove to visit her parents' farm just outside Eugene while Sky and Lila climbed up to their far-off tree platform to do peyote and contemplate the true nature of things. The rest of us remained as the farmhouse filled with the lowriders. We watched from a distance as they swilled beer and smashed their cigarette butts against any surface.

Our world was their ashtray.

While dark night crept up on us like another uninvited guest, Clint and I raided the refrigerator, but stayed in the kitchen for only a few uncomfortable minutes. All the action was in the living room, so we managed to get in and out the back door unnoticed. We then hung out in our shack and shared a late dinner of rice and beans while listening to the ruckus streaming from the farmhouse—laughter, screams, bangs, and crashes. It was as if a TV screen had gone black and only the sound remained. We could hear the show but not see it. Clint couldn't have cared less. He was drilling a detached ax handle to make a better notch, an activity which held as much interest for me as, well...drilling a detached ax handle. My mind kept picturing the goings-on in the farmhouse, but I was afraid to go see for myself.

"Clint," I said, making up a plausible excuse, "I need to get my toothbrush," which I actually needed.

"Okay."

"It's inside the bathroom...but I'm afraid to go alone."

"Carol, there's nothing to be afraid of. They're just boys in tough guy outfits. Get over yourself."

Get over myself? I was an actress. We never get over ourselves.

Maybe his egalitarianism had blinded him or maybe he was stoned stupid, but this man didn't seem at all concerned with my safety. So I gave him a look that said that if he didn't accompany me, I'd shrink his gonads to the size of malted milk balls.

"Fine!" he said, "I'm coming."

This time we entered the farmhouse by the front door. Inside the living-room, bent over the arm of the couch where Froggie and I had discussed how Buckminster Fuller's geodesic dome was based on the ancient yurt, a woman was being spanked by a man who slapped her buttocks with one hand and held a half-eaten burrito in the other. I couldn't take my eyes off the surface of her jiggling ass. She was yelping like a newborn and looked like Dr. Needleman, my old New York psychotherapist, though her nose was much smaller and her hair blonder. It was like watching an alluring sideshow—the thrill engulfing all empathy—fleshy, with the smell of beer and hairspray.

In 70's Manhattan, before cable, there were only four TV channels (2, 4, 5, and 7). To see big time, big screen porn, Clint frequented the seedy film theaters that then littered Times Square. To his credit, he always asked me to join him. But after I'd seen too many ejaculations combined with too few plot points, I begged off. Soon, he, too, tired of them and Debbie finally did Dallas without us. But on this night, despite having been Woodstocked, Clint watched the biker couplings with his old-time zest. As he headed to the beer kegs, I pushed my way through the crowd toward the bathroom to retrieve my toothbrush. Thinking the bathroom empty, I shoved open the door to find Moonlove seated on the toilet nursing a pock-marked, mean-looking biker. The man kneeled beside her, his mouth so wide open and her swollen breast so far inside it, that it looked like he would swallow her whole. "He's helping me practice my nursing technique," Moonlove giggled as her pupils dilated even further. Python man sucked harder, his gray cheeks sinking inward, his throat puffing out and then contracting. Unlike the spanked biker woman, who I didn't know and was sure I wouldn't like if I did, I cared for Moonlove. It hurt to see her so degraded. But in spite of myself, I was completely fixated on their tableau, as if watching an X-rated film instead of real life, when the man unplugged himself from Moonlove's nipple and flicked his ringed tongue at me. It was the longest tongue I'd ever seen. I tried not to imagine the wicked oral magic that tongue might be capable of, but a tingle of desire shot through me. The man, sensing my delirium, grabbed my bare arm, and slowly licked the soft inside of my elbow. It was if he were branding me with his saliva. His shark eyes had nothing inside them. I momentarily froze. And that tongue! Suddenly awakening from my stupor, I screamed out for Clint. His voice reached me from the other side of the door: "You all right in there, Carol?"

"Noooo!"

My hero crashed inside and steered me out of the bathroom, leaving Moonlove to her unfortunate fate. I felt bad about it, but not bad enough. "Sorry buddy, no harm done," Clint said to the sucking snake as we made our getaway. If Clint had been wearing a hat, he would have tipped it. Fury set fire to my belly. "*No harm done!*" I'd been tongued by a creep who'd been welcomed into our home. And just as bad, to a teensey-weensy but very icky extent, it had excited me.

"Did you get your toothbrush?" Clint asked as we walked through the living room and out the front door into the soggy Oregon night.

"No," I lied, "I couldn't find it."

There was no moon and just a few scattered stars. Clint held his flashlight out in front of us as we made our way back down the path to our shack. We could see only a few feet ahead and in that black stillness, I realized I'd reached my Jewess from Manhattan saturation point. "Clint," I said, "I can't live like this anymore."

He let go of my hand and wrapped his arm around my waist.

"Don't worry," he said, "Those guys were only here this once. They won't be back."

"It's not just them, Clint. It's this place. Greenleaf has a temporary vibe and no future for us."

"But Carol," Clint said, as he undid the rope that tied our door shut, "This is fertile land. All our friends are here and I like what we're doing together. Please, try to give it just a little more time."

But time was something I'd given enough of. The Greenleaf commune was not what I wanted. It was too open—too spread eagle in its acceptance of all.

I was done with trying to fit in. I wanted what fit me.

In Carlos Castaneda's *Journey to Ixlan,* a book Agung had recommended, Don Juan, a shaman, tells his pupil Castaneda that *"The smoke teaches you how to handle power and to learn that, you must take it as many times as you can."* So early the next morning, just after finding Clint's side of the bed empty and his sneakers gone, I rolled myself a fatty and, just like Don Juan promised, after a few pulls the answers flooded in.

I had to make Clint understand we needed our own home, not sometime in the future, but immediately. Ownership, I was sure, would give us real roots. Our land would be a place where Agung's thoughts didn't come out of Clint's mouth, where we could make our own dream come true, and where communal living would not steal sway over our own needs. We would live free, paying homage only to acts of kindness and organic land improvement—makers of a new and beautiful world. Clint would keep us alive; others, who we truly liked and trusted could join us. Sorry. But not everyone—no way.

My $3,500 hidden check was ready and waiting. I decided to beg my parents, who would surely forgive me my trespasses, for the rest.

The summer before starting Yale, while I still lived in New York, Dr. Needleman, my psychotherapist, freaked out because while waiting for my appointment, I'd stashed my chicken salad sandwich in her refrigerator without asking. Our entire session then focused on preventing food spoilage as opposed to disregarding personal boundaries. Neither of us would back down. Why, I asked, should I respect her uptight structure if it led to losing my lunch? She informed me I had a sense of entitlement that caused me to disrespect the rights of others.

After that I stopped seeing her.

Now, four years later, as clear as the lonely moon above, I saw Dr. Needleman's point. Out-of-control anarchy, without structure, could lead only to disaster—to too many visitors taking whatever they wanted and giving nothing in return.

☾

Unspeakable garbage lay everywhere. The living room couch was ruined. A burn hole in the upholstered arm was deep enough to stick my fist through. I was inside the farmhouse trying to find Clint, to convince him we had to leave Greenleaf, but he wasn't there. Dishes were broken, cigarette butts floated in half-empty glasses and the sink was filled with gray sludge. I couldn't deal with it, so I headed toward the barn. It was Clint's retreat, his place to fix and make things.

Unlike the farmhouse, the barn smelled of sweet hay and old wood. And there was Clint, on his back on the cement floor, his face protected by a clear plastic shield. A single blue flame shot out from his blow torch as he soldered a broken tail pipe onto a Harley. I stood watching, knowing not to talk to him while he was handling anything dangerous.

When he was finished, he extinguished the flame, stood, and patted the motorcycle's seat as if it were a baby's bottom. He then turned toward the bike's owner, Ed's friend, the one who knew The Young Lord's Cha Cha Jimenez.

"That outta do ya," Clint told him. "She's as good as new."

The man looked at Clint with something like love.

"Thanks, brother," the biker said in his flat Midwestern accent. They hugged in that quick way men hug and without another word, the low-riding Chicago man mounted his bike, revved his engine and took off down the road, his raccoon tail flopping behind him. He hadn't gone far when he was joined by the rest of his gang. While they sped ahead, he stopped to let his familiar-looking "old lady" climb onto his back seat. I was stunned. It was as if my thoughts had conjured her. "Doctor Needleman!" I shouted as loudly as I could. "Is that you?!" The woman turned and looked in my direction, "No, Carol!" she yelled back, "it's not." But her leather boots told me otherwise. I was certain they were the same pair I'd coveted in the shoe department at *Lord & Taylor*, but couldn't afford. Too much of my money had gone to her.

Hoping to catch my fly with honey rather than vinegar, I pulled Clint towards me and whispered into his big, red ear, "It was kind of you to help that guy out." Clint shuffled his feet and hung his head.

"I hadda do it, Carol...so they could get on the road."

"I know sweetheart," I said, aware that Clint never refused a request to fix what he could. "Let's you and I get on the road too...find our own special place. It's why we came to Oregon...don't you remember?"

"What about buying this place, Carol?" he asked hopefully "It's so fine."

I had an answer ready for him and it was the truth. "Louise told me the farmers who own it rent to rich hippies to help pay off their mortgage. They won't sell. I'm not in love with it anyway. It's too far inland and I want to be near the ocean."

"Then you'll be happy, Carol?"

"Yes," I said, "I will be very happy and you will be, too."

"I guess," he said without conviction.

Unlike my family, Clint's family had never had money. They'd lived off the generosity of his father's parishioners. On the ecclesiastical dole, they held tight to what they had, but dreamt no further than having God on their side. Not us. Not my family. Not my people. We shopped. We bought. We knew what was holy outside of the Holy Land...real estate.

"Clint," I said, "in New York when we walked around the duck pond in Central Park and you said what you wanted was to live lightly off the land in nature, that's when I fell in love with you. That's when I knew we could build a life together, because even though I loved my work, that's what I wanted, too."

"They need me here, Carol."

"But they don't need me," I told him truthfully, "and I need you."

Clint's internal clock rewound. It didn't take long.

"Then let's go," he said, looking at me with a twinkle that brightened my world. "You're right, Carol. It's time."

Sometimes Clint was as easy as Sunday morning—even if I wasn't.

CHAPTER 10

Won't You Buy Me?

December 1971 - January 1972

Private property has made us so stupid and one-sided that an object is only ours when we have it—when it exists for us as capital, when used by us... The abolition of private property is, therefore, full remancipation of all human senses and qualities.

KARL MARX, *Economic and Philosophical Manuscripts of 1844*

Dawn. A thick mist blanketed the pasture and Clint and I were ready to take off. No one else was up so we left a note saying we were going on a road trip and would be back in a month. We gave no further explanation. Our sleeping bags and tent were rolled and tightly strapped to Clint's motorcycle—mine as compact and neat as his. He'd taught me how.

Shielded from the wind by Clint's body, we rode hundreds of butt-aching miles from Portland to the North, Medford to the East, and Gold Beach to the South, my feet on the running boards, my thighs squeezing his hips like salad tongs. Glued together, we bounced along gravel logging roads and sped over highways. The rain soaked anything not covered with plastic, but the wild Northwestern coastline was worth it. Waves smashed against the jagged shore while thirty-foot plumes spewed from between enormous rocks. When angry, or even just annoyed, the northern Pacific was a watery thrill.

Clint and I tramped across abandoned farms, logged land and riverfront homesteads accessible only by boat. One moonlit night, high in the Cascades, we rode into a herd of elk that let us travel with them. The horned bucks were bigger than horses and led a pack of about thirty. To race neck and neck with those handsome creatures, their hooves thundering, their hot breath steaming in the night air, was better than opening night on Broadway...better than anything.

Finally, after weeks of sleeping in our tent on a thin piece of foam that never kept the cold, wet ground far enough away, and heating Top Ramen noodle dinners over a campfire, we found our land. Six miles off the Pacific, up Flores Creek road, past a canyon filled with meadows, rhododendron and azalea, we discovered a place that finally fit. Our mountain top had a one-room cabin nestled in a small clearing surrounded by thick second growth—part of a 160-acre homestead bordering both sides of fast-flowing Flores Creek.

In 1862, an Oregon homestead act allowed only one legal house on every 160-acre tract. More than a century later, those zoning laws still applied. The property, in Range 1 of the Willamette Meriden, near the tiny coastal town of Langlois, was six miles from the nearest phone and electrical lines, but had long views of the Pacific. The savvy real estate agent who had shown us the place buzzed us up its ruined road in her four-wheel drive. Here, in summer, we could run naked and grow whatever we wanted. Sound bounced off the surrounding mountains, announcing the approach of any vehicle. It would be very difficult for anyone to surprise us except by helicopter. Clint, devoted to marijuana growth, loved this perk. I'd wanted something more civilized, something with endless *Sound of Music* meadows, but the beauty and isolation of Flores Creek seduced me.

Only heavy trucks, four-wheel drive vehicles, and motorcycles could make it up the hill leading to the cabin.

The cabin, run-down to the point of collapse, had been built by "Shorty" (Elmer Rocksted), a local legend who had lived alone in it for forty years. Clint, I was sure, could make it new again and in my mind I was already planting geraniums in our flower boxes. It reminded me of the Davy Crocket miniature cabin I'd played in as a child at FAO Schwartz, Manhattan's most opulent toy store. I'd begged my mother to buy that cabin with its adorable calico curtains, but she assured me it was too big and would require a backyard and not an apartment. Now I had a hundred and sixty acres of backyard.

Quiet covered the land like down. A five-hundred-foot drop from the cabin, Flores Creek ran toward the ocean. Walking upstream, across black and jade rock, we felt as if we were the first humans ever to set foot on this untouched spot. Had a triceratops lumbered past us, I would not have been surprised.

☾

"Hello, Mom—it's Carol." It was the first time I'd phoned my parents in four months, but I had sent letters describing my new life and of my burning desire to own a piece of magnificent Coastal Oregon.

"Carol who?" my mother asked. "Mike," she called to my father, "someone named Carol is on the phone. Get on the other line!"

Outside Stormy's Bar and Grill, the local watering hole, I stood huddled in the only public phone booth for thirty miles. A downpour fell in sheets, the water soaking the glass cubicle's floor. There was a hole in my boot, and my feet were getting wet.

"Be careful, Minnie," my father piped in from the kitchen extension. "She wants something."

"Of course she wants something," my mother snapped back.

"She has her nerve," my father said. Then, remembering I was actually on the other end, "Carol, you have a lot of nerve. Your mother was worried sick, you could have been dead or worse and you never called."

"I'm sorry, Daddy. Didn't you get my letters? I wrote to you every week."

"Yes, we did," my mother answered, the edge to her voice softening, "and they were very nice—you write well. So how's Clint?"

"The no-good Goy," my father added.

"He's fine, Mom. We're both strong and healthy."

"Good. I'm very glad to hear it. But, if you think we're sending you any money, think again."

"Is that why she's calling after all these months?!" my father bellowed. "Is that why? Don't give her a Goddamn dime, Minnie. Not one red cent!"

"Mom," I cajoled, "land is the great commodity. We found a beautiful piece that can sustain us. Clint can build us a house; we can grow our own food."

"Fresh food is good," my mother said, her tone of voice telling me I had a chance.

"Please give me my inheritance now, instead of when you're dead," I said. "You'll be able to see us enjoy it."

"Never mind when we're dead!" my father shouted from the other end.

"But Carol, you know you're a little crazy," my mother backtracked. "You've never grown anything in your life—you're not a farmer. And all those people you live with. I bet they'll want to live there, too. And you'll let them have everything for free, just like you always do."

I angled the phone receiver toward Clint so he could hear. He listened intently, both hope and concern on his face.

"That time Daddy and I were in Europe," my mother continued, "you let that lousy professor from Yale stay in our apartment. He left us with an empty liquor cabinet and a thousand-dollar phone bill."

"All my Crown Royal," my father shouted. "That feyghella guzzled all my Crown Royal!"

"Arnold wasn't gay, Daddy."

"Gay, schmay, he's a feyghella."

A huge logging truck piled high with old-growth timber rumbled past the phone booth, drowning out my parents. Those magnificent trees, hundreds of years old, were no more.

"Mom, don't worry," I said as loudly as I could. "No one's been invited to live there. But if they do come, they'll give as much as they get. They're good people. Besides, you can gift me part of the money tax-free."

"You remember something I told you, Carol? I'm amazed. By the way, you should know Susan Shatkin is marrying a successful divorce attorney; their picture was in *The Times*."

"Mom, who is Susan Shatkin?"

"Somebody who isn't you."

After two full days of begging which involved our Coquille real estate agent (who was so eager for the sale she put us up in her spare bedroom), the head of the Timberland Realty chain, and Manny Kleinmuntz, the owner of Coquille's one shoe store and the only Jewish businessman a hundred miles in any direction, my parents gave in.

Offer, counter offer, acceptance, escrow, banks, telegrams, and for $26,000 dollars, the Flores Creek property was mine. I was twenty-three years old and had never held down a steady job, or applied for one. My mother made certain her name was on the deed, and my own. The land, they decided, would be my inheritance and their legacy.

Flores Creek dwarfed Central Park, the only other large expanse of green that I'd ever before loved. The 160-acre homestead had no zoo, but there were elk, coyotes, cougars, hawks, woodpeckers, skunks, porcupines, deer, and bear. With every second I spent looking at it, it grew more beautiful. My father had grown up in a tenement on Manhattan's Lower East Side. My grandparents, never allowed to buy property, had fled Eastern European pogroms to become fruit and vegetable peddlers on Canal Street and tailors in Flatbush. And now I owned an unthinkable amount of breathtaking Western coastal property–just like William Randolph Hearst, who was not my role model. But neither was Karl Marx.

☾

Carol," he continued, "it was the right thing."

As Clint lit the delicate filigree of our Aladdin lamp, I noticed his ears were too big for his head. In the lamplight, they glowed pink and reminded me of Mortimer Snerd, a floppy-eared, one-toothed dummy that belonged to Paul Winchell, the great 50s ventriloquist. In that moment, Clint and Mortimer were one. Then I stopped thinking. My scalp itched, too. And my crotch. I scratched both with rising hysteria.

"Lemme see," Clint said as he parted my crown and dug into my scalp; coming up with what looked like a pepper granule with legs. "Carol," he continued as he squished the tiny creature between his fingers, "you'd have danced around this forever and got everybody mad and confused. I did us a favor. You can leave no one out. It's wrong. It's hurtful. Think about it—where else would they go?"

"We all can't live in that broken-down little cabin with no running water, Clint. They could stay here."

"They won't do that."

"Dammit!" I screamed. The itch was spreading to my underarms. I snatched our sleeping bags and threw them to the floor. Clint thought I was throwing a temper tantrum and I was.

"The hell," Clint said, slapping his forehead and then changing hands to dig at the hairline above his penis. Watching him struggle cheered me up. When he stopped scratching he slid our infested mattress onto the floor and then spoke to me with a measured calm. "Carol, everyone here wants to throw in their lives with us, take the leap. There's love in that and faith."

In that moment, I cared nothing for love or faith. All I cared about was getting rid of the itch, made more unbearable by the thought that because of Clint I'd have to wake up every morning and go to bed every night with people who could irritate me almost as much. Instead of living in freedom, I'd be living in a wilderness prison, a hippie gulag where I would be both the inmate and the gatekeeper. Did Susan Shatkin, I asked myself, have to beat her lice infested foam mattress and spray it with vinegar? No way. Susan Shatkin would never get lice in the first place. She'd be living with her lawyer husband in their ten-room apartment on Riverside Drive where "the girl" came in every day to mop and iron. But I wasn't Susan and never would be. I used to revel in that, but now I wasn't so sure.

"What did you tell them about Flores Creek, Clint? Be honest. Tell me the truth!"

"I told them it was the most beautiful place on earth."

I was almost charmed—but not quite. My pubes were on fire.

"I didn't think all of them would want to come, Carol," he continued, "but they did and I was so excited about the possibilities that I couldn't imagine you'd want to stop it cold."

What I could see in that dim light was Clint's left knee, the one he'd hurt in college football. It was outsized, big, and boney compared to his right and reminded me that in spite of his strength, he was a softhearted and vulnerable man. Once, when we lived in Manhattan, we'd passed a drunk who sat shivering in a Chelsea doorway. Clint stopped to give the man his jacket; the down one I hated. This was the son of an Episcopalian priest for Christsake. Compassion was his family business.

Unable to read my thoughts, he continued with his. "I figured we had to give them all the option. Besides, not everybody will stay; it'll be too hard. Those who can't make it will be weeded out. You'll see."

I took a deep breath. It made me cough: the result of four joints a day.

"Maybe you're right Clint, but you should have asked me first. We're partners. Partners talk things over."

"Okay Carol," Clint said, "I'll tell them I made a mistake; that I didn't have your approval. We can ask the people you like in private—but I'm sure they won't come without the others."

I realized he was right. Either we had to go it alone at Flores Creek or bring everyone else along.

The *Whole Earth Catalogue*, which I'd studied endlessly, had devoted an entire page to lice. Along with the text came a full illustration of a magnified six-legged louse: "Split the hair into workable sections and drag the comb forward from the scalp. Tweezers are best for use on eyebrows and underarms."

Maybe I'd never build a wind turbine but I'd learned something about pest eradication.

"Do you have a thin comb and tweezers?" I asked.

He did, minus the beard and his ever-present joint, Clint was practically an Eagle Scout.

"It's all right, Clint," I said. "What's done is done; there's nothing we can do about it now."

His face lit up with Christian beatitude.

"It'll work out fine, babe," he said, "and you won't be sorry, I promise. We'll all pitch in. That's what we do. That's what we're here for. To help each other and get along."

For the rest of the night, neither of us got any sleep. Instead we combed, picked, swept, and scrubbed until morning when we showered and shampooed with Greenleaf's always on hand, tar-based Qwell: "100% guaranteed to kill head lice and fleas." When the hot water ran low, Clint moved over to give me the lion's share while he stood naked and shivering in the cold air, his big head covered in foam. I let him stay that way, taking my own sweet time until there was no hot water left.

CHAPTER 11

Barter

January - February 1972

Most people work just hard enough not to get fired
and get paid just enough money not to quit.
GEORGE CARLIN

While the rain turned the ground to mud, the thought of living for the rest of my life with the entire Greenleaf commune dampened my spirit. Keeping my feelings to myself and undercover, I grew sullen. And my damn molar was hurting again—throbbing with a heartbeat of pain. With my check spent and no cash, I couldn't afford to see a dentist so Clint offered to drive me to White Bird, the free Dental Clinic in Eugene, where they had a dentist who took drop-ins. Even though I was a drop-out, I didn't want to be a drop-in. The word "clinic" scared me. It said "destitute and powerless." Clinics were for people who had to wait endlessly for minimal care from doctors with little experience.

I wanted an appointment.

"What school did this White Bird dentist graduate from, Clint?"

"I donno," Clint answered. "But don't worry, Doc Webster is a good guy."

Good or bad, I wanted my childhood family dentist—Dr. Zeiss. I wanted his West Seventy-Third Street office, his framed New York University School of Dentistry diploma and his bill that my parents paid.

"You know anybody he's worked on, Clint?" I asked innocently, trying to hide my much-maligned Sutton Place snobbery. "Someone we could ask for a reference?"

"Yeah sure, Carol," he answered, "lotsa people, but none of them have a phone."

Unwilling to take a plunge into the dental unknown, I went with my grandmother Schneiderman's old home remedy: holding warm salt water in my mouth to calm the tooth's nerves. I trusted my

Grandma. Communal, country living brought her shtetl ways back.

Clint, released from having to drive me, walked down the road to collect our group mail. We all had the same address: Star Route 36; our mailbox was a fine example of hippie folk art: Warhol's giant red and white soup can sitting on the back of a unicorn. By the time Clint returned, my pain had subsided. I'd held warm salt water in my mouth and spit it into the kitchen sink so often that I could have spray-cleaned the dishes.

"Feel any better?" Clint asked.

"Yes, much," I said as I watched him place a stack of letters secured with a thick rubber band on the dining table. He looked so irresistible, with his long chestnut braid dripping water down his shirt, that I had to lean in to kiss him. When I did, I could feel the frown on his lips. I stepped back and he handed me a postcard.

"I read it," he said. His voice told me he wished he hadn't.

I turned over the plain yellow card with its printed eight-cent stamp and read: "*Your cousin Freddy is dead. He jumped off the roof of the Cambridge library. Your Aunt Lillian said it was all your fault, and she's sorry you missed the funeral—Mom.*"

My gut turned molten. I loved Freddy. One summer when I was seventeen and Freddy fourteen, my Uncle Nate let us go out alone on Hampton Bay in his new outboard motor boat. When Freddy saw that the sun was in my eyes, he reversed the boat's direction so the glare wouldn't bother me. He was that considerate and sensitive. After I turned down his plea to join us in Oregon, his parents had sent him to study with their psychiatrist friend who taught in Kent, England; the friend's field of expertise was adolescent depression and suicide. It was a poor choice—Freddy was too good a student. Maybe my aunt Lillian was right; it wouldn't have been that difficult to bring him along. I'd been selfish, not wanting the burden of his illness to ruin my time with Clint. *How could Freddy have done this?* I was furious—so mad I wanted to hit him and couldn't stop crying. Freddy was just twenty.

I crumpled up the postcard and stumbled out the back door, tripping over the rise and landing on my hands and knees. Clint ran towards me.

"Are you all right, sweetheart?" he asked, extending a hand to lift me to my feet, but I preferred to stay seated on solid ground and say nothing. "Carol," he continued, "it was your aunt's grief talking, not her. Freddy was sick and you had nothing to do with that." Clint's words barely registered because I was no longer in Greenleaf, Oregon; I was seated in my aunt and uncle's lavish Manhasset, Long Island living room with its thick golden drapes, watching Freddy's slender fingers zip across Steinway keys as he played a Bach Cantata.

From nowhere, two warm hands settled onto my shoulders. I looked up and saw they belonged to Moonlove. Apparently, she, too, had read my mother's postcard. Shrugging her off, I turned to see Joey, Lila, and Sky coming close. What was wrong with these people? Did they always read each other's private mail? Continual exposure, wanted or not, was apparently a requisite for communal living.

"My mother killed herself," Joey said as he handed me a paper towel to dry my eyes. "I thought I could save her, but I couldn't."

"Joey, I'm so sorry…I didn't know."

"Yeah," he murmured and looked up to the sky as if to find her in the clouds.

Moonlove refused to give up. She wrapped her bare legs around my torso and placed her hands on my neck. Because her belly fit snugly into the small of my back, I allowed it; but instantly regretted my decision when in her thin, high voice she sang the first lines of The Byrd's song *Turn. Turn. Turn.*

"I hate that song, Moonlove. It's so airy-fairy. My aunt's a total bitch, so just shut the fuck up!"

Moonlove stopped singing but deepened her massage. Her fingers releasing pain I didn't know I had.

"Carol, you gotta forgive your aunt."

"No way," I said as my head slumped toward my chest. "Not gonna happen."

"Her child is dead, there's nothing worse in the world."

I knew that Moonlove was right. As her fingers pressed into the crunchy knots where my neck met my shoulder, my fury lessened and my body relaxed.

"Good job, Carol," Sky said. "Now take a deep cleansing breath and release your toxicity." I didn't want to take a cleansing breath, I wanted a jelly donut. But instead I got Louise at her most kindhearted, telling me that the only life we could be responsible for in this world was our own. But I couldn't hear it. My body stiffened and Moonlove's touch felt not comforting but intrusive. The kindness coming my way, I was sure, was being given by rote with nothing underneath. No one at Greenleaf knew who I really was. I just wished they'd all go away and leave me alone.

Sooner than I expected, my wish was granted.

Despite the steady rain, everyone took off in Agung's van for a day trip to Crater Lake, an azure mile-deep hole in the earth formed by a meteor. I had to beg them to go ahead without me. Clint offered to stay, but I wouldn't let him.

In Manhattan, being alone in my apartment brought aching loneliness; on this Oregon commune, it brought relief. Only Joey remained. He was in the middle of making plum wine and funneling the dark purple juice into a five-gallon carboy when I shuffled past him.

"Hey, Carol," he called, "we're gonna have free booze, can youse fuckin' believe it?" I didn't answer. My lack of response made him try harder. "It's not ready yet so you gotta taste Louise's Santa Rosa plum jam, right offa our tree."

The sweet, tart taste was as yummy as a *Baby Ruth* bar. But then an electric shock—I'd bitten down and hit something hard. A pit. A damn pit! The pain travelled through my nose into my head. " My tooth! I think I cracked it!"

"Sounds bad," Joey said, calmly capping the wine mixture with a used cork. "Youse wanna lift to White Bird?"

"Oh yes, please...shit...take me there," I hissed, but then remembered Joey had no car and asked him how he expected to drive us. All cars, he explained slowly, as if I'd just landed in a foreign country where I didn't speak the language, were always available for an emergency. No one kept their keys to themselves, but placed them on hooks above the kitchen door—even Clint. Joey slid into a Mackintosh that had belonged to a much bigger man, then helped me into a cotton candy pink one (pink!), took my arm and walked us outside to a battered black Impala. Opening the door with one hand, he guided me to my seat. The sweetness of his gesture momentarily overtook my pain—I was touched. As soon as we were settled, he put the key into the ignition, let out a yelp of teenage joy, gunned the engine, and drove us directly into a ditch. It didn't faze him.

"Sorry 'bout that," he said. "Never been behind the wheel of one of these, but slept in plenty of 'em."

As he backed out, he told me the Impala he'd lived in was parked in a junkyard on Nostrand Avenue. "It had a primo glove compartment," he said as if remembering the best part of his childhood, "better n' a fridge for keeping cheese."

I had an image of him as a kid, curled up and shivering while all of Brooklyn seethed behind him.

While the rain grew heavier, covering the windshield, Joey stopped talking and strained to see the road ahead. With the Impala's wipers long gone, he soon plowed us into a thick stand of salmonberry bushes that lined White Bird's driveway. Unfazed, he then stretched his body out in the front seat to try and catch some shut-eye until my return.

The only other patient in the clinic's waiting room was an old Native American man reading *Glamour* magazine. Beside him was a new copy of the *Oregonian*: Democratic dove George McGovern, would be running against pernicious Republican hawk Richard Nixon. I was about to read the details when a young, topless Caucasian man appeared from behind the door to his office. As he walked toward me, a smidgeon of his scrotum leaked out of his baggy cargo shorts and threatened to drag the whole kit and caboodle along with it. His long blond dreads swayed over his bare shoulders and with a wide, guileless smile, he wordlessly beckoned for me to follow him. He was awfully cute, so forgetting the news, I did.

Except for a giant mandala that covered a whole wall and a big glass jellyfish of a bong that sat on a stereo speaker, Doc Webster's dental office was like any other. While the *Grateful Dead* played *Truckin'*, he introduced himself, shook my hand and guided me to his plush and padded dental chair. With his breath smelling of cloves and the curly hairs on his chest brushing my cheek, he told me to "open wide" and examined the inside of my mouth with his little mirror.

"Your tooth has a fissure, probably abscessed—but I think I can save it," he said in a silky Southern accent.

"Is it gonna hurt?" I mewed.

"Some, but you won't feel it."

My doubt disappeared and not knowing why, I trusted him completely. Sitting there, looking into his small spitting sink, I congratulated myself on my anti-uptight progress.

"Anise, sweetheart," Doc Webster called out into the hallway, "Maui Wowie, please. And pronto." Seconds later, Anise, a pretty woman, joined us and immediately packed his bong with deft hands at professional speed. She wore skintight jeans and, even in the cold and damp, a cropped sweater that hit way above her ringed belly button.

"You two meet yet?" Doc asked. Anise responded by leaning over the dental chair to give me an awkward hug. It was way too big for the occasion.

"Hi, Carol," she said, smashing my head into her chest, "I've heard so much about you."

"You have?" I asked as I came up for air. Before she could answer, Doc said, "Thanks, Anise, please measure the pockets in Mr. Night Bear's gums and tell him I'll be there soon to discuss the results."

"Sure thing, Doc," she said, looking at him with eyes that said she'd give him everything she had. Then, catching herself, to me, "Great to finally meet you."

"You, too, Anise," I said but didn't mean. She had known my name without introduction which made me think she was hiding something. Deciding not to dwell on it, as soon as she left the room, my attention returned to Doc. Sweat had formed on his forehead even though he was wearing next to nothing. When I mentioned it, he explained he never got too hot or too cold because a shaman in the Australian outback had taught him how to regulate his own body temperature. I was beyond impressed and staring into his protective goggles said in my most beguiling voice, "There's just one itsy tiny little thing before you start, Doc."

"What's that darlin'?" he asked, as he picked up his drill.

"I'm without funds...practically, I dare say, indigent."

Now I was Blanche Dubois, trusting in the kindness of dentists.

"No worries. I'm open to trade," he said. "Watcha got?"

"Jes two quarts of my finest blackberry jam."

Blackberries had been as abundant on bushes as leaves on the trees. Louise had canned a pantry full. She wouldn't miss a few jars.

"Works for me," he said.

How lovely. Doc wanted nothing from me except what I was comfortable in giving. The bags under his eyes, his graying brows, and wisps of white hair feathering his temple made him look owlish—both wise and ancient. His talon toenails were thick and long and when I looked down at his hairy and powerful legs, I felt compelled to confide in him.

"Doc, if someone blamed you for something you didn't do but you felt guilty anyway, what would you do?"

"I'd do nothin' darlin'. Now open wide."

Doc spread tea tree oil onto my gums and they grew numb. He then pulled a Bic lighter out of his pocket, lit his bong, took a hard toke and said, "Here, suck on this." I put my lips around the glass mouthpiece and inhaled as deeply as I could. "Now, if it hurts," he continued, "you won't give a shit."

Doc Webster's drill hummed. My mind soared. This was the nitrous oxide of ganja—the strongest I'd ever tasted. If it was laced with something more than weed, I didn't care.

There was a woman sitting in the dental chair, and I knew she was me, but my brain was having a fine time floating above her body. I heard the drill, felt a tickle—then nothing. How was all this possible? I asked myself as I nestled into a state of total wellbeing. Here I was getting expert dental care for nothing more than berries.

"Uktor, how an ouu do this an nah get any oney?"

"I was a Digger, that's how."

"Wha?"

"The Diggers, babe, we blew money off—started out in the Haight, giving away free food to anyone on the street. Not shit food. Not packaged crap, but fresh from the farm. Without us, there would have been no Woodstock. It was free food, free cash, free crash pads, free medicine, and free tie-dying."

"Oatally amaying!"

"Yup. We were a trip without a ticket and made the *Summer of Love* happen. Anybody could join, even dentists. It was all about love—the *Death of Money and the Birth of the Free...* open wider please."

Doc continued. He was on a roll. "We were making a world where there was no profit, yet everybody profited. So I shut down my straight practice and said what the fuck, I'll do what I do for nothin' and gave away all my shit. That dental chair you're sitting in, that's my old XK Jag...just a little more, we're almost done."

He squirted a thin stream of warm water into my mouth. It felt so good.

"Id ou knooo Ken Eeesy?" I asked.

With his iconic bus *Further* and his band of *Merry Pranksters*, Kesey had set the bar for "turn on, tune in, and drop out." I'd heard he was living on a commune just outside of Eugene, in Springfield. Despite having abandoned show business, I still had some star-fucker left in me and wanted to meet him.

"You bet," Doc answered. "He made it with my first wife...and my second. The man was a soul brother. *Further* was his bus and (Neil) Cassidy drove it like a mother, but the rest of us supplied the gas."

"I redhed *Un Ew Ober Da Uuuckoo's Est* eree imes," I said.

"Yup, Kesey showed us the way. Jesus. You've got a lot of fillings. What goes around comes around...as plaque."

"Erry funny."

"When I dropped out," he continued, "my blood family dropped me. My income was more important than I was. The good people you're with, they're your real family; your blood family's nothin' when they're not on your side. Now spit."

Doc Webster, I decided, was a dentist-philosopher-king. As he handed me a licorice stem to stimulate my gums, I felt the folks at Greenleaf were my tribe, my new family; there for me when I needed them—the brothers and sisters that I'd always wished for but never had. I'd been selfish in my thinking. What I'd liked or didn't like was irrelevant. It was time to surrender to the present, to share my land and build a communal life based on equality, trust, and faith.

Joey's driving improved as we drove back home to Greenleaf. The going was smooth and I was on a new high. Watching the twig dreamcatcher that hung from the rear-view mirror sway back and forth, I gained clarity and understood what had been hurtful and dark: My mother's painful criticism had come from her fear. My cousin Freddy had ended his life and she was afraid I'd discarded mine. But she was wrong; I'd exchanged it for a better one. There was no way I could love my Aunt Lillian for blaming me for her son's death, but I could forgive her. She'd had nowhere else to fling her miserable fury. My resentment was gone.

"Doc was amazing," I told Joey, as we drove towards Greenleaf. "Thanks for taking me."

"Mon pleasoir," he said. "That's French."

☾

As I morphed into a different woman, the change cost me parts of my known self, but since I didn't hold on to them too tightly, I unraveled nicely. I'd been told that to receive the gift of waking up each morning in beauty, I had to repay the hippie Gods for including me. No guru or guide told me this; it was the purple hummingbirds that had hovered over the zinnias in Louise's summer garden, the dank smell of moss on the banks of Lake Creek, the lullaby of our wind chimes in the rain. It could also have been the drugs. Okay. It was the drugs. All the world vibrated with energy and I was part of that energy and that energy was God. Karma was as real as flesh and blood, bark and sap, light and air; and I was changing mine.

Throughout elementary and junior high, my report card under the heading, "Respects the rights of others," had read NI: Needs Improvement. Fifteen years later, I learned how and improved. It's easy to be spoiled, but once you've been given everything without having to give back, it's hard not to be. Total liberation forged by communal living and tempered by weed was teaching me to step outside myself. Sweeping, and picking up what I had dropped became a source of pride. So did seeing what needed to be done and doing it. No longer grabbing for firsts, each evening I sat down with good company to a feast that continually blew my mind. The child in me that had followed her every whim faded as I became part of an everyday extended family. Having grown up alone, catering only to my own unmet needs, pitching in and sharing opened a psychic door I never wanted to close. It felt better to give than to receive. Damn. Clint's Christian temperament was rubbing off on me. If I wasn't careful, I'd soon be turning my other cheek.

On my circuitous path toward THC-induced Sainthood, I was also struck tolerant. If Froggie practiced his unstrung guitar in the living room or Joey turned the stereo up to pounding, I'd let it go without complaint or resentment. Beneath CassyJane's giggle and strut, I saw a girl using the only tools she had for survival. All Moonlove wanted on this earth was to have a healthy baby. I'd changed how I responded to what was in front of me. Living with a group, I'd also come to value silence—my own. Whenever I entered a room where no one was speaking or making noise, I'd keep my voice low so as not to disturb them. Even my irritation at being treated like a girly girl was softened by the realization that deep down, I was one. I wanted to be taken care of more than I wanted to take care of myself and had yet to turn that kind of thinking around.

Tolerance, acceptance, helping when help was needed no matter how hard or foreign the work, flowered inside me as unmeasured time moved forward. It was a perfect and necessary transition because everyone except Froggie would be moving to Flores Creek with us.

Froggie had been given a 1-Y draft deferment status due to his risk for anaphylactic shock; capitalizing on his good fortune, he'd secured, via the hippie black market, a stolen and very cheap plane ticket to Jakarta. Disguised as a Sikh with his waist-length hair wrapped in a turban, he'd flown over, not into, Vietnam. He'd written to us on thin, blue airmail stationary saying that as he'd looked down at the city of Danang (taken by the North Vietnamese during the fierce Tet offensive), he'd realized he'd been just a wasp bite away from horror and death.

Days after Froggie landed in Agung's hometown, our wagon train set out to colonize an untamed land. We were bound not by love or devotion to one another, but by parallel dreams and wild-eyed youth. When the time came to drive off, I squeezed into the front seat with Clint, next to Moonlove and baby Heaven. The others followed in Agung's van and Sky's VW. Greta, our Nubian goat, tethered to the truck railings, bleated pitifully while the old Chevy flatbed, covered with a torn army tarp and overflowing with food supplies, tools, bedding, kitchenware, and our massive dinner table, jostled toward destiny.

PART TWO

FLORES CREEK

Take my hand
I'm a stranger
in paradise.

ROBERT WRIGHT & GEORGE FORREST from *Kismet*

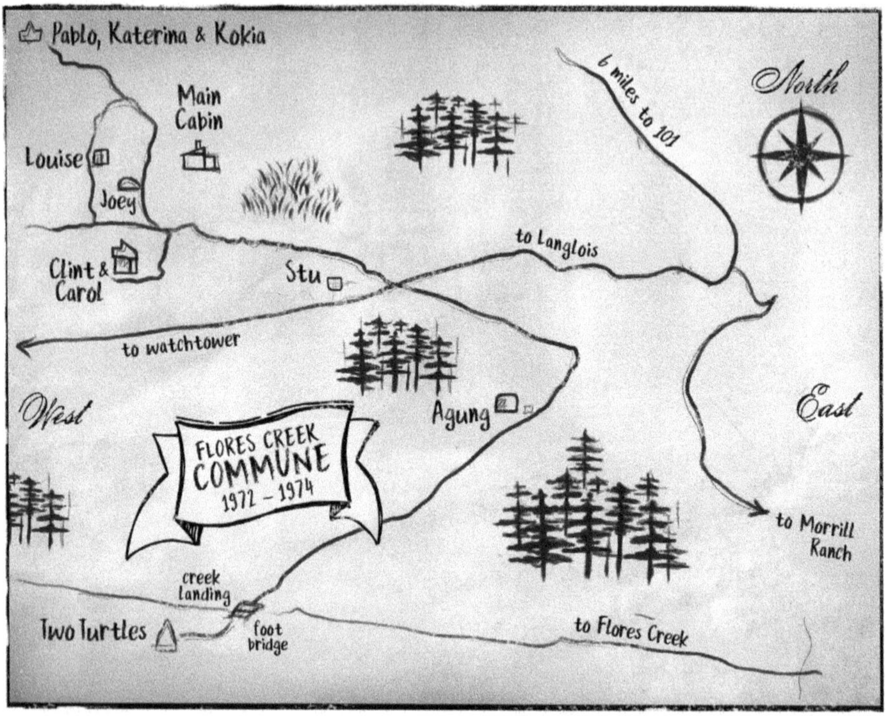
Pablo, Katerina & Kokia
Main Cabin
Louise
Joey
Clint & Carol
Stu
6 miles to 101
North
to Langlois
to watchtower
West
Agung
East
FLORES CREEK COMMUNE 1972 – 1974
to Morrill Ranch
creek landing
Two Turtles
foot bridge
to Flores Creek

CHAPTER 12

Into My Own Parade

March 1972

You can kill ten of my men for every one I kill of yours,
but even at those odds, you will lose and I will win.
HO CHI MINH to the French, late 1940s (re: Vietnam)

A hundred and twenty miles southwest, past the coastal towns of Florence, Coos Bay, North Bend, and Bandon, our caravan reached Curry County and the tiny town of Langlois—population 212. Emerald grazing land stretched out in front of us, spreading toward the ocean and fingering up valleys. The vistas ahead were a Celtic dreamland and looked as if Ireland and Scotland had mated and birthed barns and silos instead of castles and cottages. The air at Greenleaf had been fine but the Flores Creek coastal air was even better. Taking it in was like biting into a fresh-picked apple, energizing and crackling sweet.

Five miles up the county road, the blacktop ended and the gravel began. A mile later and we were road-less. Loggers had carved this route to our new home in the late 1930s as part of FDR's New Deal. It snaked ahead, rutted and ruined, filled with mud and blow-downs. It was steep, very steep. One wrong move and the Chevy would have tumbled over the edge to the forest below—a fifty-foot drop.

Agung and Sky had left their vehicles at the bottom of the hill, knowing they couldn't make it up the steep incline, but the flatbed with its enormous cargo had no choice. To lighten the load, I got out, leaving Moonlove and baby Heaven in the driver's seat with Clint. Joining the others, I trudged behind the truck on foot.

It was March and the rains would not stop till June. I'd lived in the Northwest long enough to know that getting wet was part of life. The wet was always there and the wet made the green. Once, while tripping, I'd counted a myriad shades...deep-dark evergreen, gray-green bracken fern, lemon-green skunk cabbage, bright green maple, silver-green alder, the ubiquitous black-green carpet of moss...and then lost track. Weighted down with thick sheep-smelling sweaters, I'd looped my Swiss Army pocketknife through a buffalo hide belt bought a lifetime ago at *Hammacher Schlemmer.* As I stepped through water and mud, my mink-oiled shit kickers stayed dry but my jean legs were soaked. The others, some wearing only sneakers, sidestepped the muck as best they could or walked, like me, right through.

With my Zig-Zag rolling papers tucked safely into the pocket of my rain slicker, I felt like Ma Joad, leading her rag-tag family into the Promised Land. Or into land that held promise. What the promise was, was uncertain. But I believed in it anyway.

The truck's tires were worn and sometimes lost traction, spewing pebbles and mud. But that didn't bother Clint. He was our driver and the challenge was his idea of a good time. The more he spun the steering wheel and pumped the breaks, the more handsome and godlike he became. With his long hair flowing, his fierce muscles popping up the fabric of his shirt, he became a dead ringer for the seriously cut Yahweh plastered across the ceiling of the Sistine Chapel; his arm perpetually extended to lend a helping hand. And I was first to grab it, hold on, and not let go.

In the 70s, codependency was known as "meant for each other."

Looking past a ragged meadow, the rundown main cabin came into view. Even the physically fit were out of breath. It was the first time most had seen it, and the first time I'd understood it to be my real home and not a fantasy. The homestead had been purchased as part of a dream that did not include ten adults and one colicky baby. Runoff gushed from its rusty gutter and tar paper hung in swaths from the roof. The four-acre clearing was filled with high grass, thistle, dandelion, and nettle. In the fading light, coyotes wailed in the distance: a sound I'd only heard in the movies. I was wondering how far away the coyotes actually were when I heard a scream that made my eardrums tingle.

Moonlove, with baby Heaven wrapped around her belly, had slipped, lost her balance and was about to tumble down the rickety porch steps and onto the stone pilings below. I pictured both on the ground, baby Heaven's skinny tiny body crushed and bloody beneath her mother's heavy weight. Cold fear iced me. I could do nothing. But someone could. With lightning speed, Sky grabbed Moonlove by her rain poncho and yanked her to safety. Moonlove was stunned into silence but baby Heaven howled as her monkey face turned purple with terror and rage. Although relieved mother and child had been rescued just in time, I had to ask myself what would have happened if they had been seriously hurt. We had no real medical training. Clint kept a first aid kit under the seat of his truck, but all it held were bandages, gauze, and antiseptic. Unprepared was not a strong enough description—stupid came closer. Guilt tightened my throat. Everyone had come to live at Flores Creek because of what Clint and I had offered. They'd landed on this isolated mountain top because of us. My self-confidence disintegrated. No, I wasn't tough yet tender Ma Joad, the stalwart matriarch of her migrant family; I was Carol Schlanger, an urbane Jewish woman with no survival skills and a vivid imagination. I didn't want the responsibility for anyone's life—not Moonlove's, not baby Heaven's, not even my own.

The inside of the cabin was worse than the outside. The windows were cracked and the space between the floorboards let in a damp chill. Broken jars and rat pellets covered every surface. No matter how often we primed it, no water came from the hand pump. That meant we'd all have to bed down unwashed and dirty. Clint said either mud or a water rat was gumming up the plumbing. *A water rat!* Joey offered to climb down into the eighteen-foot, hand-dug well in the light of morning to look. He didn't mind, he explained, because he was used to dead rats. In the background, I could hear Cassy Jane whisper to Pete, "I knew it would be bad, but not this bad." I had to agree with her. It was pretty damn bad.

Fumbling around in the twilight, trying to find my sleeping bag, I continued to eavesdrop on Cassy Jane and Pete's conversation. Why, she asked him, if he wanted to live in the Third World, couldn't he have picked some place warm? Before I had a chance to suggest they try Death Valley, Pete's lovely response blew me away. "Because darlin'," he told her, "what we're doing here is worthwhile and we're gonna give it our best shot." That ought to have shut her up, but it didn't. "It doesn't matter anyway," she said loud enough for all to hear, "cause we're gonna starve to death. You can't eat the scenery. This ain't no farm."

Panic.

In John Ford's *How Green Was My Valley*, a film that takes place in a Welsh coal mining community, church bells rang out when the miners were trapped by disaster. CassyJane's words sounded the same alarm. Doom was imminent. Greenleaf, with its electricity and running water was lush growing land; Flores Creek, rocky and untamed, was not. Its beauty and isolation had obliterated my concerns for rich soil and easily accessible water. I'd assumed its farming capabilities could be developed without understanding the time and effort it would take.

My haphazardly formed tribe was indigent, the result of self-induced poverty. Not one of them, not even Agung, could afford, without outside help, to leave and start over somewhere else.

Clint stopped chopping kindling for a fire.

"We won't starve, Cassy," he said. "There's plenty of meat on the hoof—bear, elk, and deer."

"Please don't kill the animals," Moonlove, our only vegetarian, begged as she sat cross-legged on a nasty piece of old foam, nursing baby Heaven. Sky patted Moonlove's head and told her not to worry. We wouldn't have to resort to hunting because there was much to forage: miner's lettuce, huckleberries, lemon grass, and dandelion greens. Her food stamps would buy all the protein we needed. By summer, he assured her, we'd be scarfing down the bounty of our garden. But his assurance had no effect.

"Not the four-leggeds, Clint. Please don't!" she whimpered as if she herself were the prey.

"Moonlove," Clint said in a stern voice I'd never heard him use before, "If I have to kill for meat, I will."

This from a man who hand-fed squirrels, on whose shoulders birds landed, and who gently picked up spiders rather than squash them. Slowly reality crept up on its little cat feet and bit me hard: we were about to drop a thousand years of civilization and become hunter-gatherers. I knew how to gather (mostly in Thrift stores), but not hunt. My aim was terrible. Nonplussed and in the near dark, always-competent Louise found our broom and swept away the rat droppings, allowing the rest of us to lay our sleeping bags on the floor around a converted oil drum that served as a heat stove. It was a rusty relic left by Shorty, the leprechaun-like old hermit who had owned the land before us. He'd built the cabin by hand and lived alone in it for forty years. The original deed, signed by President Garfield, said that the 160-acre Flores Creek homestead was sold in 1904 for six dollars to the Smith family. I'd choked up when Shorty presented it to us saying he was "pleased as punch, cause we were jes the right folks," to come live on the place he'd so cherished. A serious car accident had left him partially crippled. His truck had gone off the road, rolled into a ravine, and pinned him under it. He wasn't discovered until three days later. "So you youngins take care," he said, "'n watch out fer each other." I assured him we would.

It seemed we'd soon have a fire for the cold night ahead. But despite Clint's cedar shavings and a carefully constructed twig teepee, the wet wood would not catch and he was forced to pour kerosene onto the dying embers. As the blaze rose and the logs burned, a cloud of heavy smoke poured from the blocked stove-pipe and filled the room. Baby Heaven wailed while the rest coughed and choked. Lila, Louise, and I tried to force open the windows, but they were nailed shut. Pete pushed open the huge front door and fresh damp air filled the room. Able to breathe, but too exhausted to cook, we all climbed, fully dressed, into our sleeping bags—snug as ten hippies in a rug.

Nightbirds: swallows, and robins, warblers and sparrows sang, the wind blew, bodies rustled while the coyotes howled at the cloud-covered moon. Clint's body gave me warmth and soon the darkness became a friend. This was my new home. I was drinking in the bitter-sweet reality of it when Louise sneezed. The high-pitched, door mousy sound irritated me. Over that tiny, repressed sneeze, I heard Cassy Jane say in her little girl lisp, "Petie Weetie, I'm freezing wheezing." I wanted to shove my footsie wootsie down her throatie woatie.

So much for new-found tolerance.

The wind outside rose and blew between the floorboards.

We were sleeping head-to-toe in a star pattern. If I rolled too far onto my side, I'd find a heel in my face or a toe up my nose. If I turned and the person lying next to me was tall, I'd encounter a buttock or crotch.

"Come on over here, Cassy Jane, honey," Sky said, loud enough for all to hear, "let yer ole uncle Sky warm you up."

Having sex took less energy than cooking and Cassy Jane often coupled with anyone who'd respond, but always returned to Pete who was stoic about her trespasses.

"Don't go, Cassy," Pete said as he cracked his knuckles, first one at a time and then all together. I cracked mine, too. Knuckle cracking, like yawning, was infectious.

"I'll do whatever I want, Petie," Cassy Jane said, "and I've always wanted to fuck Sky."

"Thank you, darlin,'" Sky said.

This adolescent interchange annoyed me no end. Equally dismaying, Sky's lover, the calm and gentle Lila, said nothing and was silent.

But thankfully, Louise, despite her inhibited sneeze, wasn't: "Will you please shut up," she hissed. "Some of us are trying to sleep!"

"Fuck me tonight, Cassy," Pete whispered, ignoring Louise's request while simultaneously trying to honor it, "and tomorrow you can fuck Sky." Pete was a wiz at placating and controlling Cassy Jane at the same time. When tomorrow night came, he knew she'd have forgotten all about it.

"You promise me, Petie?" Cassy Jane said, sounding like the helpless twelve-year-old she most definitely was not.

"Sure, Cassy. But you've gotta be with me tonight," Pete said.

Then, from a spot on the other side of the sleeping circle, came a voice that did not whisper. It was Agung: "Way to go, Pete! Reign in your woman. Let her know who's boss." Louise disregarded her own demand for silence and echoing my own thoughts barked, "Nobody here is the boss over anyone, Agung!"

"Just kidding," Agung said in hushed voice. But he wasn't.

The thumping began. Pete and Cassy Jane were going at it. Listening to them was like hearing chalk on a blackboard, a nail file on a nail. I dreaded their orgasms in the same way I would have dreaded Monday morning if I'd ever have held a steady job—knowing it would come, but wishing it wouldn't.

I'd pulled my sleeping bag up over my head to block out the moans when without warning, the ceiling and walls shook while the windows spewed glass. It felt as if a bomb had hit. Screams and gasps were followed by a mad scramble for flashlights and matches. Not one of us had been hurt but through the dust beams we could see the floor covered with jagged shards. A dead limb from an overhanging Maple tree had hit the roof, its branches poking through the shattered windows. We were lucky it hadn't impaled one of us. Clint, without missing a beat and in a burst of unparalleled optimism said, "Well, now we'll have lotsa good firewood."

What, I asked myself, was wrong with him?

After picking up the broken glass as best we could and piling it in a far corner, we all retreated into a weary silence. As we bedded back down, covering ourselves with quilts and sleeping bags, only the suck-suck sound of baby Heaven nursing broke the quiet. Clint hugged me to him but his body gave no warmth; it was as cold as mine. Then it came the way it always did—unexpected and cleansing—my laughter, belly deep and unstoppable. The moment was too outrageous—unimaginable just months before in my big-city life. The crash, at first terrifying, felt absurd, but in a startling way, it was life-affirming.

This new life was better than being in an action movie because it was the movie. Better than reading history because we were making our own. Back in New York, I could have been lying in my nice warm, fluffy bed, eating chunky peanut butter from a jar and watching *The Late Late Show* while slowing dying. Instead, I was in the deep, dark woods living the grand adventure. I was Nelly Bly, Louis and Clark and

Marco Polo, Christopher Columbus and Sacajawea. So what if trees fell and men were hairy and macho. So what if we had no toilet, no phone, no running water, no electricity, and had to live like hippie sardines. So fucking what. The vibe hit us all —a little like magic, but more like family. Everyone joined in. The sound of our mutual laughter gave more warmth than central heating. We all felt the same. We were one. Together and howling louder than the wind.

CHAPTER 13

Sacred Outhouse

Early April 1972

Obey the nature of things, your own and nature and you will walk freely and undisturbed.

RAM DASS

The next morning, dawn came but not whole heartedly. All was dark gray. Since no one wore a watch, it was impossible to tell the time but it felt like 4 AM. The pale sun looked too weak to rise above the still apparent moon. We were in various stages of undress: cursing, rubbing our hands together, and hopping from one foot to the next. The chill had made getting out of my sleeping bag an act of courage. The real torture came when I put on my jeans. They were stiff with cold and sent everything below my waist into shock. Then the unthinkable happened: I had to go to the bathroom and had to go bad. Hidden in the trees, across the four-acre meadow, was an old outhouse. It wasn't visible from the cabin but I knew it was there.

As I stumbled forward, the high, wet grass bunched around me, leaving in my wake a path of broken stalks. When I reached the edge of the meadow, there it was: a small and very compact structure. With my warm breath steaming in front of me, I opened the latched door and stepped inside. It smelled all woody and clean, like the inside of a cedar closet. A fresh roll of toilet paper sat in a coffee can on the tightly grooved floors. Next to the can, dried corn cobs waited for those willing to wipe and compost at the same time (Ouch!). A tin bucket filled with lime and ash hung on a peg. To break down waste, the ash was to be poured, post-dump, into the five-foot hole below. Dropping my jeans was as heart-stopping as getting into them. Once they were at my ankles, the cold air swept through my legs, thighs, and delicate lady caverns. I didn't dare look into the dark abyss below my exposed butt. Even though I'd been assured there were absolutely no poisonous snakes in Western Oregon, I imagined a nest of vipers slithering beneath my naked flesh. Then, as I looked through the moon-shaped cutout in the outhouse door and saw the encircling forest, my mind flipped: This was God's sweet but freezing outhouse and evil could not lurk here. Shorty had built it as a present for his young, pregnant wife to spare her from having to squat in the woods. Love and kindness were embedded in its timbers. Inside it, I was surely safe. Outside it... not so much. Tragically, Shorty's bride had not been able to use his considerate gift for long. All of Flores Creek, including the homestead, was open range. No rancher in Curry County had to fence in their livestock and all could roam free. Shorty told us that while she was picking wild iris, his wife had been gored to death by a wandering bull: "My red-haired gal was pretty and feisty, just like you, 'bout the same age, too. Never did get hitched agin after that." The wooden box that held the toilet seat was etched with little hearts and crosses. The outhouse was sacred. I touched down on its icy seat with much trepidation but also with reverence.

I'd been gone from the Main Cabin for what felt like only a few minutes but must have been longer because on my return, I found the inside had undergone a dazzling transformation. Sawdust covered every surface. All our belongings: duffle bags, bedding, furniture, clothes, mattresses, and books were piled in a haphazard mound. Above my head, hammering obliterated all other sound. Sky, Clint, and Pete, our master builders, were constructing a sleeping loft. Heat, they explained, rose and if they finished in time, our next night together would be cozy and warm. Sky flew down the ladder, wearing a leather carpenter's belt. His sleeves were rolled up and sweat slid down his face. Without his usual "Howdee," he grabbed a bucket of nails and immediately climbed back up to join Pete and Clint. The three moved in a construction ballet, graceful and synchronized: arms, legs, bodies bending with strength and purpose. I was thrilled by their forward momentum. It was all happening. We were moving like Kesey's bus *Further.* Further into our collective future. Further ahead.

All the broken windows had been covered with old sheets and towels. At the sink, Louise, with her usual speed and purpose, was priming the hand pump. I watched as rusty water spit forth from the spout; a few more plunges of the handle and it turned clear. I cupped my hands to catch some. It was as sweet as water could be, with no bitter mineral aftertaste. We would not have to carry water a mile up from the creek to drink and bathe. It flowed into our new home, free and beautiful.

"Check it out!" Joey shouted as he came through the back door holding a dripping and dead water rat at arm's length. "Bettcha its been floating around down in the well for days!" The rat was bloated and hairy, its nasty head falling limp onto its chest.

"Hey Guys, I got the mother-fuckin' rat!" Joey shouted up to the loft.

The hammering stopped.

"I got the water rat—fished it out!"

"Good work, Joey!" Clint called back. "Why don'tcha come on up and give us a hand."

Joey thrust out his chest like a rooster, so proud he'd been invited to join the master crew. He'd just reached the first rung of the ladder, when Moonlove saddled up to him holding an empty cigar box. "Please put it into this," she said. "We can't just throw the body away, we have to bury it proper, it's God's creature."

"Sure thing," Joey said gently. "We can do that."

Inspecting the rodent's bloated belly Moonlove's eyes filled with tears. "It had a mother and a father, too."

Moonlove's heart had been broken so often that everything, even a dead rat, broke hers.

Cassy Jane stopped sweeping. "Nobody gives a rat's ass about a dead rat," she said, "including its mother." I had to agree with this blunt farm girl so accustomed to critter life and death. Soft-hearted Joey, however, was moved by Moonlove's sadness. So instead of joining the men to hammer and nail, he held the little rat coffin while Moonlove placed Heaven, her sleeping daughter, on top of a duffle bag and covered her with a frayed blanket. Moonlove, in whatever gear she could find, then stepped outside into the pouring rain with Joey to dig a rat grave. It was a gesture I expected from a child, but not a grown woman—her compassion felt overblown and absurd. Where, I had to ask myself, did respect for life begin and where did it end? I was searching for an answer when Louise's voice sliced my thoughts: "I need a goddamn sponge!" Louise was bent over the sink, angrily scrubbing it with a rusty scouring pad that left a trail of rusty fibers. The metal disintegrated under her steam and in moments the pad was no bigger than a quarter. "Is there anything wrong, Louise?" I asked, knowing full well it was a bad idea.

"I can't talk now, Carol," she snapped. "I'm working. Something you might actually consider."

"Louise, no one can keep up with you."

Louise shook her can of Ajax so furiously that the powder not only covered the sink, but also the wooden sideboard. Her elbows flew as she spoke, as if she were an agitated bird, flapping her wings: "That's just wonderful, Carol, how you turned it around to blame me."

"Turn what around?" I asked innocently, even though I felt guilty.

"Doing jack while all the rest of us haul ass!"

Being blindsided was ancient and familiar to me but a grain of self-esteem, countered it. My thoughts, I assured myself, surpassed Louise's logical, neatly organized mind. I was an artist, a visionary, and could see beyond her simple goal-oriented myopia. Even when I was doing nothing, I was doing something.

"That's not fair, Louise," I said. "I do plenty."

"Bullshit! I'm sorry, Carol, but someone had to say it. Clint won't. He treats you like a princess."

My response had no weight, but was all I could manage, "You're the one married to a prince, Louise. Not me."

Louise said nothing but grabbing the pump handle with both hands, pumped water into a tin bucket with self-righteous fury. When the bucket was full, she set back her slight shoulders and hauled it over to Agung who, at the other end of the cabin, was standing over our converted oil drum stirring a cast iron pot full of graying, day-old rice and beans. When he noticed Louise struggling with the bucket's weight, he pushed the pot to the rim and grabbing her bucket's handle, helped her lift it onto the stove. He then turned towards me. "Hey Carol," he said, "we sure could use salad greens. You up for finding us some?" I thought I caught him looking knowingly at Louise. Were they complicit? I wasn't certain, but it didn't matter.

"Sure thing, Aggie," I answered. "I'd be glad to."

Could it be more obvious how willing and helpful I truly was? In addition, salad was in my blood. My mother had juiced in an industrial sized juicer and also served buckets of fresh lettuce, arugula, kale, and parsley to her customers at Kubies. When business was slow, she had let me help. Mom bought her produce from organic farms in New Jersey. But I wouldn't have to. Foraging for it would be like shopping in God's supermarket.

"Do you need me to come with you?" Louise offered. I was sure it was a conciliatory move, only half meant. But even though I didn't want to venture into the deep woods alone, I refused her. Flores Creek was my home. To own it meant to know and work it with or without fear.

I was halfway down the cabin steps, when Clint stepped onto the front porch. "Carol!" he called out. "Don't forget your knife!" After my imaginary viper experience, I went nowhere without it looped to my belt. "Got it, sweetheart!" I called back.

Clint beamed like a proud papa: I was prepared.

Just a few feet into the forest and a canopy of alder treetops covered half the sky. I pulled my knife from its sheath and tested the blade. It was razor sharp. Clint had instructed me, when in the forest, to slice slivers of bark off the trees on my pathway, so I could follow the markings, retrace my steps, and find my way back home. The thin bark came off easily and the white inner cambium stood out against the darker silver. I was blazing a trail and had made three markings when I discovered a giant patch of miners' lettuce. Moonlove had taught me how to recognize it. Growing everywhere with small, fat leaves, it was a luscious, deep green and tasted like spinach—only better.

Free food—I loved it.

Anyone who knows their mushrooms will say what happened next was impossible but there they were, just a few feet ahead: a golden circle of Chanterelles mushrooms, lightly dusted by fir needles. Their unique fluted underbellies were a dead giveaway: an exact replica of the mushroom photos I'd studied in *The Wonderful World of Fungus*. Chanterelles, seemingly knowing their own high value, hid themselves in the dark earth. They were out of season, a little soft, but still edible. If by chance I was mistaken, all who ate them could die a slow, liver-destroying death. But even though my previous experience with fungus had been limited to toenails, I was sure. Taking the biggest and firmest, I cut off only the head and a small part of the stem. Leaving a stump in the ground assured regrowth. Not many ex-Manhattanites were privy to that information. In fact, I might have been the only one.

The sun was still flitting through the trees like a strobe light and even though I'd had just one early-morning toke, I was transfixed by the beauty of the forest floor. Dead leaves and rotted twigs mixed with myriads of mushrooms: spotted red, neon green, and witchy black—all phallic and wondrous with their meaty round heads and silky stems. A huge orange and edible hen-of-the-woods stuck to a distant log and looked like a petrified omelet. It was irresistible. I tore off chunks and stuffed them into my paper sack. Visions of sautéing the golden bits with garlic and butter danced in my head.

Birds! They were everywhere and singing like an avian orchestra. One outstanding, high-pitched trill reminded me of my father. He'd loved to imitate birds and somehow during his youth in a tenement on Manhattan's Lower East Side, he'd heard and copied their songs. I could almost see him in his black cashmere coat and silk scarf, as, later in life, he whistled on his way to work at our health food store. But I wasn't on East 57th and Lexington, I was deep in the Oregon woods and the sun had suddenly disappeared. The temperature dropped and a light drizzle began. Foolishly, I hadn't worn rain gear as it had been sunny when I started out. The damp cold came at me like a slap. Then I was hit with something even worse: Without sunlight, my tree markings were invisible. Every direction I took led me deeper into the unrecognizable, but I didn't panic until I heard the crashing sound. Something was moving through the underbrush towards me. A bull! No. I reminded myself, bulls don't stalk, they charge. At worst it was a bear, at best an elk. A cougar was unlikely because, I'd been told, they were silent and attacked from above. You didn't hear or see a cougar until it was too late—until it had bitten through your neck and was chewing off your face. Scrambling down a narrow deer path, I dropped my precious bag full of mushrooms and greens and shouted for the only help I knew to depend on: "Taxi! Taxi!"

None came.

Only a deer who took one look at me and fled.

Every direction I took led nowhere. All paths dead-ended. Every tree was unmarked. The wind rose and rain poured down in sudden, relentless sheets. With my body trembling and the assurance of impending hypothermia, I ran, not knowing where I was going, just knowing I had to go.

Then, above the whistle and roar, I heard a reassuring sound. It wasn't a voice asking "Where to, Lady?" No, it was a sound I'd grown to love: hammering. Pushing my way through the bracken fern and thimbleberry bushes, I followed that sound and with each step it grew louder. Having come full circle, I landed at the edge of the forest and could see smoke rising from the cabin chimney.

Saved.

Dripping wet, I pushed open the cabin's huge wooden door, stepped inside and was greeted by Clint's warm and open arms. Sky and Pete were still working on the loft, but Clint, Agung, and Joey, dressed in full rain gear and carrying flashlights, were about to set out to search for me.

"Jesus, Carol," Clint said, "We were getting worried."

"We sure were," Louise added. "You better get out of those wet clothes or you'll catch pneumonia." I threw off my jacket and peeled off my soaked jeans. Cassy Jane handed me a dry towel, Lila made me a cup of hot peppermint tea from her private stash and Agung clapped his hands saying, "Shit woman, we're glad you're safe."

The warmth of the cabin, the caring of my tribe, the coming together of what had seemed impossible, formed a warm ball at the center of my chest that felt like love. These people, these friends; where would I be without them?

"I lost the salad," I sniffled.

"Hey," Agung said, "tomorrow's another day."

"And so's the next," Clint added.

We were at Flores Creek for the long haul.

Nothing in the cabin looked the same—the chaos wasn't gone and never would be, but it was cleaner and more orderly than when I'd left. Books and Ball jars lined the shelves. Colorful clothes hung from the rafters like Tibetan prayer flags. And most amazing of all—our cast iron pans dangled on hooks above an enormous, bow-legged porcelain cook stove. With its double oven, six burners, and clawed feet, it was undoubtedly the biggest and the most beautiful wood cookstove in the known universe. The word "Superior" was emblazoned across it.

"The stove," I asked, "where did you get it? How'd you get it here?"

"Took some doing," Clint answered. "Got it from Woody, an ole farmer livin' down the road. Cost us in trade. We're gonna help shear his sheep come June."

They'd hauled it, Agung explained, "like a tiger after a hunt." Two guys on one end, three on the other, all staggering under the weight.

Our combined energy, when in force, could do great things.

Together, I realized, we'd survive.

CHAPTER 14

Bless Your Beautiful Hide

Mid April 1972

The great way is not difficult for those who have no preferences.
RAM DASS

For weeks we cleaned up the foot-deep muck and time capsules of debris that Shorty had left behind. Tangled masses of rotted wood, forgotten clothing, broken glass, soup cans, and old newspapers; all had to be buried deep and covered with dirt. My shovel was outsized, bigger than all the rest because I'd grabbed it first. Its thick handle felt solid in my gloved hands. I loved how it helped me scoop up a huge load to be carried and dumped into a fresh-dug hole far from the Main Cabin. Sweat dripped down my forehead and into my eyes. I wiped it off with the back of my hand, proud to help make my...our new home, a place for all to live.

Under the porch we found depression-glass medicine and milk bottles, antique blue Ball jars, five-gallon Hudson oil cans with rusted 1930s logos, rotted high-button shoes, old *Life* magazines (one with a picture of Lauren Bacall on the cover), Louis L'Amour paperback Westerns, rusted saws, disintegrating saddles, bridles, harnesses, and tack. Most were soaked and almost ruined by the rain, but we oiled the handsaws, rubbed wax into the old leather, and used the bridles and harnesses to decorate the cabin wall. Clint and Sky hung a six-foot hand saw over the porch. It gave the cabin a purposeful rustic look. I scrubbed years of scum off the delicate glass medicine bottles and placed them on the window sills so the sun could shine through their prisms and project rainbows into the dust.

The simple life was complicated. Everything in our (my) forest home took time, effort, and cooperation. To cook or to boil water began with gathering wood or cutting down a tree, sawing the tree into logs, then rounds, then splitting the rounds with a wedge and finally chopping the half rounds into a size that would fit inside a fire box. Once the fire got going, the damper had to be turned down so the wood did not burn too quickly; but not so slowly that the fire would go out. Tending the fire was like surfing or sailing—adjusting to the forces of nature to ride the wind and waves—a hell of a way to bake banana bread. A single mistake, like using slow burning wet fir instead of dry cedar, could stretch the task out endlessly.

In this "chop wood, carry water" existence, patience became a survival mechanism. The simplest tasks, which in the outside world required only minutes, could take days or weeks or were just impossible. I learned to wait and accept what was and what couldn't be.

Gas cost money and we did our best to conserve both. We had only one or two running vehicles, making coordination a categorical imperative. A "town trip" into Langlois called for deep cooperation. As many as six people drove in together, all with individual agendas but with the same group needs...food, medical and farm supplies, communication, gas, and vehicle maintenance. This required time and goodwill, but our time was not money—our time was our time.

Clint had been so right. We needed everyone. In having less, we appreciated each other more. And there was music. Moonlove played her flute and a man called Two Turtles joined us. Tall and lanky, he was a friend of a friend; after spending two weeks with us, he asked if he could stay indefinitely. The vote, although not formal, was unanimous. Everyone liked Two Turtles. He would not sleep in the cabin but in a tent down at the creek. Two Turtles knew how to shop for bulk foods and was happy to share his few food stamps, a serious perk. The man was accustomed to communal living and roughing it. He was handy and thorough and, to the delight of all, he played the guitar. Soft nights, gentle music, a warm fire. It was peace on earth. Only tribal opened-heartedness could give us this forward momentum...and music.

My thinking had come full circle, made a 360 degree turn. I was thankful for anyone with skill who chose to join us. All that mattered was that they would add to the whole rather than detract. Even if they'd robbed an occasional bank, it was cool with me as long as when one of us was bleeding, they'd stanched the flow. Murderers and crazies aside, only opened heartedness would keep all of us safe. Nothing between us could be bought, only given freely.

Living tightly packed presented a new learning curve. Lack of personal indoor space required careful consideration of one another. Inside the main cabin, this included: lightness of foot (not stomping around and making a lot of noise), avoiding body contact (bumping into someone invaded their territory), and even staying out of one another's sight lines. At night, we hung sheets and blankets between our mattresses in the sleeping loft— private space had become golden.

After Two Turtle's arrival, we had three vehicles but they rarely ran all at once and always needed parts. Joey, our Brooklyn boy, made friends with Stumpy at Stumpy's Local '76 and Stumpy (Stumpy not because he was missing a limb, but because he cut down trees, leaving their stumps) traded us his gas for our weed. It took ten fat joints to fill up Clint's truck—and seven for Agung's VW bus.

The tiny town of Langlois was six miles west and two miles north of Flores Creek. The name Langlois came from "L'Anglois," the French word for "The English." One-hundred and fifty-two families lived in and around Langlois. Every local mispronounced the name and Americanized the French: *Lang Loyze*. Even though I wanted to, I didn't correct them. Nobody wants to be told they don't know how to say the name of their own hometown, especially by a former New Yorker.

Langlois had a Texaco Station, a Feed and Seed store, a post office, a bar, a public telephone, and Miss Suzy's Diner—open for breakfast and late lunch. Miss Suzy was eighty-one. At least that's what she told us. She served mostly truckers and her hours were between 5 AM and 2 PM. Watching her serve her griddle cakes and eggs was a life lesson in true grit. The stuff of pioneers, she wanted no help, but it was impossible to just sit there. You had to get up from your seat and lend a hand.

She reminded me of the hard-working, strong women I knew in my beloved N.Y. support group. With her bowed legs and hairnet, Miss Suzy would be a great character to bring to life. I had to share her determined independence with the best of my old friends:

Dear Ellen,

There is an elderly woman in town who I know as Miss Suzy. Miss Suzy is our only source of forbidden white flour and white sugar. The griddle cakes she serves from her trailer/truck stop are to die for. Ancient but spry, she moves from stove to table, with full-plated breakfasts riding up her arms. If you try to help her she says, "Sit yer butt down and lemme get on with it." I love her. Big hello to Claudia, Stockard, Faith, and Katherine and all the ladies back in the Big Apple.

Xoxo Carol

To reach our mountaintop on our return trip, we passed through the Flores Creek Valley. Our creek water was crystalline and delicious. No human lived above us. Big mammals did, but never ever, Clint assured us, took a dump in the creek. They preferred dry land. The creek itself flowed a mile below the clearing. Downhill, it was an easy reach by foot, but the uphill return was excruciating, particularly if you carried anything besides your own weight.

The valley below our mountain home was dotted by ranches, ranging from 160 to 2,000 acres. They had been handed down through generations. Most living in these isolated areas had never seen a black man, an Asian, a Jew, or even an Italian in the flesh. At an animal auction in Bandon, which was as close as we came to live entertainment, a reclusive rancher discovered there were Jews among us (Louise, Joey, and I) and asked to see our horns. I didn't laugh. Prejudice or, more aptly, mistrust of anyone not like them was so ingrained that breaking through was impossible. They had a particular dislike for Native Americans, particularly the Siletz, Siltcoos, and Coquille who had lived in Coastal Oregon and were now displaced and stuck in poverty on the local reservation. While the small local farmers were comparatively liberal and accepting, the large ranchers resented the hippie population for invading the territory they considered their birthright. Some of their men, rarely, if ever, travelled beyond their homesteads and had never seen the ocean or women other than their mothers or sisters. The most cloistered among them, alone and isolated, did actually fuck their sheep and saw our hippie women as near animals. We stringently avoided them. Nearly insane but not evil, they were sexually starved beyond their own endurance.

Sounds: giant woodpeckers the size of poodles pecked at trees with a rat-tat-tat as loud as any riveter; the cry of the cougar, as plaintive as the wail of a lost child; limbs cracking, caused by wind or unseen bears as they climbed trees and ravaged beehives.

Dear Mom and Dad,

I am living with a delightful group on our beautiful wilderness estate and I have acquired much knowledge and very useful survival skills. Did you know that when you encounter a cougar, the safest course of action is to reach for the sky to appear taller and to slowly back away? Never, I've come to learn, turn your back on a full-grown cougar. Tell that to Susan Shatkin who just married Robert Weiss in the Persian room of the Plaza.

P.S. Please don't send me any more of your friends' daughter's wedding announcements. I don't want to ever get married but I am happy and healthy and hope you are the same.

Love, Carol.

☾

When I looked around me, I could not believe that the lush forest, the magnificent trees, and the creek were mine. And they weren't. A letter that Chief Seattle of the Squamish tribe wrote to President Franklin Pierce held the truth: *The Great Chief in Washington sends words that he wishes to buy our land. How can we buy or sell the sky, the warmth of the land? The idea is strange to us. We do not own the freshness of the air or the sparkle of the water. How can you buy them*?" Having a big city with a space needle in the middle of it named after him would not have been of consolation to Chief Seattle.

At Flores Creek we were living in the past to find our future and everything started from ground zero. The first step in cooking meat, foul, or fish, required the creature to be dead. Louise and I murdered our first chicken together. We rounded up our free range, skinny squawking bird and I pushed its neck against a stump while Louise held the ax. Just before she made the chop, I realized that if she missed—goodbye to my left hand.

"Louise, don't! There's gotta be a better way."

"Yeah? What??" she asked as she dropped the ax to her side. I closed my eyes and tried to summon up a method I'd read about in the *Whole Earth Catalogue.* But the only thing that came to mind was how to make buttons out of goat horn. "Butcher a goat. Saw the horns into cross sectional slices and drill holes into each disk." Useless. As Louise waited, my memory finally kicked in. I handed the freaked-out bird to her, found two nails and hammered them close together on the stump. Louise watched in disbelief; I'd always been more chaos than solution-oriented. Grabbing the bird, I pushed its neck through the nail bars and holding onto its feet, stretched it out like an accordion. The ax blade would come nowhere near my body.

One swipe from Louise and the chicken's head rolled to the porch floor. Nerve endings dangled from the hole where its neck used to be. The body ran helter-skelter until it figured out that something had gone terribly wrong. It then collapsed into a dead chicken puddle. Holding the bird corpse at arm's length, Louise carried it into the cabin and plunged it into boiling water to remove the feathers. Next came the truly nauseating part—scooping the offal and feces from its still warm insides. The smell of fat and guts lingered on my skin long after I washed and only for a split second did I remember I was once a girl who'd splashed herself with Jean Nate cologne and could order lunch in French from a menu at the Brasserie. Lesson learned: Slaughtering an animal is stinky; growing a vegetable is sweet.

"Bruschetta de Flageolets s'il vous plait."

☾

The 1954 musical *Seven Brides for Seven Brothers* stars Howard Keel as Adam, a bearded Oregon lumberjack, who finds and marries city girl Milly (Jane Powell) in a heartbeat. The next day he takes her to his farm in the woods. The place is a pigsty. Milly is forced to cook, clean, and take care of Adam's six younger brothers. In the end, the brothers get their own wives and everybody lives together in the woods as one big happy, dancing, and singing family. Adorable Russ Tamblyn played one of the dancing younger siblings, but my heart belonged to burly and bearded Howard Keel, the eldest. I loved his deep baritone and thought him the sexiest man on earth. Big Epiphany: A 50s romantic musical, not the "Revolution," had provided the roadmap for my back-to-the-land life.

At age thirteen, I'd sat in palatial RKO's Loews' theatre on Fifty-Ninth Street and Third Avenue and skipped school to watch the film repeatedly until it was replaced by *The Tarantula*, a drooling giant spider that ate goats, dogs, and people. As the second fattest girl in the seventh grade at Simon Baruch Junior High 104, I'd survived only because I knew that somewhere beyond the Rockies, something other than the food fight at Leonard Handelsman's bar mitzvah was waiting for me. The enchanted life of the Brides and the Brothers had burrowed its way into my unconscious and stayed there; dormant but alive. But the words of my feminist girlfriends in Manhattan haunted me: "Carol, you're negating everything the Women's Movement has stood for. It's a daddy-take-care-of-me choice." For me, and for the rest of the women at Flores Creek, the physical battle for dominance was easily lost because in the woods, expedience was everything and the men had the muscle power and we did not. Not one of us had ever worked out or been athletic–nor did we have the inclination to become more so. The longer I lived in this wild and natural world, the deeper I fell into a conventional female role. And, Goddess help me, I liked it. What my urbane friends could not know was every morning when I opened my eyes I saw beauty and, while the wind howled, my nights were filled with the warmth of sleeping in a good man's arms.

At night, we played cards and chess, sewed, made art, conversed, and read. To sit in our one tattered rocking chair by the fire and read was nirvana. Our book shelves included copies of the *Mother Earth News* and *Mother Jones, Build Your Own Windmill, Portnoy's Complaint, The I-Ching, Nine Circles to the Moon, The Tassajara Cookbook, Be Your Own Wilderness Doctor, The Iliad, The Red and The Black,* and everything by Meher Baba. Our massive farm table and matching benches brought from Greenleaf dominated the one room in our open concept dining/ kitchen/bedroom. Due to our limited amount of running water, we had no bathtub or shower and had to adapt a new standard of cleanliness. Without direct access to hot water our relationship to dirt changed drastically. It was easy to tell how long a person had lived with us by the state of their clothes and the hue of their skin. We dirty hippies were not dirty by choice.

CHAPTER 15

Too Much for the Money

May 1972

"The first duty of a revolutionary is to get away with it."
ABBY HOFFMAN

There were eleven of us: Clint, me, Agung, Louise, Sky, Lila, Pete, Cassy Jane, Joey, Moonlove, and Two-Turtles living at Flores Creek when April turned to May and daffodils sprouted on our mountaintop. Adorable leaping lambs covered the rolling hills of the 500-acre Sullivan ranch below. The rhododendrons had pink blossoms as big as a head and the rain grew lighter and warmer. White buds flowered on wild blackberry and orange-tipped salmonberry bushes promised future fruit. Except for Moonlove, all spent more time outside. Moonlove sat inside the cabin all day, every day, staring into space, playing her flute, nursing her baby, and washing the rags she used as diapers. While the rest hiked and explored, tripping on the giant ferns, she suckled and dreamed. To help with chores, she tried sweeping the floors and washing the dishes but usually forgot what she was doing. Whatever she cooked came out soggy or burned.

On top of being a colicky baby, Heaven's lower body was covered with a mean rash that no goldenseal poultice could cure. When anyone else tried to pick her up, her cries increased. When awake, she flayed her skinny arms and legs while her screams turned her face radish red. Sky had never claimed her as his child, even though Moonlove felt certain he was Heaven's father. Sky and Lila had become deeply involved in an enlightenment correspondence course with the Mahari-Ji in Malibu, and Moonlove and Heaven had dropped off their radar. A tight couple, they were kind and generous to Moonlove but stopped making her part of their lives. Moonlove's eyes grew sadder. She never complained—just rolled more and bigger joints.

Moonlove said she didn't want to go; but feeling the impossibility of her situation, announced she had to return to her hometown of Sugarland, Texas. What awaited her there no one knew, but she'd surely have to go back to being called Betty. Clint had been right; life with an infant in the wilderness had proven to be too much for her. A less stoned and more stalwart woman might have made it, but Moonlove was no Sacajawea. We had done all we could to keep her and her baby warm, but it wasn't enough. We weren't child-centered. We were our own children—centered on ourselves. No one, not even Agung, tried to talk her out of leaving. I felt shamefully relieved to see her go.

The morning they left, the wind blew wet billows across the clearing. Mother and baby were seated for the last time in the cab of Clint's pickup, waiting for him to drive them to North Bend to be dropped off at the Greyhound bus terminal. As the rain let up, a miracle: Moonlove had just rolled down her window to receive a last well-wish when Heaven smiled. The smile stayed on her tiny face and widened into a grin. Maybe it was because she had gas or was pooping, but for the first time Heaven seemed happy. Moonlove held Heaven's tiny hand in her own and with it, waved "goodbye."

"Be careful, be safe, we love you," we called to her. And as the old Chevy chugged down the road, no one seemed glad or sad, just contemplative. Lila and Sky were missing, they were deep in meditation inside the cabin and nothing, not even Moonlove's departure, could disturb them.

"She really liked rats," Cassy Jane said.

"Yeah," Louise added. "It's too bad she didn't get to bury her placenta in the ground the way she wanted to."

Not now Louise, I thought to myself, hoping she'd shut up.

"Whadda ya mean?" Joey asked her.

"Carol gave Moonlove's frozen placenta to the Highbridge commune," she answered, "as a Solstice present."

"Hey Louise," I said, "it was an accident. I thought it was a steak. They were both in the Greenleaf freezer and looked the same to me."

"Everybody at Highbridge freaked out," Louise gleefully added. "They figured it was some kind of ceremonial thing and we wanted them to eat it."

"That's foul," Joey said.

"Why did Moonlove want to bury her placenta anyway?" I asked, trying to change a subject that amused everyone but me.

"The Navajo believe that if you bury it under a tree, it binds the tribe to the land," Agung answered, his eyes still on the road even though Clint's truck was out of sight. "And it promotes future fertility."

No one questioned his explanation; instead, while dead leaves swirled around us, Joey, as if punishing himself for forgetting something vital, slapped his own forehead with the palm of his hand: "Shit" he muttered, "Moonlove's gone and there goes the food stamps. How we gonna eat?"

"We're not," Pete said

"No more American cheese?" Cassy Jane asked incredulously.

"No more," Louise answered.

The loss of Moonlove as a communal member lasted only minutes, but the loss of her $180 dollars a month in food stamps lingered. Not only would there be no more American cheese, there would be no more honey, no more molasses, no more granola, soy sauce, peanut butter, almonds, raisons, olive oil, or tuna fish. It was scary. Someone else had to procure as many food stamps as soon as possible. But who? Getting caught lying to the federal government could mean a stiff penalty or even jail time; someone brave and daring had to come forth, someone with chutzpah and guts, someone who didn't mind cheating and stealing for the common good.

"Hey guys! I'll do it," I said. "I'm very good at fooling people." Joey rolled his eyes. Sky cleared his throat and Cassy Jane stared at me while her sometimes lazy eye drifted towards her ear. Everyone had known I was right for the job and were practicing restraint while waiting for me to volunteer. Surely, I told myself, a good government that cared about "the people" should subsidize an experimental lifestyle that insured a lighter footprint on the earth. We were environmental revolutionaries, experimenting with simplicity, community, and natural alternatives to a chemical world; doing for America what America would not do for herself. It was simple. The system had no room for radical change, so, like Gandhi said, we'd become the change. This was my big chance.

Stealing came naturally to me. I'd been shoplifting since I was nine: jacks, pick-up-sticks, Spaulding balls, and double-bubble gum. At fifteen, I was caught swiping an Angora cardigan from *Orbach's.* Charges were not pressed but they contacted my parents. When I got home, my lawyer mother gave me her best professional advice: "Carol, what's the matter with you? Never do anything illegal, where there's a chance of getting caught. You have to weigh your odds." I took her deeply maternal advice to heart and stopped for years. However, my propensities were reignited after reading only three pages of Abbie Hoffman's *Steal This Book.* Ripping off corrupt institutions and corporations was my patriotic duty and, as a good American, I was happy to volunteer.

Martin Buber, the kind and wise Jewish philosopher who in his *I and Thou* reminded me of my own grandpa Schneiderman, would not, I was certain, have approved of my dishonesty. Buber told us we should do nothing we wouldn't want the whole world to do. What if everybody ripped off everybody else? That would be cosmically wrong, but that was what was happening. Every government, big corporation, and billions of people were stealing from and lying to each other. Those who were ethical had trouble surviving. They were the fall guys.

Lying and cheating the Federal Government was my mandate to help keep my tribe alive. And at last—a chance to act, to use my long dormant chops. My character motivation was already there, my hair was perfect, and I couldn't wait to figure out what to wear.

Up against the wall motherfucker! No. Sorry. I meant...all we are saying is give peace a chance.

☾

Louise was at the wheel waiting for me. Since she had to drive us two hours to Gold Beach, she'd decided that she, too, would give food stamps a try. Earlier that morning I'd snuggled up with Greta our goat and rubbed my body against her back and flanks. Except for trying to eat my rain hat, she didn't seem to notice. For her interview Louise had on her best jeans, a bright shirt, and had polished her shit kickers. The outfit was so wrong. Louise was a straight woman in hippie clothing—a lifetime good girl. I, on the other hand, wore a tattered blouse, filthy sneakers, and a disintegrated hunting jacket I'd found under a log in the woods.

"Jesus, Carol," Louise said as I climbed in next to her, "you reek." She rolled down the driver's window. The goat odor went beautifully with my back story—I was a mentally challenged backwoods housewife with four young children and a blind husband. Inspired by Country Joe (of *Country Joe and the Fish)* who had named his daughter Seven, my make-believe kids were named One, Three, Five, and Eight.

"And your children's names, please," the befuddled interviewer would say.

"One, Three, Five, and Eight."

"I'm sorry, perhaps you misunderstood me. Not their ages, their names."

"One, Three, Five, and Eight." I would repeat, keeping a straight face.

I was never asked this question. It was so disappointing. For the required proof of residence, I carried no traceable ID, only a letter addressed to my alias of "Laughing Heart Goldman" at the group post office box: Star Route 93, Langlois, Oregon. I had sent it to myself before we left Greenleaf, just in case.

The dim florescent lighting and the gray walls of the Curry County Welfare Department packed a heavy institutional wallop. As soon as I stepped inside I had to fight off the wish to flee. The wooden benches seemed purposefully uncomfortable. Louise sat on one side of me, her face pinched with worry. On my other side was a woman who looked older than I was—but wasn't. Her cheek was dominated by a flowering black eye that extended to her ear and down to her nose. It went from dark brown, to purple, and then to yellow at the edges. Her nails were bitten to the quick and dark dried droplets of blood popped out of the exposed skin on her fingers. A dirty-faced little boy of about two sat asleep in her lap. His nostrils were encrusted with snot and more viscous stuff bubbled out of him as he breathed in and out. They were so sorry-looking that I wanted to share my discomfort with Louise but couldn't get her attention; she was too deeply buried in her application handbook—studying hard.

A big clock sat on the wall. Louise and I had nothing to do but listen to it tick. Being poor, our time was no longer of value; we had forfeited it. We would have to wait until our turn came—many hours if necessary. The place was crowded. Curry County had fallen on hard times. If we didn't score, we might have to live on berries and deer, wild and rotten vegetables, and an occasional squirrel.

I pulled an ancient packet of chewing gum out of my jacket. It was still in the wrapper and stiff with age. The woman sharing the bench with us introduced herself as "Boston Mary," and asked me for a piece. A voice within told me Mary would more than appreciate any kindness given to her, so I took a leap of faith and gave her the whole Juicy Fruit pack. One after the other she unwrapped the pieces and stuffed them into her mouth, tossing their silver paper on the floor. That's when real inspiration hit. I offered her a pair of pink plastic imitation pearl earrings I kept in my jeans pocket for special occasions. She could have them I told her, if she'd let me carry in her toddler for my interview.

There were two certification counselors, each sat tightly boxed in two separate cubicles. We could share Boston Mary's little boy if I was called into one cubicle and she was called into the other. The time element was important; we'd have to go in at different times.

All Mary's son had to do was not wake up. "Sure thing," she said as she screwed on the earrings. They brought out the azure in her black eye. I was about to ask her son's name when a voice called out:

"Number 43. Laughing Heart Goldman?"

"I see you left your address blank," the welfare worker said as she pushed her chair as far away from me as she could. The goat stink had done its job. Her distaste spurned me on. She had a bloated body and light blue hair. Living all her life in this remote ranching area of Southern Oregon had not prepared her or her agency for the growing hippie invasion. I glanced under her desk, saw her stockinged ankles were swollen and felt unexpectedly sorry for her—this was her job, she'd probably taken it to comfort and help others while supporting herself and her family. A caring and responsible woman, it wasn't her fault our government thwarted forward thinkers. But I'd come this far and had to do what I had to do. So, I let a little wad of spit form at the corner of my mouth and slowly glide down my chin. It was a subtle drool, nothing over the top.

"We're six miles up the crick, jes pass the big Myrtle," I answered, wiping my chin on my sleeve. Boston Mary's boy was fast asleep in my lap, enveloped in a cloud of urine. I adjusted my leg to cradle him at the knee. He coughed but didn't wake up. My interviewer pretended he wasn't there. "What creek is that, please?"

"I...fergit"

"Maybe you'll remember later," she said, not believing it herself. "And your husband's occupation?"

"He's a goatherd...Nubian. But their teats went bad with the staph infect and all's that wuz good eatin' got et."

She looked down at her desk, shook her head and certified my six-person household for six hundred dollars for three months. Three months! Six times three was eighteen hundred dollars' worth of free food! Visions of sesame seed butter danced in my head. This was the score of all time, more than anyone had ever received. Surely I deserved real acknowledgement: "Ladies and Gentleman of the Academy, I am deeply moved and deeply grateful..."

When I got back to the waiting room bench, Louise was sitting there, looking glum. She'd received only forty dollars in stamps and had been told to come back in a month if she wanted recertification. I floated on her disappointment. What had she expected? As well-organized and giving as she was, she didn't have the chops. I knew what I was doing was against the law, but believed I was serving a higher cause. We would have golden raisins and virgin olive oil, dark buckwheat honey and carob powder for months. My acting classes at Yale had born fruit—literally. Thank you Stella Adler, "the method," and your little dog Muki, too. Best of all, this lucky hit did not stop at food. With Stumpy's trade agreement, giving us gas in exchange for food stamps, we'd be able to fill the truck's tank.

The food stamps themselves were lovely things, coming in little pastel booklets of fives, tens, and twenties. I shuffled them with my free hand, as thrilled as if I'd just broken the bank at Monte Carlo. Boston Mary watched me as she reached for her little boy. Just waking, his eyes widened as he looked up at me and saw I was not his mother. His response was to take a full handful of my long hair and pull it as hard as he could. Mary had to unwind his fingers one by one to make him let go.

"Hey," she said as she slapped her son's grimy hands away when he tried to grab on again, "Where's my cut?" If I had thought the earrings had sealed the deal I was sadly mistaken. Quickly opening a booklet, I tore out a twenty and handed it to her. She stared at me with such contempt I immediately handed her three more tens. "Jew," she mumbled and walked toward the exit taking my exhilaration with her. No matter how far my wandering people went, no matter how deep into the woods, hatred followed us. In my mind I saw Boston Mary smashing windows during Kristallnacht, then laughing as my people, shivering and naked, walked into ovens. "Nazi," I shouted back at her, but it was too late. Boston Mary was already out the door but her prejudice stayed and hurt. Yes, I was a Jew—the best kind. The kind who provided for her family, who used her wiles to survive—just like Naomi, Ruth, Rebecca, and Sarah. Despite Mary's horrid invective, victory was mine: because, of all the food stamps ever scored by anyone, at Greenleaf or Flores Creek, my score was the biggest. And just like that, I had a solid identity, a content within the context of my new life: I was liberator of funds, a lady bountiful who served the needs of her tribe and once again, a successful actress.

☾

After our windfall at the Welfare Department, Louise drove us thirty miles North to McKay's supermarket in Port Orford. As we stood in line to pay the cashier, Louise bent over to hide her stamps from the person standing behind us on line. She'd been brought up to give to, not take from the poor and it embarrassed her to be on the dole. But not me. I felt I'd earned them. Next we hit the '76 station in Langlois. Above the pump a sign read, "We take food stamps." But it didn't say what for. Stumpy took a hundred dollars' worth of our blue stamps and put seventy-five dollars, all real green tens and twenties into my hands. The cash, even though wrinkled, felt rich and cool to the touch—reminding me there were those who relied on it, worked for it, and worshipped it. As we headed North to Dick's feed and seed, holding that money in my blistered hands felt empowering and in spite of myself, I wished I had more.

Dick's was owned and run by Deputy Sheriff Dick Labin, whose family had been in Curry County for generations. They operated a successful thousand-acre cattle and sheep ranch. Dick's father was the mayor of Langlois, his sister the elementary school principle, his brother ran the Bandon livestock auction, and his mother was the town librarian.

Dick greeted us with unexpected warmth, "Good afternoon Ladies," he said. "What can I do ya for?"

"We need some garden hose," Louise said, getting straight to the point.

"Betcha you hippie gals need mulch, too," he said winking knowingly at Louise, who was the only one of us who had nothing to do with weed.

"And some chicken scratch," I said, trying to affirm our legal farming activities.

"Jes drive round the back," he said, "and I'll load 'er up for you."

While Louise wandered off to inspect a stack of new rubber boots, Sheriff Labin continued, "Say, don't mind if I pay you all a friendly call one o'these days, do ya?"

I was glad Louise hadn't heard him. She might have wet her overalls.

"Anytime Sheriff," I lied. "You're always welcome."

"The feelin's reciprocated, Miss...

"Schlanger."

"Schl..."

CHAPTER 16

I'm In Love with Chekhov

Late May 1972

Three o'clock in the morning. The soft April night is looking at my windows and caressingly winking at me with its stars. I can't sleep, I am so happy."

ANTON CHEKHOV, *About Love and Other Stories*

Naked. We were all naked and I didn't like it. Not when I was standing outside on a wet, chilly afternoon because the water supply from our twenty-foot deep well was fine for drinking and dishes, but not plentiful enough for bathing. There was another reason I didn't like it—my belly. I'd gone twenty-five years without a waistline and had never recovered from the experience of having too much flesh; no matter how lovely my face, how shapely my legs, how searing my intellect, that bulbous thing stuck between my hips had always hindered me. The sense of failure I'd faced ever since my mother first took me to Lane Bryant's, the department store for the miserably chubby, had never left. How many parties and auditions had I gone to thinking I wasn't good enough? *"Hello, I'm imperfect. Would you care to humiliate me?"* Now I was a hippie for Chrissake. I'd been bare-assed in front of these people more times than I could remember, but the old shame was still there. I was supposed to feel free and unfettered. Instead, I felt fat. It was stupid. I felt fat and stupid.

One after another we stepped inside a low geodesic dome framed with bent alder and covered with transparent plastic. Clint, Sky, and Pete told us they'd used the Native American Sweat lodge as a prototype, which made it not only utilitarian, but cool. In the center was a three-foot wide hole filled with red hot volcanic rock. This special rock would not crack or spit shrapnel and came from the Three Sisters mountain range in Eastern Oregon.

Once cooked, the glowing rocks were shoveled into the pit by someone strong and steady on their feet. Sky, who was both ripped and graceful, did the job as well as any real Arapaho—or Lutheran jock from Galveston, Texas. All our men: one Muslim, one Jew and a few not-born-again Christians, were seated on one bench, opposite the women seated on the other. This arrangement reminded me of when, in high school, I visited a Jewish orthodox temple-Beth Israel on West 34th street where men and women could not sit together. Now, in the Oregon wilderness, I considered that this ancient seating rule, initiated by Hebrew men who blamed women for having spiritually distracting bodies, might have actually had a root in nature; and I almost forgave those bearded, davening guys in their yarmulkes for not allowing women to pray alongside of them—almost, but not quite. Even though it was apparent that the sexes did not always want to be physically close and separated—instinctively, my orthodox brethren thought of us as unclean, treif...not kosher...like pork.

Pete placed a sprig of sage on the rocks and it sizzled, Joey dipped into a bucket with a tin cup and poured the cold water over the rocks. The steam rose. Rivulets of grime ran down our arms, chests, and legs. There was only a sliver of soap between all of us, but it didn't matter, the steam did the work. This was the real Rapture: getting clean.

I could still make out a few faces and if I looked directly at any one man, he looked back at me with a wide open, friendly grin. There was nothing sexual about it. We were just glad to be getting clean. After the first go around, the steam disappeared. We waited, limp and happy, for more red-hot rock to be added to the pile. Clint opened the flap and stepped outside. Cold air hit and I could clearly see the lineup of male genitalia directly opposite me. I tried not to stare, but, I asked myself, how often did I have this opportunity? I'd never seen so many clumped together, dangling like so much fruit on the vine. If I'd wanted to, I could have reached over and checked each for quality and firmness, but I preferred to compare and contrast. It was an old habit left over from having to write too many college essays.

Sky's penis was much bigger than Two Turtle's and this struck me as very odd because Two Turtles was much taller. But in a way it made perfect sense. Sky, when standing, had a straight, proud back; Two Turtles, lanky and lean, hunched over. Sky was a woman magnet. Two Turtles (whose real name was Alan) had to work hard to get what he wanted and, even then, his liaisons, he'd told us, didn't last long. He was the only one of our six men who wasn't circumcised and his hooded fellow looked like a country bumpkin that has forgotten to take his hat off at dinner. Agung's member, my favorite next to Clint's, was almost too large for his compact bronze frame but totally in sync with his outsized personality and hefty intellect. His penis was calmly assertive—the way only a self-assured man can be. Joey's was short and chunky and matched his pugnacious insecurity. If his member could have talked it would have said: "Please sir, can I have some more?" It reminded me that Joey, the former Red Hook street urchin, had been dumped on us from a passing hippie bus and allowed to stay only at Agung's insistence. When Clint came back inside, I could again see that in comparison, his was straight and regular—a no-nonsense, "Let's roll," kind of guy.

No one talked. The heat was too overwhelming. Just before more steam rose, I leaned forward to take a quick look at the seated women. It was only fair. Louise had a hairy bush whose thick foliage climbed down her thighs and in a thin straight line up to her belly button. It stood outspoken and determined against her well-organized body. That was Louise all right—always together, always prepared. Lila and Cassy Jane had barely visible blond pubes, but while Lila's subdued down covered her vagina like a summer cloud, CassyJane's did not. Lila was always clear and forthright, entirely without frills. Cassy Jane was anything but; her pink and puffy missy was hairless, as bare as a baby's bottom, as childlike and provocative as she was. Not wanting to exclude my own sweet pudendum, I bent forward and looked. It was like my head: covered with dense, flaming auburn hair: outspoken and impossible to ignore.

More steam. Hot. Hot. Hot. Sweat dripped down my neck and back. In the half light, my mind expanded with my pores. Then it hit me: Nothing about me was defective. I was perfect. Everybody was. Both beauty and imperfection were here and it was impossible to tell which was which. Big, small, dark, fair, we were all human animals cleaning up our act and washing our coats: pedigrees and mutts—some Cocker Spaniels, others Great Danes; never meant to be the same with a single standard for beauty. All were "Best In Show."

When as a little girl, with only an indiscernible but very naughty twinkle in my eye, my grandma Schneiderman sat me down in the bathtub, looked at me, clapped her soapy hands and said, "Sheyna medele" (my beautiful child), I thought nothing of it. She was my grandma. When Steven Levine, my college lover, watched me hurry into my clothes and said, "You just don't know, do you?" He was right. I didn't. And Clint...seeing me naked for the first time said I looked like "one of those hot Renaissance women," I dismissed his opinion because he ate bologna sandwiches with mayonnaise on white bread.

To be human was to be beautiful. I'd heard it said before, but never believed it, not until that very moment.

Then just like that, my rebirth party was over.

There was a rustling outside. A high-pitched voice asked "Is any there room in there?"

"Sure thing," Clint answered. "There's always room for you." He'd recognized the female's voice but I hadn't. It was familiar, but I couldn't place it. The flap opened. The woman's head appeared. It was nothing special, flat and oval with stringy dark hair, but then followed by her outrageously amazing body. It was Anise, Doc Webster's former nurse and ex-old lady. Doc Webster was the cannabis-loving dentist who had repaired my abscessed tooth and worked for barter. Everybody loved the Doc, including Anise's best friend Pasture. Through the hippie grapevine, we'd all heard that the good dentist had dumped Anise to be with Pasture, a large and fertile woman whose name invoked a leisurely graze. Wounded and on the rebound, Anise had, earlier that morning, arrived at Flores Creek in her bright blue Jeep and had taken a long walk to heal among the dripping, fragrant firs. Now she was in our sweat bath. As Anise squeezed in next to me, the other women were forced to move closer together, thigh touching sweaty thigh, to make room for her.

Life can be hard and lonely for a single woman who does not want to be single. It can be even rougher and lonelier in the isolated rural Northwest. Just before Anise sat, she deliberately pointed her firm, melon ass at the men's bench and any sympathy I had for her, evaporated. As her buttocks encroached on mine, I saw that her vagina with its sparse bargain-basement pubes, was ordinary and dull. According to my interpretive genitalia theory, if it reflected who and what she was, I had nothing to worry about. The woman was a snore. But in an instant, that notion proved bogus. Anise had the most exquisite breasts I had ever seen. I tried my hardest to remember how beautiful and human I was, how I could sing *Anchors Away* in Latin and how my analysis of *Uncle Vanya* caused the dean of Yale Drama to suggest, before he grew to hate my guts, that I might consider becoming a theater critic. Instead, I sat riveted by Anise's pink, perky, and perfect orbs— 36 Cs with no drop or droop. In comparison, mine lay on my chest like two flat, undercooked pancakes. Even worse, my nipples turned inward toward each other—freakishly cross-eyed and looking like what they did all day was spit tobacco and wrestle swamp alligator.

The atoms in the steam bath realigned. Our nice and clean became Anise's raunchy and desperate. Her need took over the whole space. She was a female in heat, her tail lifted, her glands dripping their irresistible musk. She let her legs drop open, her thighs saying "ENTER HERE." The male organs hanging across from me awakened; one after the other they lifted their Cyclops heads to get a better look.

Slowly, oh so slowly, Anise dribbled water over her chest. She then took the soap and cupped herself, lifting first one tit, then the other, slowly—oh so slowly, carefully scrubbing beneath each. As she touched herself, her nipples responded. Through the parting steam, I watched as those two miniature pig snouts quivered upward, chocolate-colored and plump.

Our female warning system went on alert; Anise wanted one of our men. It didn't matter which: Sky, Agung, Pete, Two Turtles, or even Joey, but I knew she was doing her dance mainly for Clint. He was so movie-star masculine and...such a total shit: his penis was growing bigger, flowering like sea money in water. Clint's and Anise's eyes locked. Their look lasted only seconds, but was the way a man and woman stared at each other just before he pinned her against a wall and ripped off her panties.

When Clint caught me watching him, his penis recoiled. He closed his eyes and inhaled deeply, as if merely enjoying the steam. I told myself the powerful attraction I'd seen the two share was my imagination. I'd always had trouble separating illusion from reality and this had to be one of those times. That's what I told myself, but I wasn't listening: "Clint!" I hissed. His eyes popped open and he looked at me with such unexpected tenderness that my fear melted and I blew him a kiss. He blew one back and with it, I could feel his arms around me even though they hung at his sides. Despite his attraction to Anise, I was sure he loved me and always would.

The steam was gone. The rocks had grown cold. Sky opened the flap and the rest of the men ran out into the meadow, yelping and hooting, exuberant with youth and First People's folklore. We women followed, less audibly ecstatic but equally free. The cold air hit my overheated skin, but I hardly felt it. What I felt was wonderful. Of all the life choices to be had, I was sure this was the best. Here was where I belonged, where the wind shook the trees and the very air had a primal juju.

Minutes passed—I was freezing.

"Didn't anybody bring a towel!?" Cassy Jane screamed.

"They're all gone, Greta ate them," Louise said as communally, we sprouted goose bumps. Greta, our goat, had pulled all our towels off the front porch and chomped them to bits.

"It's so not my fault she did that," Joey said defensively. "Last week was my turn to feed and tether Greta; this week it's Agung's."

"Don't pin it on me. Your timing is off," Agung said. "Today is Sunday. It's not a new week yet."

Joey turned toward Clint, begging for backup. "It's Monday, right Clint? Tell Agung that I'm right."

Even a good mind, which Joey's was not, loses a sense of time when always stoned.

"Maybe it is, maybe it isn't," Clint answered as he hurried to get dressed; he had no idea what day it was, but would not let on.

Anise ran ahead to her jeep and bolted back with a stack of fluffy, clean towels.

"Please everybody," she said. "Take one. I always carry extra."

Despite not trusting her, I grabbed a towel and threw it across my shoulders. It wasn't scratchy and stiff but soft and comforting, reminding me of a life lost, of a luxury that remained in the world without me.

☾

Dinner was over. Inside, the cabin was illuminated by the soft glow of kerosene lanterns. With Anise's help, the dishes had been washed and put away. All of us relaxed into the evening, playing chess, reading and talking softly. Pinned to the wall, our calendar, a gift from Stumpy's Garage and Auto Parts, told us it was February even though it was late in May. No one had flipped it for two months. I looked up from reading *Black Elk Speaks* and saw Clint sharpening his hunting knife on a whetstone. Anise was knitting what looked like a small shroud. Neither registered any interest in the other. Relieved, I turned the page:

The Wasichus (white men) had slaughtered all the bison and shut us up in pens. It looked as though we might all starve to death. We could not eat lies, and there was nothing we could do.

I loved Black Elk, he was so Chekhovian.

Hours later, when the lanterns were doused, we all climbed into our sleeping bags side by side in the loft. Anise chose a spot on Clint's other side. I was on his left and the tit monster was on his right. Clint and I shared our sleeping bags. The softer down on top and the fiber bag over our yellowing foam. We curled up in our usual spoon position with my back cuddled against his belly. All was dark and warm and lovely. Clint undulated against me. The motion turned me on but as my feet touched his, I discovered a third foot—Anise. I turned to face Clint and the power and size of his erection stabbed me in the stomach. "Come on baby," he said huskily. "It'll be liberating...the three of us."

"What?!" I honked.

"Carol, I'm not hiding anything from you. I'm sharing the experience—it will be ours."

Clint had mentioned that he'd like to "experiment" before, but I knew my boundaries and they were not to be crossed. These were my thoughts on "free love": No way. Love wasn't free. To be with Clint, I'd given up my identity, my home, my art, and my career. I'd done it willingly and with high hopes, but for a high price and not without regret. Historically, women had made that choice in numbers far greater than men and as my woman's group had insisted, it was retrograde. But I hadn't cared until this moment; lying on my back in the dark on thick cedar planks and realizing Clint expected to pay nothing, to get all of me for free and play at love without risk—with all odds stacked in his favor.

Clint was kissing my breasts, second rate though they were.

"Baby, please, try it just this once...for me."

Anise's hand was on Clint's penis. I felt it as I grabbed for the one thing I knew I could control, but she'd beaten me to it.

"If you don't like it, we'll stop. Carol, I promise." His voice was so thick with desire that I almost felt sorry for him.

"Okay, sweetheart, okay." I said. The words ran out of my mouth and I couldn't catch them in time to shut them up. But where my mind had faltered, my body took over. In a flash, WHOMP! I kicked him hard in the gut. Accustomed to the dark, I watched him double over in pain. "I'm sorry, I'm so sorry Clint," I whispered. My leg had had a life of its own. Clint didn't respond. He didn't hurt me back. "I'm sorry, too," he said and turned away from me. Not that I'd won, but he'd lost. Now Anise had something to say: "Carol, you're wrong. This isn't the way to hold onto Clint."

"Yes, it is Anise. So, move your fucking sleeping bag somewhere else."

"But Carol, I want to be friends with you both."

"Yeah? Well, my friends don't grab Clint's dick. Call me crazy, but that's just the way I see it."

"Maybe in the morning," she said, "I hope you'll see things differently."

"Anise, I come from a five-thousand-year-old-matriarchy, so I can assure you, I never will."

"From a what?" she asked.

I didn't answer. It wasn't my job to improve her vocabulary. I'd captured my Semitic, girl commando power. Clint said nothing. His idea of a three-way did not extend to conversation.

Just after sunrise, without even staying for breakfast, Anise headed out. I figured she wanted to visit another commune, one with more available choices. I was going to suggest to her she try Black Bear in Northern California. Compared to Black Bear, Flores Creek was Levittown bourgeois. We hooked up in couples for as long as possible. In the name of sexual freedom, no one on the Black Bear commune was allowed to sleep with the same partner for more than two nights in a row. The place seemed like a perfect match for Anise. God knows she had the towels for it. But I held off. Black Bear was ultra-natural and Anise still used lavender-scented stick deodorant. Before she drove off, she hugged me goodbye. She was so small and slender that I could have knocked her over with a well-aimed rock.

"See you next time, Carol." she said, waving her hand.

"Not if I see you first, Anise."

It was a tired old joke, but she giggled anyway, a sweet, vulnerable giggle—so needing to be loved.

She was just another woman.

"I really wanted to be with you too, Carol, "she said. "You have such great skin."

"Thanks, Anise," I said. Then incapable of stopping myself from being a wise-ass, "But I'm in love with Chekhov. Along with Clint, they're as much as I can handle right now."

"Chekhov? Is he here at Flores Creek?"

"No Anise, he just visits. He's in Medford with the Hoe Dads, planting trees. But I think you'd like him if you met him."

"I would?" she asked, her face brightening.

"Yes. I'm sure you would. Everybody does."

CHAPTER 17

Bucky Fuller Blues

June 1972

When we Indians kill meat, we eat it all up. When we dig roots, we make little holes. When we build houses, we make little holes. When we burn grass for grasshoppers, we don't ruin things. We shake down acorns and pine nuts. We don't chop down the trees. We only use dead wood. But the white people plow up the ground, pull down the trees, kill everything...The White people pay no attention...How can the spirit of the earth like the White man? Everywhere the White man has touched it, it is sore."

WINTU WOMAN, 19TH CENTURY

If you blow it, it's blown.

STEVE GASKIN, *The Farm*

As the months passed, the fabric of life at Flores Creek changed with our visitors. Anise was just one of many. We all hoped that anyone who arrived would bring something positive into our circle and anyone who left would do so as a friend. That was not always the case. Bitterness and anger, always unexpected, cut deep. Not only with those who visited, but also with those who had stayed.

"No way. You can't do it. Not gonna happen here," Clint said as he watched Cassy Jane and Pete rip open a ninety-pound bag of cement. The powder was the start of an indestructible Buckminster Fuller-inspired dome they planned to build. The four of us stood in a clearing surrounded by silver Alder, their leafy umbrella heads touching the sky. Pete stared at Clint in disbelief.

"Hey man," Pete said. "We sunk big bucks into this. It's gonna be like an igloo that won't melt. We'll stash our stuff inside and split."

"Pete," Clint said, "we don't want it here." Pete tipped his wheel barrow, poured the cement into it and said nothing more. The color drained out of Clint's face but turned his big ears an angry red. "I'll have to bust it up, Pete, and haul it off. The damn thing will scar the land. We live lightly on the earth, you know that."

Pete remained silent while Cassy Jane dug her shovel into a pile of pebbles and spilled them into the barrow. The veins in her neck stood out, her arm muscles popped.

"Stop it, Cassy," I said. "You heard Clint."

"Like I give a shit," she said under her breath.

I wanted to bloody her pug nose. This was my old man she was disrespecting. While preserving the forest and maintaining the top soil, Clint did everything with care and exactitude: digging up intrusive plant species and insisting only standing dead trees be cut down. He considered himself to be the prime protector of the 160 acres of Flores Creek land. And he was. During Clint's seven years in the Naval Air Force, he'd been assigned to oversee the "parachute loft." If a parachute in his squadron of two hundred men was deployed and turned out to be defective, he was responsible. The buck stopped with Clint and the lives of the men he watched over were in his hands. Helping others came naturally to him, but at Flores Creek he'd wearied of being the go-to guy—tired of burying everyone's garbage, tired of fixing every broken machine, tired of adding rock to the overused road. Being left with a mass of cement to haul away was his tipping point.

CassyJane's trespasses had always irritated me. The woman bought Crisco, Cool Whip, and white sugar with our food stamps. Without thinking, I said, "Maybe this is the wrong place for you, Cassy. Maybe you should live somewhere else."

Pete spit into the barrow. His wad darkened a spot in the gray powder. I watched its tiny bubbles sink as it spread.

"You're telling us, Carol," he said, "that if we don't do like you say, we have to leave? That's bullshit."

"It figures," Cassy Jane added, as her pretty pink face turning an ugly red. "We put in everything we had into this dumbass place..."

"Shit," Pete broke in, "my Dad asked me what I'd get out of living here and I told him 'a new life.' I should have told him 'nothing'—cause that's what we got, Carol. Fuckin' nothing."

"I'm sorry you feel that way," I answered, still not biting my tongue, "but this is my land. Not yours."

As soon as I said those words, I knew I'd unleased a demon and said the unsayable. No one owned Flores Creek except me—game over. I'd confirmed my power.

I was the bad guy.

"I knew it! I fucking knew it!" Cassy Jane suddenly screeched, her hands flapping like fish, her head shaking from side to side. Something was very wrong with her. Pete kicked the wheelbarrow, held Cassy tightly to his chest and when her movements lessened, turned to Clint. "We're out of here!" And saying nothing more, they hobbled away. I turned toward Clint, dumbfounded.

"They're both epileptics." Cassy Jane and Pete, he explained, were "petit mal," and stress could bring on a seizure. Being different together had led to their mutual devotion and turned them into our kind of freaks. Clint considered Pete a dear friend. They'd met through the South Coast Collective and both had studied architecture at Yale. It was Pete, the epileptic, who first told Clint, the dyslexic, about the wonders of Oregon.

"It's gonna piss folks off, Carol," Clint said, "knowing you have say over their lives."

My stomach dropped. I didn't want too much power; I just wanted what was right for Clint and me. A neon green caterpillar inched its way up my shoulder toward my neck. Clint picked it up and placed it on a leaf.

"Pete and Cassy will leave," he told me. "They weren't going to stay anyway. This will just get 'em goin' faster."

"But I shouldn't have said..."

"No, Carol, you had good reason. Gettin' right with each other is important, but respect for nature comes first."

Was Clint telling me that how we treated the earth was more important than how we treated each other? I wasn't sure, but knew the two were interconnected; locked in a survival handshake.

"Who said that, Clint?"

"Me...and maybe Thoreau." Clint took his rolling papers out of his pocket and neatly sprinkled a line of marijuana across it, rolled it tight, lit it, and sucked hard. Again, I admired the easy way he held a joint, his thumb against his lips, middle finger just touching the paper. As we walked toward the main cabin, he took my hand. His was twice the size and covered with calluses.

A dust storm rose from the front porch ahead. Louise and Lila were furiously beating rugs that hung over the wood railing. Between thwacks Louise spun round and laid into me. "Carol, Pete and Cassy told us. Now what? If I do something you don't like, you're gonna get rid of me, too?"

"Louise..."

She didn't let me finish because she wasn't finished.

"This is totalitarianism, Carol. And guess who's Stalin?"

"Not me, Louise. I'm Trotsky."

She didn't laugh.

"Louise," Clint offered, "Pete and Cassy Jane were going to split anyway."

Louise stopped and leaned her broom against the railing. She spoke to Clint without looking at me.

"Carol never liked CassyJane."

"You didn't like her either, Louise." I said.

Louise turned in my direction, her eyes blazing.

"I don't like you right now, Carol, but I still have to live with you. You're so spoiled. You have everything, the rest of us have nothing."

"That's crazy, Louise. You have just as much as I do."

"Go ahead and hide from the truth, Carol," Louise continued. "You're good at that."

Louise's broom fell from the railing, hitting the floor with a bang. Lila picked it up and in her calm, celestial voice added, " Cassy Jane and Pete are being sent where spirit takes them."

"Gimme a break," Louise said.

No one felt good about it. A Pandora's box of power, ownership, and private property had been opened and before Clint and I knew it, Pete and Cassy Jane were gone; Agung told us they were headed for Hawaii and said that he was happy for them. In response to the incident, he began a discussion about just how we'd ask people to leave Flores Creek. Everyone agreed it had to be a unanimous decision. Louise motioned that anyone who had lived with us for two consecutive years could not be asked to leave without a trial. I abstained, but the rest voted "yes," and it carried. I owned the land, but the Flores Creek commune owned me. And I didn't mind. Not one bit. It was liberating and took the onus of decision-making out of my hands and gave it to the group. Or so I thought.

Clint's ancient tractor helped him bury the indestructible, rock-hard cement bags that Cassy Jane and Pete had left behind. The rain and sun had gotten to them.

Three weeks later, Lila and Sky decided to also leave to follow their Guru, the Mahariji, to Malibu. It was time, they told us, for them to move on to a life more focused on prayer and meditation. I thought it was because of how Clint and I had dealt with Pete and CassyJane, how the dream of a new way of life was tainted by my ownership. But they assured me that their time at Flores Creek had been "magical," but they needed more sunshine than Oregon offered.

Our numbers were diminishing. The four who left Flores Creek were smart, strong, and part of our collective past. Even though our differences were monumental, I'd appreciated not liking, then loving, them for the great adventure we'd shared. However, our communal flow was moving toward the future and all who remained had to go with it.

☾

More people, as unexpected as they were inevitable, came and went. Some were relatives, others friends of friends of friends. In a total reversal, I was grateful to all for showing up and found myself no longer wanting exclusivity but welcoming any hippie, no matter how down or dirty, as long as they brought us an open heart and a strong back: "Hi, nice to meet you...here's a shovel."

One morning, when it wasn't yet hot but soon would be, Louise and I were sitting on the porch skinning young alder trees to make teepee poles. We each held a draw shave, an ancient two-handled tool used to strip the bark. The strips came off like potato peels. As soon as the sun stayed a while, we planned to stack the poles for curing. While the thin slivers floated to the ground, my mind first wandered to Manhattan. A year ago, I'd been seated in a red leather booth at Sardis's sipping a martini amidst women in fox and mink, their toenails lacquered, their hair coiffed, talking theatre and politics.

Now all I knew of current events came from copies of *Newsweek* and *Time* I'd found in the Langlois library. From them I'd learned Carl Bernstein and Bob Woodward had tied President Nixon to the infamous Watergate burglary scandal. I wanted to kiss them both for bringing the bastard down. And Jane Fonda, aka "Hanoi Jane," an actress whose bravery and commitment knocked me out, had won an academy award for her role in the film *Klute*. Devouring the details of that event, I imagined the glitterati, rising to their feet in the dazzling Chandler Pavilion, to give her a standing ovation and saw myself standing with them, truly believing that somehow, someway, I'd get there, too.

The old dreams, drive, and ambition were still inside me. My motor was still running but I had no road map. At Flores Creek I felt both lost and at home: no longer who I was, but uncertain of what I'd become.

The voices brought me back to reality. They were speaking in a language I didn't understand. Through the high Timothy grass, I saw a little boy sweeping the stalks aside and running toward us. He shouted something unintelligible to a man and woman who followed behind him. When they came close, I could see both the man and the boy had dark almond eyes and girlishly handsome faces. Their boots looked new and their backpacks clean and unused. The woman was tiny and doll-like with long copper hair flowing down her back. Just a head taller than the boy, she appeared to be a Renaissance Venetian in mountain gear.

"English, Kokia!" she ordered. "Use your English!"

"We're here, Mama! We're here!" the boy shouted to her in a voice that had only a slight accent. "It's the little house in the woods!"

The Xandakis family had arrived.

Louise and I put down our drawshaves. Clint burst out of the main cabin.

"It's Pavlo and Katerina!" he shouted. "They made it." He threw his arms around the man. They bear-hugged for a long time and when they ended their embrace, gave each other hard and manly back slaps. The love they had for each other was clear. "Hey buddy," Clint said. "Welcome! What did you do with your car?" Clint's mind, after scant preliminaries, always turned to machines. Since I was not a carburetor, he'd omitted telling me his best friend Pavlo, who was avoiding the Greek draft, Pavlo's very young wife Katerina, and their four-year-old son Kokia, were coming to live at Flores Creek until Greece's war with Turkey ended. Pavlo and Clint had been close at the University of Houston and at Yale. Both preferred buxom red-headed women.

Clint held the cabin door open and with Kokia in the lead, the little family stepped inside. In contrast to the rest of us, they were so clean, colorful, and new. "That's some fancy gear you got there," Joey said, staring at them while he scrubbed a stunted carrot at the hand-pump. Having come from the street, Joey, a hippie by default, never had the chance to reject the material world like the rest of us; anything costly impressed him.

"Yes," Pavlo answered as he slipped off his backpack, "they have anti-gravity zippers, aluminum suspension bars, and foam shoulder straps."

Joey's jaw dropped. "You betcha."

Not awed by top-of-the-line camping gear, Clint launched into the subject that most concerned him.

"Pavlo," he asked, "where's your Nash? You drove it here, right?"

"That is a very sad story my friend," Pavlo answered as he helped Katerina lift her oversized backpack from her shoulders. "When we tried to get it up that rocky road of yours, it blew a tire. I'll buy a spare and fix it immediately; I can assure you of that." Clint scratched his head. Pavlo's response apparently worried him, but I had no idea why.

Weary after the climb up our hill, Katerina sat down on our worn rocking chair. Kokia climbed into her lap, his body taking up half of hers. I was afraid they would both go through the tattered seat to the floor, but it held. The wife and mother looked despairingly at the shabby sixteen by twenty-five-foot cabin.

"I love it here, Mama," Kokia said. "It is just like I dreamed!" He then slid off her lap and dashed out the open back door. "Be careful, Kokia!" Katerina shouted after him as he walked toward the grass that was as tall as he was. Watching him go, her face brightened and I could see that if Kokia was happy, so was she.

"You guys can sleep up in the loft. You'll be comfortable there for the short run," Clint told Pavlo, "and when you're settled, we can scout for your building site."

"Really?" Pavlo said. "We can build a house here?"

"You bet," Clint answered, relishing his own magnanimity. Then remembering, quickly added, "If that's okay with you, Carol...and the rest."

It was more than okay with me. I was delighted. Clint had introduced me to Pavlo at Yale and I knew him to be a careful and considerate man. His wife and child were new to me but I felt certain I would like them.

"Thank you brother," Pavlo said. "You are very kind." In that moment, the two men, slight Greek and large Texan, brown-eyed and blue, did seem like brothers. While Pavlo climbed the ladder to the loft to inspect their new living quarters, Katerina unzipped the side pocket of her pack and took out a tightly-wrapped cardboard box. "The secret is rosewater," she said with a playful smile and handed the box to me. And what was the rosewater a secret to? I couldn't wait to find out. "They are my grandmother's recipe," Katerina continued. "I think you will like them very much." Too excited to conserve the wrapping for future use, I ripped it off and clawed open the box. As soon as I lifted the lid, a honeyed perfume filled the room. Baklava squares—dozens of them. Even before I popped one into my mouth I could savor their feathery crispness and toasted Mediterranean sunlight.

Nothing in this life or the next will ever taste as good as that heavenly mixture of layered filo dough and walnuts dripping with butter and honey. As we passed the box, Pavlo descended from the loft. No one else moved. Even Louise, who could be counted on to offer tea to our more welcomed guests, stayed where she was. The exotic pastry kept us all riveted. Finishing one brought on an insatiable desire for another—stopping was impossible. Without hesitation, I took the last remaining square.

At that very moment, Kokia burst through the door holding a little striped garter snake.

"Look Mama," he said. "Isn't he beautiful? I am particularly fond of the white stripe that goes down his back." While Katerina did her best to appreciate the writhing snake, Kokia turned toward the empty pastry box. I was holding half of the last piece between my fingers and chewing the rest. The crunch in my ears could not shut out his wail: "Mama, I didn't get any! The fat lady took the last piece!"

Fat!!

"Shush, Kokia," Katerina whispered.

"It was mine, Mama! You promised to save it! She steals from children!"

"Kukla," I said, my mouth still full, my lips dusted with golden flakes "the baklava was a gift from your mother to us."

"My name is Kokia!"

"Kokia, I do not steal from little boys."

"Yes you do! I saw you!" he screamed. "You are a big liar!"

"Kokia!" Katerina said sharply. "You must apologize to Carol. This is her home and we are her guests."

Before I had a chance to tell Katerina that no apology was necessary, and that she could consider Flores Creek her home, too, Kokia shrieked, "I will not do such a thing, Mama! I will remember this all my life! I hate her!"

He hated me? My anger ran neck and neck with Kokia's. His shining hair was precisely cut, his face scrubbed clean, his jeans and Tee shirt a perfect fit. It was clear his mother spoiled and adored him. I instinctively knew Katerina saved the best and last part of any and everything for her little boy: the wishbone, the marrow—the butter cream rose on the cake. It was his undisputed birthright—just as it had been mine. "Well, Kokia," I snarled, "I'm not particularly fond of you either."

I was being maligned by what looked like a kid but was really a vindictive old man. I was the five-year-old.

"Kokia, that's enough," Katerina said. "Have manners, please."

Kokia puffed out his chest and gave it his best shot: "You can hold my snake if you want to," he told me, "but it might poop on your hand." Before I could respond, Pavlo, seated on a low rung of the ladder, pulled Kokia to him. As his son buried his face in the crook of his father's neck, Pavlo reminded him that hate was a bad word, a word that started wars. "If the Greeks did not hate the Turks, Kokusky, and the

Turks did not hate the Greeks, we could go home and eat mama's baklava until we couldn't eat any more." There was something wonderfully wise and considerate about this man. As Pavlo hoisted his family's sleeping bags up to the loft, I noticed a small gap between his two front teeth I found oddly attractive.

Sympathetic with Kokia's dismay Louise patted his slumped shoulder and cooed, "Kokia sweetheart, do you like chocolate?"

"Yes I do," Kokia answered. "I enjoy it very much."

"Well then," she said, looking directly at me, "you're in luck because the gas station in Langlois sells all kinds and I know that Carol will buy you a big, yummy bar. You'll do that, right, Carol?"

I wanted to wring Louise's goosey neck.

"I guess so."

Kokia's big brown eyes brightened. He was as handsome and regal as any royal.

"That will make you feel better, won't it, Kokia?" Louise asked, her compassion endearing her to both the mother and child. She was tricky, this woman who I thought to be my best friend.

"Absolutely," Kokia answered. "I prefer Hershey's with almonds."

It wasn't too long before I understood the look on Clint's face when Pavlo spoke of his flat tire. Slow-moving and languid, Pavlo never got around to replacing it. After a few weeks, their immobile Nash Rambler was mysteriously gutted and stripped by local scavengers; leaving the Xandakis family forever stranded without their own transportation and dependent on the group. Along with their vehicle, they, too, deteriorated. Despite Katerina's devotion to cleanliness it soon became impossible to tell them from the mud-stained and hairy rest.

Equally slow as a builder, the pace at which Pavlo erected his tent platform and picked out a house site was painful for all of us. His family slept and lived in the Main Cabin for what seemed like an eternity. Evenings inside lost their charm and were no longer filled with lively discussion, laughter, and music because Kokia and Katerina needed their sleep. We were forced to behave as caring adults, putting the health and welfare of a child and his mother above our own amusement. For some, aware of this necessity, the adjustment came as a natural course of events. For others, not so much. Whenever I was excited or even just engaged, my big voice, which could break glass, grew painfully loud. One night, not long after the Xandakis'arrival, we were arguing over Lyndon Johnson—whether he was ridiculous or very smart. Excited, I shouted, "That picture of him on the cover of

Newsweek pointing to the scar on his naked belly after his bladder surgery—what a buffoon!"

"Carol...shhhhh!"

The silencing hit me hard. Unable to control myself, I stopped participating in our heated nighttime discussions. Instead, I took to reading alone in the loft. By kerosene lamp and flashlight, I devoured every book about Native Americans I could find: *Sitting Bull, Seven Arrows, Black Elk Speaks, Bury My Heart At Wounded Knee, Geronimo, Crazy Horse, Tecumseh, Standing Bear, Hungry Wolf, and Ishi*—the Native American authors were concise, their voices quietly poetic. I tried to follow their example in real life, but when the controlled voices of the others below me broke through my reading, I had to join in and voice my concern. One night, I thought I heard them plotting a dangerous and foolish scheme and couldn't stop myself from screaming: "What! Are you crazy?! No pointing guns!! No shooting at Weyerhaeuser helicopters!" It was believed that Weyerhaeuser, a giant logging company and our next door neighbor, while spraying their alder trees to make way for their more valuable fir, rained poisonous chemicals down on our soil and water supply.

"We're just talking. Anyway, Carol, it would be to scare them."

"No! No pointing guns!!"

Then came the inevitable: "Carol...shh! Shhh!!"

CHAPTER 18

Hello Darkness

June 1972

Our sanity is not true sanity, a sensitive person, pushed by an unhealthy environment, escapes into another world so as not to deal with the disconnectedness and horror of the consensual reality.

R.D. LAING, *The Politics of Experience*

"A hundred pounds of rice gone." Louise and Katerina were taking inventory of our staples, but there was little inventory left to be taken. Sitting on wooden stumps, Louise with her glasses tipping at her nose, Katerina with a speckled child's notebook in hand, their faces were grim in the sunshine. The warm weather had brought us constant visitors. What had usually taken us a month to consume, had disappeared in days. I was looking past our empty storage bins and out the window, trying to remember the date of my next food stamp appointment, when I saw them spilling out of the woods: eleven adults, two rams, and one child—the entire Elephant Rock Commune. They'd hiked ten miles across the rugged Coastal Mountain range that separated us. Furiously beating the Djembe drums strapped to their shoulders and tooting flutes—they were the Von Trapp family on acid.

High not only on LSD but also on Amanita Muscaria, the precious hallucinogenic mushroom that grew in our coastal pastures, Rachael and Robert, their leaders, stood on our front porch and told us they'd come because they'd burned down their newly completed two-thousand-foot white cedar cabin. It had taken all their resources and almost a year to build, but on completion, they had discovered it had been infected with evil karma and had to be condemned to death. After a few chilly nights, and finding they had no bedding, tents, food, or protection, they decided to move in with us and stay through the winter. Inept hunters, all were bone thin and had been sustaining themselves on insects, grasses, and any seemingly edible mushroom they could find. It was a wonder they weren't all dead. Louise, Katerina, and I could not turn them away; they were our communal brothers and sisters. Always planning ahead, Louise, as soon as she saw them, hid our last jar of raisins under the sink. I hoped they'd find no evil karma at Flores Creek. Our cabin was all we had.

Elephant Rock's commune was located five miles up the Sixes River and south of Flores Creek. The land they lived on was owned by Rachael, a young, dark-haired Jewess, (aside from our hair color and sanity level, we shared a common ground) and her wealthy East Coast family. Named after an elephantine boulder in the middle of their eighty acres, Elephant Rock was Paleolithic in mindset and little inclined to plan ahead. They rarely lit a fire because their uncovered wood was always wet; subsequently they ate fish, meat, and vegetables raw and strongly believed in the health benefits of their diet. When agitated, Rachael developed a tic that went from the side of her mouth down to her neck. Her throat then made a clicking noise like a Chiclets hitting against tooth enamel. A mass of dark, uncombed curls framed her face. Her full lips were always wet with saliva because she covered them with spit when she spoke. What she said was often difficult to understand because her thinking was never simple, but convoluted and heady.

Moments after walking into the Main Cabin, Rachael stripped naked and without asking, took what pleased her out of our communal clothing bin. Her own rags lay in a pile on the floor and had a heavy, metallic smell. Katerina, Louise, and I stepped away from her, while Rachael kicked her rank mess into a corner—she was on her period. "The microcosm of the human body is the macrocosm of the universe. We can find the entire galaxy in one drop of blood," she told us as she wiped her blood-stained thighs with an old sock. I thought her theory brilliant but was distracted by a small slab of skin hanging from her vagina and could not stop myself from asking her if she was a hermaphrodite. Nonplussed, Rachael explained she was not. What I'd seen, she said, was a sliver of her insides that had protruded from her labia after she'd given birth. She'd delivered her son Streamer herself while squatting over a dugout and hanging onto a rope attached to a tree limb. It was, she continued, the most ecstatic experience of her life and well worth the slight disfigurement. Even though I thought her one carrot short of a stir-fry, I couldn't help but admire her dedication to the primal and shared her belief there was no inherent defectiveness in the female birth machine. Hanging onto a tree limb while birthing was revelatory—far-fetched, yet heroic.

"It's an elegant solution," she explained. "Gravity works in your favor, not against you. Not like it does in hospitals that harm babies and mothers with their stupid rigidity."

"But what about the umbilical cord, Rachael?" I asked. "What if the baby is dangling over the hole in the ground and is still attached to your body...then what do you do?"

"Bite it off. Jeez, Carol, if a chimpanzee could figure that out, so could you."

Rachael then dug into her backpack and coming up with a newly skinned deer hide, threw it across our dinner table. Wordlessly, she whipped her flint knife from its sheath and scraped off the guts and membrane still stuck to the animal's skin. Then, with the flat of her knife, she wiped the gray globs on the table's edge. This was too much for Katerina: "You cannot do this where we eat. You must take that filthy thing outside!"

Rachael continued scraping, intent on her labor. Her lack of regard for sanitation and for Katerina's command caused Louise, the doer, to spin into action. She grabbed the hide and yanked it off the table and holding it out in front of her body, demanded Rachel scrub the table's surface clean with soap and water. All Rachael said was, "I got no time for this shit," and yanked her awful deer hide out of Louise's hands. Rachael then strutted out of the cabin, deliberately leaving her son Streamer behind. The poor abandoned, little fellow looked up at us with his sad, four-year-old eyes and greedily licked the rim of our open honey bucket.

What time, I asked myself, didn't his mother have?

Later that day, when Katerina suggested to Kokia, who was a year older than Streamer, to play with him, Kokia refused saying, "I will do no such thing, Mama. He poops on the ground and then dusts it with dirt like a dog." It was impossible not to pity Streamer, or not to be vexed by his mother whose ecstasy at giving birth did not extend to child care. She paid no attention to her little boy unless he was screaming or bleeding.

"Rachael's out of her mind, you know that don't you, Carol?" Katerina whispered, making sure Streamer was far from ear shot.

"I know Katerina, but America is crazier than she is. That's why she's here, that's why we're all here–to not have to adjust to a sick society."

"That may be true, Carol, but she's still not normal."

Our mop shed strands of mop hair as I pushed it along the cabin floor, trying to clean what Rachael had left in her wake.

"Normality, Katerina, is a construct defined by fragmented people who have lost their souls."

"Carol, you sound just like her."

"I am like her, Katerina. We're all freaks—light years ahead—seekers."

"Perhaps you are a freak, Carol, but I am not."

What she said was true. Katerina had no freakiness in her.

"What are you then, Katerina?"

"I am Greek."

"Open the door!" Joey called from the porch. "Hurry-up, before she sees me!" Louise slid the heavy wooden latch and pushing the door ahead of him, Joey hobbled inside. He'd sprained his ankle, he explained, trying to escape Rachael. His big mistake, he elaborated, was that in running into her, he'd smiled and said "hi." She'd mistaken his intentions and licking her lips, had pulled down her pants and as Joey put it: "Diddled herself right in front of me." In his haste to escape her, he'd tripped over a gopher hole. "She's sick," he informed us, "like totally nuts!"

Rachael's mental illness wasn't the only kind the Elephant Rock commune exhibited, but sadly, was the most benign.

Late the next afternoon, Robert, Rachael's lover who was AWOL from the marines, slaughtered their youngest ram for our summer solstice celebration. I could not watch but heard its death shriek. Clint and Sky built a bonfire and when the flames had died down, placed the animal, its head still on, its eyes a gelatinous white, on a five-foot alder home-built rotisserie. The hours passed slowly as both men hand-turned and basted the roast. All of us, including those who ate raw, were driven slightly mad by its fantastic aroma. When it was done, the vision of twenty-four hippies, slicing off thick, savory chunks of meat to eat with their hands while the bonfire glowed red, was a throw-back in time—prehistoric and medieval. As the music began and dusk descended, those sated or still gnawing ram off the bone, became a swirling mass of bodies dressed in astounding rags, dripping with the salty juice of youth. The party felt like it would never end.

With a full belly and my hands clapping to the rhythm of bongos, tambourines, and flutes, I looked up and saw a sky covered with stars. I'd never seen so many except in the virtual skies of Manhattan's Hayden Planetarium and fully expected a booming male voice to point out the Seven Daughters of Atlas and the Big Dipper. As shooting stars fell, I watched their tails disappear into the darkness and flashed from the Planetarium to the Museum of Natural History, to the Met, the Frick, the Guggenheim, to hot showers, high heels, stockings, and to my old friends at Yale Drama. They were working on Broadway, in film and in television and becoming the solid professionals they'd trained to be.

I was becoming a pagan.

Couples were peeling off and disappearing into the woods. Others were sitting around the coals of the bonfire. Clint was nuzzling my ear. Peering over his head, I saw Streamer trip over his oversized rain boots as he tried to tear off a hunk of meat. Unable to steady himself, he was about to fall into the glowing coals. It was terrifying but before anyone could make a move, Kokia flew to Streamer and helped him stand upright. Our little Greek hero then took out his beloved pocket knife, cut off a slice of meat and handed it to Streamer, a child so stunted in growth, he almost looked like a toddler. Streamer tore into the pink-gray flesh. He was the only one at our celebratory feast who had not yet eaten. After Streamer had had his fill, Kokia took his greasy little hand and guided him toward Pavlo and Katerina, his own watchful parents. Both adults had been seated on a huge log at the opposite end of the fire, too far away to help but close enough to see. Pavlo turned on his high beam flashlight, Katerina took Streamer by his other hand and the two adults and two little boys walked together toward the Main Cabin. In the soft darkness, I knew for that night at least, Streamer would have parental concern and wondered if Rachael knew or cared where her son was or what he was doing. Calling for her, we received no answer. Once again, life without structure or boundaries led to a "Nothing-Left-To-Lose" empty freedom, especially for the innocent and helpless—children.

The next night, after we'd found Rachael and Robert and had returned Streamer to their far-away hidden tent, I curled up in the sleeping loft next to Kokia to read him a bed-time story. "Let the wild rumpus start!" I shouted with abundant feeling. No "Schhhhhhh," came. Not from anywhere. Or anyone. I continued, "Oh please don't go. I'll eat you up. I love you so!" Hearing Maurice Sendek's words, Kokia threw his little boy leg over my chest and said he was "extremely delighted" to be my friend. His compact body felt as sweet and as warm as a fresh-baked muffin. My new pal and I were alone together *Where the Wild Things Are*. From then on, I loved him, and not just a little.

CHAPTER 19

The Sky with Diamonds

Late June 1972

The man who walks through the Door in the Wall will never be quite the same as the man who went out. He will be wiser but less cocksure, happier but less self-satisfied, humbler in acknowledging his ignorance.

ALDOUS HUXLEY, *The Doors of Perception*

All of Elephant Rock was still with us and Rachael's lover Robert was washing his feet in Katerina's mutton stew. She had added carrots, wild onions, garlic bulbs, and a special virgin olive oil just sent from Pavlo's family orchard on the Greek island of Limi to the leftover ram meat and after letting it simmer for hours, had served it for dinner in a large cast-iron pot. I'd been anxiously waiting my turn to have her fill my bowl, when Robert climbed up onto our table, giving me a close-up view of his matted ankle hair and the dirt between his toes. No one moved or spoke. We'd grown inured to outrageous behavior and were like emergency room attendees; nothing about the human condition surprised us. At first, I thought Robert was just being playfully exuberant. Fred Astaire, when doing a happy dance, had jumped on top of chairs, tables, and even climbed walls—Gene Kelly, too. My theory vanished when I saw Robert's eyes darting around in his in his head like tadpoles.

The deerskin pouch he wore around his neck, always stuffed with peyote, shrooms, and acid tabs, hung flat and empty against his chest. He'd ingested it all. Seemingly impervious to the heat, he had lowered his foot into the steaming stew and then had quickly retrieved it to hand scrub his sole, toes, and ankle down with bits of meat and glistening fat. There were gasps. Not coming from Robert who registered no pain, but from everyone else. They could not believe their eyes. "Get the fuck off the table," someone screamed, but Robert just sat down next to the stew pot, crossed his legs and blew on his blistering foot.

Only Agung could talk him down off the table, and wrapping his arm around Robert's waist, led the dazed man out the door.

Dinner was over.

Filled with disappointment and disbelief we remained seated while Rachael explained that Robert had been downing tabs of Window Pane acid every day for a month, self-medicating because he was depressed by the sudden death of his beloved German Shepherd. A lucky few scraped the bottom of our peanut butter jar, but the rest went to bed hungry.

In the morning, as we searched for eggs, we discovered our new milking goat was nowhere to be found and our chicken coop empty and covered in feathers and blood. At first, we thought the birds had been victims of a bobcat, but when questioned, Robert admitted to the slaughter.

"They know what is happening to them and after the terror, there is acceptance. There is beauty in acceptance." He'd hung the dead carcasses in the woods to cure, he explained, to later surprise us with a new feast. When Robert was out of earshot, Smoke, the Elephant Rock Rastafarian and the only black man for a hundred miles in any direction, told us that Robert had lied to Rachael about his dog. When it wouldn't stop howling, he'd hacked the poor thing to death with an ax.

That did it.

Hunting knives at their side, led by Agung and fortified by Clint, our men formed a power circle around Robert and told him he had fifteen minutes to gather his belongings and leave. Clint, Agung, and Joey would drop him off on highway 101. Robert went without argument—as if accustomed to being run out of town on a rail. He said that he would not return to Elephant Rock, but instead would go back to Winnetka, Illinois, his hometown.

With Robert gone, Rachael and the rest decided it would be best for them to walk back over the mountains and return to their burned-out commune. Streamer begged his mother to allow him to stay with us, but Rachael would not leave him behind. Only kindhearted Pavlo tried to convince her to remain. Her way of saying "no" was to kick him playfully in the nuts. Kokia gave Streamer a pair of sneakers he'd outgrown. Streamer put them on his hands and slapped them together as if they were cymbals. Watching them leave, less spirited but still musical, I felt proud of my own tribe. The Flores Creek commune was sane. When real trouble came, we could gather our forces and address it. Elephant Rock was not so lucky.

It could have been a few weeks but more likely a month later that I ran into Rachael at the back lot of Vons Supermarket. We were both scouring the garbage bins for unsalable produce. I'd gone to Yale and now I was competing with a lunatic for rotten zucchini and soft tomatoes; not only that, but Rachael was better at it. She'd found a single, still edible pineapple. I tried to trade her a bunch of blackened bananas for it but she was immovable. The pineapple was hers. As a consolation prize, she offered me information about Robert. He'd made it back home to Winnetka but had stayed for weeks curled up in a fetal position in his childhood bed. No one could get him to move. One morning, to entice him, his mother served Robert his favorite breakfast of buttermilk pancakes and bacon. After he'd finished, he finally moved, grabbed a kitchen knife and stabbed both her and his father to death. The wounds he inflicted were in the hundreds. Sent to prison for the criminally insane, Robert would never get out. The good news was that he didn't have to face a court martial for desertion. Lucky guy.

☾

It was R.D. Laing's *Politics of Experience* that convinced me mental illness could be transformative—that aberration could illuminate. Insanity, I understood, flowed from blood, enzyme, and cell chemistry. Hallucinogenic drugs could take a person in any direction, from enlightenment to death. It could turn the sane into mad men and seekers into gurus—and as with any intoxicating cocktail, the outcome depended on the mix.

Wavy Gravy, Aldous Huxley, Carlos Castaneda, and Timothy Leary, whom President Nixon called the most dangerous man in America, were the pied pipers who opened the doors of perception and lunacy for thousands, if not millions of my generation. It was commonly believed that acid was a mind detergent capable of washing away years of social programming, a re-imprinting device, a tool that would push us up the evolutionary ladder. Perhaps even a gift from God , given to mankind in order to save the planet.[1] Well, who didn't want to save the planet? Dropping acid was an ethical choice. Something we had to do to change ourselves. It allowed some to "break on through to the other side," to grow spiritually and open their eyes to a compendium of Eastern religions. For others, like my cousin Freddy and Robert, it sent them straight to hell.

[1] Stevens, Jay. *Storming Heaven: LSD and the American Dream*. New York: Grove Press, 1998.

On my own few but astounding acid trips, I dissolved, lifted off like a flame spinning into infinity to become at one with the universe. I saw glowing colored auras around people's heads and bodies and understood their spirit. The circular light reminded me of the halos that classic artists drew around images of Jesus, the saints and angels—apparently, they, too, were in touch with a higher light vibration.

Once, as I floated in another dimension, a chatty ladybug trying to climb up a leaf told me she was having a hard time getting a foothold because the damp had caused her arthritis to act up and asked if I could give her a little push. When I gently moved her with my finger she told me she'd "always trusted in the kindness of strangers" and had a secret to share. To hear her better, I brought her closer to my ear and was surprised to see she had Vivian Leigh's face. Her eyes were a remarkable shade of azure that stood out against the black dotted red of her shell. In a whisper, she told me that my cousin Freddy had committed suicide because he was gay and it had hurt him too much to live in a world that didn't understand. I thanked her and then shared that I, too, was a Tennessee Williams fan and had always wanted to play Blanche DuBois, but felt it was out of my reach because I was too hefty. She said she'd had the same problem except that she was a bug.

Sadly, this was my last interspecies conversation. A few weeks later, the close encounter with patricidal, matricidal Robert of Elephant Rock did for me what on August 9th, 1969 the criminally insane *Charles Manson* family had done for hippies everywhere: ended our age of innocence. I never took acid again.

CHAPTER 20

Car Song

July 1972

Life has got a habit of not standing hitched. You got to ride it like you find it. You got to change with it. If a day goes by that don't change some of your old notions for new ones, that is just about like trying to milk a dead cow.

WOODY GUTHRIE

In 1918 my namesake and grandfather Carl Schlanger's horse-drawn vegetable truck was knocked off the Brooklyn Bridge by a drunk in a Model T. Grandpa Carl tumbled to his death with his onions and carrots into the murky waters of the Hudson River—it was stuff of family legend. Subsequently, I came from generations of non-drivers. We believed that had God meant for us to drive to Lake Mahopac, New York, he wouldn't have given us Grand Central Station. I saw the automobile as a noisy cockroach that plagued the landscape while emitting noxious gasses. So, not surprisingly, aside from Katerina, I was the only one at Flores Creek who didn't know how to drive and it kept me a beggar—a second class communal citizen who was never allowed to be in the driver's seat, who never had control of the wheel. It was more passivity than I could handle.

One night, after sex, as Clint and I kissed, thanking each other for the stellar ride, I begged him to teach me to drive. Too open and too happy to say "no," he agreed. But I knew his heart wasn't in it.

The next morning, we were rolling along, our thighs touching and his hands overlapping mine at three and nine o'clock on the steering wheel. I was doing my very best when the first swipe came. It was light and not meant to hurt but was Clint's way of getting my attention—as if I were a puppy who'd peed on the carpet. I let it pass. He'd been right about my mistake: I'd forgotten to use my turn signals. The second "tap" came a little harder and a little meaner with more anger behind it. I told him to "quit it" and felt a sour taste rising in my throat.

When the third arrived, it took all I had not to slap him back. In trying to get up a steep incline, I had gunned the engine and the truck had skidded, coming close to the edge of the ravine. After my heart stopped pounding, I let him have it. "Clint! You do not hit women. It doesn't matter what happens or how wrong you think we are...us, you do not hit!"

He was not apologetic. "You practically drove us off the road, Carol! You wanna live or you wanna die?!"

I threw his anger back at him: "You have to use your words, Clint, not your hands!"

It felt as if I was reprimanding an out-of-control little boy...and I was.

After that, Clint refused to look at me but instead fixated on his belt buckle. It was embossed with a big horse's head with a flowing mane. "Just hand me a J," he said.

"Get it yourself."

Banging open his glove compartment with his fist, he took out a fat spliff and lit it. As I sat stunned and silent, I realized the love of my life felt he could train me like a pet and knew I'd never ask him to teach me again. But I had to learn to drive even though cars frightened me and for good reason—my body rarely knew in which direction it was headed. Differentiating between my right and left was also a problem. Like my grandpa before me, the automobile could send me to an early grave.

But I would not give up. The next morning, ignoring family history, I was sitting in Clint's truck repeating for muscle memory, the five "H" positions of the stick shift...1st, 2nd, 3rd, 4th, and reverse, 1st, 2nd...when Agung climbed in next to me. I'd been too focused to see him coming. His vibe felt certain and altruistic. Something good was about to happen. Something great.

"Hi," he said, taking a pull on his fat joint and passing it to me. "Up for a spin?"

"You're gonna teach me to drive? Is that what you're saying, Aggie?"

I couldn't believe it. All the others had refused, citing their desire to live. Aggie was volunteering.

"Yes, Carol, that's exactly what I'm saying. All you have to do is pay attention and do what I tell you to do, you think you can manage that?"

"Totally," I said. However, I knew there was a stumbling block. Magnanimous Aggie had given away his VW bus to Pete and Cassy Jane and now he'd need to borrow Clint's truck to teach me.

"But Aggie," I reminded him, "Clint's Chevy's his baby. He won't lend it if he knows I'm driving."

"Don't worry," Aggie reassured me. "It'll be cool."

We had only to follow the mounds of dirt and the noise. Clint was in the far pasture digging post holes, jumping up and down on the digger as if it were a pogo stick. He didn't stop when he saw us. That was no surprise. Clint never stopped in the middle of anything and always finished what he'd started. We waited. Sweat dripped down his face in rivulets and caught in his chest hair. When he was done, I wiped his beady forehead with the palm of my hand just to show him how much I loved him, and then stood mute while Agung asked for the permission we needed.

"I'd like to, Aggie," Clint said, looking me and smiling, "I really would, but I can't. Carol rode my brakes so hard, she wore out the pads. It cost me plenty. I don't trust she won't do it again."

But Aggie was not a man to be put off. What he said next brought me to tears. He promised Clint that no matter what I did, no matter how severe the damage, he'd reimburse him—I was worth the investment. My self-confidence soared. If Aggie believed I could learn to drive, then so did I.

Clint took Aggie at his word and agreed.

With one swipe of his arm, Agung cleared the truck's front seat of an empty oil can, a socket wrench and a wad of greasy rags. He then passed me a joint to help me focus. It worked. My mind quieted and as we came off the mountain top toward the cow-dotted pastures below, I drove in a smooth straight line. An ocean breeze drifted into the cab, cooling my skin. Aggie and I were alone together for the first time in months and he confided in me like the old friend he'd always been.

"My chauffer taught me how to drive," he offered. "We were very close. He had eleven children."

"Wow"

"Carol, you know I'm here because I didn't want the future my family wanted for me: to be a big man and run a large corporation or a small country."

Envisioning Agung as a benevolent dictator waving to the populace, I drove us into a deep pothole. "Just pull out slowly," Agung advised, and continued on as if nothing had happened:

"The funny thing is," he said, " I was groomed for Harvard and Yale, but being there convinced me to join the Revolution. Without the Ivy League, I wouldn't have dropped out."

"Me either, Aggie."

The education both of us had fought so hard to acquire had turned us against achieving conventional success. It was a cosmic joke and weed made it funnier. Through our laughter, with the blue Pacific in the distance, happiness and pride engulfed me. The brilliant prince and I were part of the same brother-sisterhood, and with him as my teacher, I knew I would learn. Cautiously putting the truck in reverse, I backed out and we were on the road again. In no time or maybe a week, Agung assured me I'd passed my alternative driving test and that the timing was perfect because he had had to stop our lessons and leave Flores Creek to meet his father in Eugene. Mr. Tannudjaja was taking a detour on his way to a conference in Brussels to spend time in Oregon with his son. Agung couldn't wait—he left for Eugene the next morning.

The first time I stepped onto the Chevy's running board, swung into the cab and grabbed the steering wheel was like the Bat Mitzvah I never had. A right of passage. When I put the key into the ignition and the eight-cylinder engine rumbled beneath me, I became one big truckin' mama. Yeee haaa! I turned on the radio. COOS country was playing Tammy Wynette's *Stand by Your Man.*

Tammy and I knew—our hard-riding almost-cowboys could be both brutal and kind; no matter, we stayed.

With my seat adjusted and my foot on the gas petal, I was about to take off for my first solo ride when Louise came running in my direction. As soon as she plopped in beside me, her scowl buried my mood. "Agung's fucking someone else," she blurted. I turned off the motor. All went quiet except Louise. "He's lying, Carol. His father isn't coming to Oregon and Agung isn't going to meet him in Eugene, he's going to Rainbow to fuck another woman."

Louise used the word "fuck" harshly, spitting out the word's consonants, as if to make sure there was no love involved.

"I think you're wrong, Louise."

She had to be wrong. She and Agung were one. A unit. A pod...unbreakable now and forever.

"Carol, you think you know Agung but you don't. Beneath that big heart of his, he's heartless."

"But Louise, you and Agung belong together. You're like me and Clint...a great team."

"We're not, Carol. Not anymore."

I didn't want to believe her but had to. Agung did not return.

☾

It was difficult to say how long Agung had been gone, but July was ending. Best friends again, Louise and I were sharing a pair of work gloves. As we cleared the pasture of thistle and ragweed, she wore the right hand and I the left. Ragweed had a stubborn and deep root system but the purple prickly thistle was more insidious. It produced thorny flowers that called out to be touched; but if you did, they pricked. The whole plant was like bad sex; irresistible at first, but resulting in pain.

Louise looked strong and provocative in tiny, tight cut-offs and high, clunky work boots. I thought the shorts a poor choice as she could have been badly scratched in tender places, but since Agung's departure, she'd been asserting her sexuality—hairy thighs and all. Her nights, she told me, were so long and desolate that she'd taken to sleeping with an old tabby cat, rhythmically stroking its soft underbelly until she fell asleep.

A rustle in the high grass. We both looked up and watched as Agung walked toward us. Through the dry stalks we saw he had an oversized rucksack strapped to his back. It went from his neck down to his knees and made him look like an Asian turtle. When he reached us, he seemed sorry he had. Without saying hello, without extending a hand or a touch, he spoke with no feeling or emotion. What he said caused Louise to drop her thistles to the ground.

"Louise, I'm leaving you. I'm in love with another woman."

The skin on Louise's face slackened. Her lips plunged toward her chin and in seconds her face was no longer young. "What are you saying, Aggie?!"

"I can't be with you anymore, Louise. It's over."

Louise moved toward him. He didn't back away. All fire and fury, Louise stomped the ground with her heavy boot as if it were Agung's face:

"Who is she, you motherfucker?!"

"Skybird," Agung answered, his voice as impersonal as a train conductor's announcing the next stop, "We're gonna live together at Rainbow."

The Rainbow commune was headed by Jarrett Beck, the son of Judith Melina and Julian Beck, the founders of the Living Theater. Word was this commune dropped acid continually and was lysergiclly openhearted and welcoming to all. If Agung lived there with Skybird it might be a long time before any of us saw him again.

"Skybird!" Louise shrieked, "That flake who wears a red dot in the middle of her forehead even though she's a total wasp—that Skybird. That zombie?!"

Skybird, as I knew her, was nothing like Louise's description. Skybird was beautiful and serene, an anti-Louise, always high and wise with a fantastic color sense. I liked her, but I liked Louise a lot more.

"Goodbye, Louise. I'm sorry to hurt you," Agung said, and walked away from her. In a flash Louise vaulted onto his back. The howl that came out of her was a wail from the deep. With her war cry and her hair circling her shoulders like a whirlpool, she wrapped both legs around Agung's torso and pounded him with her fists. Agung did not protect himself or fight back, he just stood and took her blows. Louise was taller than Agung, but Agung was much more muscular. Unable to just watch, I grabbed Louise and tried to pull her off him. For my effort, she elbowed me hard in the stomach. I'd never seen any woman as furious as Louise; fighting for what she wanted even though she knew there was no win to be had. Agung covered his face and head while she continued to shriek and beat him. When she'd finally exhausted herself, he silently continued on. Louise quickly undid her boot and threw it at his head screaming, "No you don't! You don't leave like that, you little shit, you deal with me—with meee!" She missed. The boot fell at Agung's feet and he continued on down the road, still saying nothing. Louise hobbled after him. He didn't turn to look at her, but just tightened the straps of his rucksack, shifted its weight between his shoulders, and walked out of her life.

Louise sat in a heap on the grass, sobbing. I put my arms around her and hugged her to my chest.

"I'm proud of you, Louise," I whispered. "You gave the bastard hell."

I couldn't help but think that all marriages should end like this; with a boxing match. Louise didn't want to kill Agung, she just wanted to hurt him. As I saw it, she was right-on. The man deserved some pain. He'd discarded Louise like an old pair of jeans and the act shook my foundation. It was a reminder that families dissolve, that nothing in life was permanent and any relationship could end. The thought that Clint might someday stop loving me and leave was chilling. I never wanted to live in the woods without him. Not on my own—ever.

The sputter of an engine: a truck started—Clint's truck. He sat in the cab ready to take off. I let go of Louise and ran toward the road, determined to stop him, pissed off at all men. As his truck neared, I waved my arms and screamed for him to stop.

"Whadda you want?" he shouted back at me.

"You knew Aggie was with Skybird! You knew!"

Not only didn't Clint answer, he changed the subject:

"Move yer butt!"

Furious with Clint's refusal to move in any direction but his own, I grew certain he'd known about Agung's affair with Skybird, but had kept it secret. They were cut from the same cloth: men—loyal to each other. But surely, I told myself, Agung could not leave us for the long term; he belonged at Flores Creek and nowhere else. The main population of Rainbow had little or no higher education and knew little of the international. Agung would have no one to engage in heady discussion, no one to inform about the world stage. He was our royalty, our prince, and his global perspective put us a cut above the rest. Agung made us stronger by his presence. We couldn't lose him. No. Not forever.

Clint's truck had come to a standstill but his motor was running.

"You think Aggie will ever come back, Clint?" I begged rather than asked.

"I'm gonna give him a lift," he answered. "If you want, come along and ask him yourself."

I knew Clint's offer was empty. He didn't want me along. I'd never be welcomed inside their impenetrable man-to-man force field. I shook my head "no" and his engine roared back at me. Macho asshole that he was, Clint would drive Agung three hours to the Rainbow Commune. As I watched his Chevy jiggle down the road, black smoke pouring from its tail pipe, I accepted that when he returned to Flores Creek, it would be without that prick Agung, who I loved like a brother.

The vibes traveled quickly. Louise's anger and pain hit us all.

"He's a control freak," she fumed, "a fucking Svengali. He wants every woman to change to suit him. I couldn't. I wouldn't!"

Kokia, Katerina, and I were lying with Louise in the tent she had shared with Agung. Kokia was drawing banana slugs while Katerina patted Louise's back. Tears ran down Louise's face. Her bile flowed with them. "I was just a phase in his life, that's all. First there was Muffy from North Carolina—the Kappa Kappa Gamma nympho. Then he switched over to a Black Panther. Her hair was bigger than his body. Then me—the political Hippie Chick who cooked and sewed but wanted a career. Now it's Skybird, his acid fairy flake. Fuck them all!"

Her walrus sobs returned.

"I should have known," she cried. "Agung could talk anyone into anything."

"He never talked me into anything, Louise," I said.

"That's because you never listen, Carol."

Kokia stopped drawing and pressed Louise's hand to his chest.

"Don't be sad, Louise," he said. "I'll be your husband even though

I am a child."

Given the chance, Louise might have waited for him. He was that endearing.

"I'm not sad, Kokia, sweetheart," she said. "I'm just a fool...a stupid fool!"

I couldn't disagree with her. What woman in love wasn't?

CHAPTER 21

Nobody Knows, Nobody Sees

August 1972

Our laws of men change with our understanding of them.
Only the laws of the Spirit remain always the same.
HYEMEYOHSTS STORM in **Seven Arrows**

The cool thing about weed is that it is a weed. It grows like Jack's beanstalk, thumbing its five serrated edges at vine choke and blight. Almost nothing can stop it. Anyone can grow it, but has to know not to let the plants cross-pollinate and become androgynous, or even worse—males.

The rich forest soil at Flores Creek hadn't been turned in fifty years. Lovely aerating worms called it their home. Our money was growing on bushes. A pound would trade for a good running vehicle, an ounce, new tires or a pair of boots. Only the men grew it because it took real muscle power to haul 10-gallon tin water buckets by foot into the forest and none of the women cared enough to try. This division of labor didn't bother me. I was happy to live with an endless free supply and the men lived for it. Our old Greenleaf homegrown with its big sticky buds and sappy residue that stained my fingertips black was fantastic. It had been, according to us, best in Lane County. The Flores Creek crop was bound to be just as fine.

Being an outlaw turned me on, but the consequences were frightening. The penalty for possession was a harsh fine plus possible jail time but the penalty for cultivation was worse. It included confiscation of land. Agung and Clint had calmed my fears by assuring me their marijuana would be grown only on adjoining Bureau of Land Management and International Paper acreage, not on my one hundred and sixty. Anyone, a logger, a hunter, a local farmer could have cultivated it. No one could prove it was us. We hippies knew what the powerful old white men who ran everything did not: weed was an ancient proven remedy for many ailments—a curative and not a harmful drug. It was better than a vitamin, and we knew its illegality was wrong, but United States law did not agree. It was our moral imperative to break it.

Agung, who, when it came to economics, had everyone's attention, had theorized that in growing marijuana we were merely mimicking the U.S. mint. Our government, in its great fiscal wisdom, printed dollars when its coffers were low on gold-backed capital. We had no printing press but Mother Nature had provided us with our own renewable tender. Since we had decided not to exchange marijuana for money, but only for goods, we would not become dealers but traders—just like Davy Crockett. What could be more American?

Louise's loss was our own. Without Agung, a void opened that was impossible to replace. Something vital had gone missing. When I stuck my hand under the warm, feathery butt of Lillian, our laying hen to retrieve her eggs, the act felt more like a chore than something magical. From, "Look a chicken! Look an egg! Yes, there is a God!" to…"Okay, so here's an egg…so what." The man who could hold disparate views and personalities together to make things work was no longer with us to lend meaning to our anarchy. The Revolution, the framework, and the fire were gone. Since he'd dropped Agung off at the Rainbow Commune, Clint had changed, too. He'd stopped asking me to join him on long discovery hikes or help him gather rounds of fresh-cut fire wood. Even when we held hands, his grip was no longer as firm. Clint had always done for me what I couldn't do myself; but no more. If I needed his help starting a fire or carrying a heavy water bucket, he did so, but begrudgingly. What, I asked myself, had Agung said to Clint during their three-hour drive to make Clint feel differently towards me? Clint was easily influenced, I knew that—maybe Agung's pulling out had given Clint permission to pull away. Maybe my dependence on him had become a burden Clint no longer cared to shoulder. For the first time I understood our future together was not indestructible and that the ties that bound us all could unravel. Living a life that defied containment made certainty impossible.

The unpredictable Flores Creek tide, having drifted out with Agung, brought in Stu, Clint's younger brother. A Vietnam vet, broke, ragged, but still cowboy handsome, Stu had spent the previous winter as a ski bum in Breckenridge, Colorado. Flores Creek was at the bottom of his downhill run. A day after Stu's arrival, I'd slept late and awoke alone. Clint's side of the bed was cold; he'd been gone for hours. In the distance, I heard a vehicle climbing our hill. It sounded too new and fast to belong to anyone living with us. I scooped up the jeans off the floor that I'd worn for three days running. It was time to start a fire under the huge caldron we used for communal washing and dump them in, but that chore would just have to wait; I was too curious to see who had driven up our road. Once out in the sunlight, I saw a note pinned to the tent flap: "Watering the girls, see ya later—xoxo." Clint had gone into the forest with the other men to spend time with his female marijuana plants. His love for them, unquestionable.

As I ran uphill towards the Main Cabin, even though I smoked four joints a day, my breath was no longer labored. A shiny black and white four-wheel-drive with a gold star emblazoned on the door was parked at the clearing. Unable to stop myself from looking through its tinted window, I saw a walkie-talkie and a 30-06 rifle and freaked. Once on the porch, I opened the front door and heard a smooth voice say, "Care for a cup of Java, Sheriff? I've got some made up fresh." And there was Stu, holding our enamel coffee pot and smiling like a Cheshire Cat. "Don't mind if I do," the Sheriff's said as his eyes scanned the room. What he saw was a sink piled high with dirty dishes; windowsills covered with shells, rocks, dried snake skins; and a dining table decorated with dead daisies. When his gaze landed on me, he licked his thin lips and said, "Howdy, little lady. Hope you don't mind the intrude. Told ya I might show up."

"Sure thing, Sheriff," I answered. "Real nice to see ya."

As nice as swallowing a toad.

Sheriff Dick Labin was no longer behind the counter at his hardware store—he was *The Law* and Stu and I were the only ones around. Luckily, the stink of Stu's morning cigarette masked the ganja odor that always filled the room. Stay calm, I told myself, the sheriff's just visiting. He isn't going to bust you for cultivation. He can't. He won't. Agung and Clint planted it on BLM land, not yours. They hadn't gone to Yale for nothing.

Stu's eyes guffawed as he handed the sheriff our steaming "Jesus is my Savior" coffee mug.

"Cream or sugar, Sheriff?" Stu asked.

"Jes black for me, thanks," Sheriff Labin answered politely. Too politely.

The Sheriff knew what The Law always knew—where there were hippies, there was marijuana and plenty of it. We never ran out. For us, as they would say, "it was always better to have dope in times of no money than it was to have money in times of no dope." It was stored in our tents and everywhere in the Main Cabin: in empty coffee cans, in Ball jars, under the sink; none in plain sight, but in two months, the new crop would be hanging from the rafters to dry. The sheriff understood cultivation and had sold us all our growing supplies. We were loyal cash customers. He also knew it was too early in the season for mature plants and not far away, our adolescent ganja was growing up. At that moment, our men were deep in the forest, watering and fertilizing their sequestered patches. (Clint had once rented a single engine plane and flown over them just to make sure the patches could not be seen from the air.) I purposely never learned their exact location in order to be convincingly innocent if they were ever discovered: "What? Where?"

"Fine weather we're having, huh Sheriff?" Stu said.

"You betcha, real fine."

The sheriff's grin matched Stu's tooth for tooth. There was something about these two men oddly similar—their age, their compact bodies, their quiet country drawl. The big difference was Sheriff Labin packed a Colt 357 Magnum on his hip while Stu held up his pants with a frayed rope. I stared at the Mother-of-Pearl handle of the sheriff's pistol and kept my mouth shut, unsure of how to ingratiate myself with a western lawman. Stu, however, who'd seen action in Phnom Penh, was all charm. "Nice piece you're packin' sheriff—five and a half barrel?"

"You bet. Had it made up special."

Cool. Stu was talking man-gun-talk with our unwanted guest. He seemed so in control that the butterflies in my stomach settled and the hand holding my coffee cup steadied.

"You shoot it much?" Stu asked.

"Much as I have to," the sheriff said, his grin going south.

Stu stepped toward the sheriff; the sheriff stepped toward Stu, the sheriff's crisp uniform contrasting with Stu's moldy jeans. Neither took their eyes off the other. Stu placed his hand on the sheriff's shoulder. The sheriff looked as if a big bird had just splat on him.

"Mind if I hold her, get a feel?" Stu said.

The light air in the cabin did a backflip. You could have cut the tension with a chainsaw.

Had Stu lost his mind, asking the sheriff to let him feel his gun?

"Sorry son," the sheriff said, moving out of Stu's reach, "can't let you do that. She's got a real light trigger. You jes breathe on her and she goes off."

Stu's lips turned down into a sneer.

"I'm not your goddam son!"

Oh no! I looked out the window toward the porch. The edge was lined with empty whisky bottles. Stu was drunk. It was almost high noon and Stu was smashed.

The sheriff slowly walked the floor, his boot heels slapping the wooden plank. The walls shook. He opened the bread box. Inside there was nothing but bread—homemade and slightly moldy. The law man shifted his focus towards me. "You sure done Shorty's place up different."

We sure had. Shorty had never tacked a picture of Angela Davis, her thighs straddling Richard Nixon's head, on the wall of his cabin.

"It's lookin' more girly," he continued, "more cleaned-up."

"Thank you," I said, smiling like a brand-new Miss America. "I think we did a great job maintaining the original fixtures and mountain-man ambiance. Don't you?"

"Yup. You done ole Shorty proud."

"'Nother cup Sheriff?" Stu said, moving back toward the stove, as if his nasty blowup had never happened.

Forget *as if*—in moments, Stu had forgotten it entirely.

"Best be on my way," Sheriff Labin said, gulping down his dark brew. "Mind, if you folks run into any trouble, you give me a holler. Not everyone round these parts likes hippies as much as yours truly."

"We sure will, *Dick*," I said, emphasizing the double meaning of his name to let him know I was a fun girl with downhome sass.

"Now that wasn't very nice, was it little lady?

His reply felt like a noose around my neck. The butterflies were back. I'd misjudged him.

"Jes playing with you Sweetheart," he said, chewing on a toothpick he'd taken from his shirt pocket. "Everybody calls me Dick and everythin' between. And if you're growin' illegal, don'tcha worry none cause I got more trouble in these parts than I can handle. Sides, it's bad for business."

"You got that right, Sheriff."

"Sure do, little lady. Be seein' ya real soon. Chicken scratch you been asking for jes came in. Better hurry 'fore it's all gone."

With that he tipped his hat and was out the door. I had a feeling he'd be back. Stu made a damn good cup of coffee.

☾

Marijuana was not the only weed growing on our mountaintop. Beautiful purple and pink digitalis, a flowering heart stimulus, blanketed the hillsides. Shaped like pixie hats they swayed in the wind and our life took on their rhythm. We all were building, each with the idea that a tent site could be replaced by a tiny house. Help was given wherever it was needed. No one struggled alone. No one ate alone. Few slept alone. We all did our best to do our best. I learned how to chop wood. The solid heft of a good ax in my hand satisfied me almost as much as a clean, straight cut. The fragrance of fresh cedar was better than Lancôme.

Living with light as our alarm clock, going to bed at dark and waking with the sun, all of us were embraced by the beauty, cruelty, and kindness of nature. The primitive became deeply satisfying. Rain and sun on our skin, the wind and fine air in our lungs, the fragrance of earth and wood gave both energy and peace.

The great Native American tribes of the Northwest: The Salishan, Siletz, Klamath, Coos, Suislaw, Alsea, and Kushetunne—we were experiencing their umbilical connection to the land and its wildlife. An ancient Hopi prophecy states: "There will be a time when many youths, the sons of the white man, grow their hair long, wear beads, smoke medicine weed and live together as one tribe. Their name will bear a name of the same sound as my people (Hopi) and they will not be like the white men we know now who are cruel and greedy."[2]

Our time had come and we were right on schedule.

Food, shelter, weed, and clothing—that's all we needed and that's all we had. Throughout summer and early fall the gathering and production of enough to carry us through winter was always on our minds. Our garden had failed, our water tank leaked and was abandoned but it was of small consequence because apples, pears, and peaches could be purchased for pennies a pound and blackberries were everywhere—thickets so dense you could grab a fistful in seconds. Our marijuana bushes were dark green and lush. Hanging to dry from the cabin's rafters, its perfume filled the air. Everything smelled like weed—even the dishcloths.

Clint and Two Turtles built a milking pen for Greta and our new goat, Margaret. Both supplied us with milk to make yogurt and curd. Along with Joey, whose quick hands made him our best milker, I learned how to force either lady to remain still while I grabbed her full teats to slide, pull, and squeeze. If I milked her incorrectly, she'd turn and give me a filthy look, or even worse, kick over the milking bucket. If milking was delayed, her teats engorged and her goaty bleat became plaintive and almost human. Only later would I understand her pain.

Woody, our nearest, friendly rancher, let us keep meat in his walk-in freezer in exchange for helping him shear his sheep. Our men had

[2] Waters, Frank, and Oswald White Bear. Fredericks. *Book of the Hopi:*. New York, NY: Penguin Books, 1991.

no hunting permits but had guns and the woods were filled with game. After a deer had been shot and killed, we did our best to use the whole animal—the meat for eating, the brains for tanning, and the skins for clothing—just like the Sioux, the Cheyenne, the Kiowas and the Cherokee. Coming in a far second to the First Peoples, we never got the tanning process right. Our hides came out stiff. Our leather made better placemats than leggings.

We did better with meat. Very lean deer and elk tasted a little gamy but a lot like steak, especially the much-coveted back strap. Bear had the flavor of pork cooked with old gym shoes. Even when smothered in wild onions and baked in tomato sauce, it still tasted like bear. Rabbit was similar to chicken, but sweeter. Killing a bunny rabbit involved bashing it over the head with a bat: so long Mopsy, Flopsy, Cottontail, and Peter, hello rabbit stew. And squirrel, well, I never ate squirrel; it was too much like a rat. Two Turtles, an avid scavenger who'd developed a taste for the bushy little rascal, once offered me a bowlful of his squirrel stew. Inside the thick brown mush, I saw a tiny black toenail.

"Sometimes I miss a part," he said when I registered my complaint. "Come on back tomorrow, it's always better on the second day."

Within this earthy, funky, animal-to-vegetable world and back again, my human-to-human relationships blossomed. Clint and I found we didn't have to rely on each other for what neither of us had to give. If I wanted a heady conversation about books, art, or politics, there was always Pavlo who loved to talk theory, and Louise, who prided herself on turning theory into logic. Clint and I, unlike a boxed-in nuclear couple, received from the other the best each offered: his gifts coming from his hands, mine from my mouth. It felt ideal—this dedication to one person while remaining free to find day-to-day intimacy with the others.

Our togetherness was all inclusive and we faced mutual survival like links on a chain, like tethered climbers reaching for the unseen summit. Each day I stepped more outside myself to make the whole stronger. Liking or disliking a person, no longer mattered. All that mattered was that he or she was there—to talk to, to work with, to provide another voice and a needed hand. Even when physically separated, we were together. During both tiny and tidal occurrences, each of us was exposed. Selfishness, anger, pride, joy, love, desire, envy—all showed. During long periods of harmonious living, surrounded by astounding beauty, all our lives were elevated. But hard times hit when that connective cord was broken and our own nature turned us against ourselves—then we ran in circles and tried to bite off our own tails.

CHAPTER 22

I Left My Mind Behind

Late August, 1972

We are all just walking each other home.
BABA RAM DASS

The day I had a nervous breakdown was sunny and hot. The eggshell blue sky pushed the almost edible clouds into relief. A gentle wind was blowing off the Pacific, causing the evergreens surrounding our clearing to shiver. As the temperature rose, shimmering rings of heat appeared around our woodpile. Barely willing to move, I tried to summon up enough energy to drive down to our neighbor Woody's swimming hole. But the group had a better idea—a decision reached without debate: "Let's split to the ocean."

A ride to a deserted stretch of sandy beach, six miles west and ten miles to the south, would be a fun outing and a good way to cool off. We could pack lunches and make a day of it. But I hesitated to join the party because Georgia, a med-school graduate and good friend of Sky's, was visiting and leaching all joy from my life. She and her stacked psychic friend Sharon had decided to stay at Flores Creek for as long as possible. Georgia worshipped the sun. Each morning she practiced her naked sun lion yoga in the middle of the clearing and in full view of everyone. Her downward dog, her butt high in the air, her legs spread, had a rutting element. Our culture attracted exhibitionists. Or maybe it was the other way around.

Georgia had a pert little face, a bouncy blond Dutch-boy haircut, thick bottle eyeglasses, and with her tight round tush, was a dead ringer for *Playboy* magazine's comic book heroine, *Little Annie Fannie.* Clint could not keep his eyes off her. She was from Austin, a Texan home girl who spoke his language and even worse, had interned in the Alaskan outback tending to Eskimo tribes and isolated loners. God—the woman was both competent and altruistic: a nightmare. Where, I asked myself, was my ego reduction, my loss of self, my ability to go with the flow? They didn't exist. When it came to Clint relating sexually to other women, they never had.

Unlike Anise, who wanted only inclusive experimentation, Georgia was edging me out. Each time Clint looked at her with stupid, entranced eyes, she'd glance at me, her face announcing victory. Overriding my presence, she'd press her body hard against his to "release" his shoulders. Their lips sought each other as she rubbed his earlobes between her fingers and then manipulated his neck. Next, I figured she'd stick a rectal thermometer up his ass and pull it out with her teeth.

Deciding I couldn't leave them alone together and needing a break from the heat, I crammed into Stu's pick-up along with twelve others. Stu had offered to drive us to the beach because he had errands in Bandon, a seaside town twenty-five miles to the north. In three or four hours, he promised to return and drive us back home. Bouncing down Flores Creek Road, seated on a ragged army blanket that covered the holes in Stu's upholstery, I recalled Chekhov's warning that having thirteen at the table was unlucky. Loaded up with thirteen, Stu's pickup was our table and fate, I feared, would ruin the party.

Sunlight danced on the gray-blue Pacific. Human scavengers had carried away all the portable driftwood from the shore and only huge sea-soaked giants remained. The water was so cold that if you stood in it for more than a minute, all feeling left your feet. Looking down the shoreline I could see Clint and Georgia, walking with their arms around each other, entwined like a tomato on a stake. I tried to focus on a pelican as it swooped down into the sea and then zoomed up like a feathered rocket, holding a flapping fish in its bill, but could not find relief from my miserable insecurity. Georgia was a perceptive and funny woman; we'd chatted at the dinner table and done our wash together. How, I asked myself, could she do this to a "sister"? And what could I do to stop her? I gasped for breath and grew dizzy. My mind splintered, tearing off in so many directions it began to rip.

"Can you believe the government exposing our Vietnam troops to Agent Orange and our soldiers are getting cancer?" I asked Katerina or a tiny sand crab crawling sideways along a tide pool. I heard no answer.

Clint's body and spirit answered something so primal in me that it had changed my body chemistry. In the part of my brain that was no older than three, he wasn't a strong, gallant and silent Texan; he was my mother and father combined. He was Minnie and Mike Schlanger, two forty-something New Yorkers who ate bagels and lox on Sunday mornings and went to work every day leaving their only child with nannies or my delusional aunt Ruth who confused her elevator man with Harry Truman.

Clint, my hero, my fortress, my forever-love was actually blowing me off? Yes, he was.

Daylight faded. The air and sand turned cobalt. Those who'd had the good sense to bring jackets put them on and waited for Stu. The wind, always strong on the Oregon Coast, pushed through my light sweatshirt. Clint appeared and walking toward me wearing the face of a stranger, sat down at my side. I curled into his body, but felt no warmth. He wasn't with me anymore.

"You're attracted to Georgia, aren't you?" I asked.

"Yes."

"Does that mean you are going to sleep with her? Is that what that means?"

"Maybe," he answered, as if the hundreds of sweaty nights we'd had together never existed.

"Please don't," I pleaded without shame. How quickly I'd turned into a beggar.

"I can't promise you that, Carol. Try and get some sleep."

The Clint I'd known had disappeared and his body had been taken over by an elusive spirit, vexatious and cruel, over whom I exerted no control. Not only was my heart breaking, but the wind was turning my body to ice. We had matches but no kindling. Lighting the huge pieces of wet driftwood was impossible. Dusk and then darkness set in and we huddled together in groups of twos and threes. I closed my eyes, curled myself up into a tight ball beside Clint and slept fitfully for what I thought was a few minutes. When I awoke he was gone. Freezing, I crawled toward Katerina and Pavlo, seeking their body warmth. They had found protection behind an enormous uprooted tree. The roar of the Pacific was everywhere. My body shook and my teeth chattered. I could not cry, I could not move, all I could do was try to keep warm and pray for the sun to return.

I awoke at dawn. The sky was a thrilling yellow and pink and my body was stiff with cold. Pavlo, Joey, and Clint stood nearby, rubbing their hands together and slapping their thighs. They'd decided Stu had been in an accident or had gotten drunk and that all of us would have to hitch back to Flores Creek. The heaviness had not left my chest and I felt as if I were in a tunnel, floating. My feet could not feel the ground.

As I walked alone up the steep embankment toward Highway 101, Clint chased after me.

"Wait up!" he yelled. I ran ahead.

"Come back, don't be like that, baby!" *Baby?* There it was again—that horrid diminutive.

"Go...to...hell!"

"Hey! Stop. I don't want you to hitch alone, it's dangerous."

His voice was calm, too calm—detached.

I increased my speed, desperate to get away from any kindness he offered. His pity was more invasive than the wind. And suddenly, there was Stu's pickup, parked where the highway ended and the sand began. He opened the driver's door, got out, and walked toward us, his baggy eyes squinting in the sunlight.

"Stu, where were you?!" I screamed.

Stu mumbled something, his face like an old hound dog resigned to abuse.

"You left us here all night!"

"Sorry Carol, I forgot."

"You forgot! How could you forget twelve people? How could you do that, Stu?!"

"Guess I had too much to drink."

"I guess you did, Stu," I said, resigned to what was. "I guess you did."

No one knew what to say to Stu and no one wanted to talk to him. Of this I was certain: I couldn't trust either of them—Stu or his big brother. Texans—short on words, long on pain.

☾

In the slow-moving days that followed, Clint and I slept together at night but did not make love. In the morning he'd get out of bed and leave without telling me where he was going. If I asked him, he was elusive: "Just checkin' things out," he'd say.

Obsession took over. I couldn't think, sleep, or eat without picturing him with Georgia. Leaning next to the Main Cabin door, I discovered an old baseball bat that someone still into conventional forms of recreation had left behind. I took it and searched for Clint and Georgia in the forest and tall grass, deciding if I found them making love, I'd clobber and separate them like stuck, rutting dogs. That's what I wanted to do, but part of my brain told me violence was not the answer. But how I'd loved playing Lady Macbeth back at Yale, how I'd embraced her female power, her thwarted ambition, her fury and determination. Having murdered for her indecisive husband, her karmic demons got the better of her and she couldn't stop washing her blood-stained hands. In the end the deranged woman was left with only a severe obsessive-compulsive disorder.

Murder on stage was fun, but in life it took a real toll.

The sexual revolution I had welcomed with open arms and orifices was turning against me. Living free, without makeup, hairy and animal, was liberating. But sexual freedom without responsibility was, as Kris Kristofferson told us "just another word, for nothin' left to lose." There was always a price to be paid. I'd wanted to create a heaven and instead created a hell.

Georgia was lying nude on the back porch and sunning herself like a lizard.

"Georgia...."

Hmmm?

"Georgia, you and Clint...please stop, I can't take it."

Getting into a shoulder stand, with her small breasts and glasses remaining in place, she said, "How can I stop what exists, Carol? Clint and I want each other."

I sank down to the ground, my face level with hers. Through her thick lenses, her blue eyes looked enormous.

"Go away, Georgia. This is my home, not yours."

"I'm sorry, Carol, but that's not possible."

"Why not?"

"Because," she said, "I don't want to."

On the land I thought I owned, but actually owned me, I could only ask, but not force. Georgia was not insane Robert, or imprudent Cassy Jane. Georgia had squatter's rights.

I was the one who would have to leave.

CHAPTER 23

Kiss the Sky

September 1972

The unnatural, that too is natural.
JOHANN WOLFGANG VON GOETHE

It took only a day for me to pack my backpack and find a ride to Highbridge, a commune ninety miles to the northeast, near the town of Swisshome. The world, as I saw it was out of focus and wrapped in gauze. I bumped into things, tripped over my own feet, and felt my whole body had been injected with Novocain. I either hitched or caught a ride with whomever was headed toward Eugene. It might have been Louise—or Joey.

Highbridge lay on the far bank of the Suislaw River, which was impassable in the winter. No actual bridge to their land existed; it had been washed away during a thirty-year flood. To get across the river, they'd constructed a cable car between the banks and used it to transport themselves and heavy supplies. Attached to a huge fir pole that supported the cable line, a threatening sign read: "Ring bell. All trespassers will be shot at." Not shot. Just "at." It was an empty threat. They had no guns. The sign was a warning because, paranoia aside, they had much to fear. Their strongest member, Billy Trumock, an original member of the East Village "Motherfuckers," gave them an outlaw panache, but their reputation far exceeded their reality. Angry locals had set fire to their out-buildings, believing this commune harbored Black Panthers, Weathermen, and draft dodgers—which they did. All of Highbridge had then been forced further back into the woods, into the "second clearing."

Where at Flores Creek we'd quietly skirted the law, Highbridge flaunted their disobedience. They were a real "Living Theater."

Standing on the shore, I hoisted my rucksack over my shoulders.

I'd packed a frayed towel, the Oxford American dictionary and two mismatched hiking boots, one mine, the other Clint's. I'd accidently taken his instead of my own and when I opened it, felt a tinge of happiness, knowing how hard he'd search without ever finding it. The feeling evaporated when I realized it would be harder for him to live without his left boot than it would be for him to live without me.

As the sign instructed, I pulled the rope. The attached church bell rang out. A pack of emaciated yellow dogs immediately gathered on the far bank, barking and howling. The two largest tore at each other. The dogs, I reassured myself, were not vicious, just hungry, so I searched my jeans pocket for the remains of a beef jerky that I'd bought at a 76 station, but all I could find was a greasy cellophane wrapper and a tiny packet of salt. I ripped open the packet and threw the salt over my shoulder for good luck—an old Yiddish custom. As the dogs turned into a swirling, canine tornado, a deeply tanned man wearing a beaded loincloth appeared on the other side of the bank. His straight black hair hung down to his waist.

"Who are you!" he yelled. It amazed me I could hear him over the din.

"Carol from Flores Creek!" I shouted back, "I'm a friend of Talisa's!" The man jumped into the trolley car and, placing one hand over the other, pulled himself up along the cable line toward me. Then—Whoosh! And there he was—on my side of the bank.

He was handsome: his face flat and gentle, his dark hair so smooth and shiny that it fell down his back like satin drape. I could not keep my eyes off his loincloth. It was made out of chamois deer hide and sported an exquisite, intricately beaded red rose in full bloom. A chicken hawk's foot dangled from his ear—it had been painted blue. This was Flaming Rainbow, the first real Lakota I'd ever met, and queer.

We back-to-the-land hippies did our best to connect to the lives of Native Americans—they were our rock stars, so smart and so cosmic. Who could own the rocks, the sky, the stars, and the rivers, they asked us, having no word in any of their languages for the word "own." They understood that the earth owned the human race and not the other way around. The White Man was so stupid and anthropomorphic that he even had a name for it—anthropomorphic. Flaming Rainbow drew me to his chest and gave me a bear hug.

"Welcome, sister," he said in a soft monotone. How fine it was to again feel a hard, friendly chest pressing into my breast. I'd always been a woman who loved men who loved men. Although my heart still felt like a boulder, its weight lightened. Tossing my rucksack into the trolley cart, Flaming Rainbow gestured for me to follow—just a flick of the wrist and silent point of his finger. As I waddled onto the wooden floor of the cart, my weight caused it to lurch toward the water below and I slid helplessly across it. The cart hung from a hook attached to a cable line. The cable itself was suspended high above the river and it seemed impossible that the flimsy wooden cart could travel across it, holding two full-sized adults.

"I don't think I can do this," I said as I gasped for air, heaving like a caught fish; not only because I was terrified but also because the love I'd given up everything for was no longer mine. Flaming Rainbow kneeled and as I lay splayed across the cart's floor, looked down at me with his pitch-black eyes and said, "Do not be afraid, sister. When the river is high, we carry big fat cows across and they do not fall." I was not comforted.

Once I regained my balance, I tried to help pull us up the cable line so we could swing across the river, but only burned my palms on the thick wire instead. When I spit into my hands and shook them in the cooling breeze, I realized that if anyone wanted to leave Highbridge in the winter, they'd need strong arms; otherwise they'd be in for a long stay.

The cart hit dry land with a thud, throwing me to the floor. Flaming Rainbow helped me to my feet, tossed my rucksack into the tall grass and said, "I will not see you again, sister, I am leaving this place."

"Where are you going?" I asked him, feeling as if he were an old friend deserting me.

"To Wyoming, going back to the Rez. It's time for Sundance and the love I wished for in this place was not possible."

"I'm sorry to hear that," I said, wishing we could pass the talking stick and speak from the heart. Rainbow however, was stoic. Without another word, he drew himself up on the cable wire, swished back across the Suislaw, and was gone.

The emaciated dogs stopped fighting each other and encircled me, sniffing and yelping. I could see their ribs sticking out beneath their scruffy, pale coats and smell their meaty mushroom breath. Picking up a large stick, I held it above my head. Instead of establishing my dominance, the action caused the biggest dog to leap into the air to grab it. His waxen teeth and muck-colored gums flew toward my outstretched arm. My *New York Times* obituary flashed in front of me: "Carol Schlanger, born December 28, 1945, in Brooklyn, New York, died being devoured by a pack of wild mongrels." (Very Tennessee Williams.) "In lieu of gifts, please make donations payable to the New

York City Animal Shelter, 326 East 110 Street." I threw the stick as far as I could: "Fetch! Fetch! Go fetch you fuckers!" I screamed in a voice that had broken glass. It worked. As the dogs ran off, I caught sight of a bare-breasted woman squatting in the tall grass, urinating while balancing a large woven basket on her head. When she stood, I walked toward her, taking in her earthy smell of rosemary and weed. Mounds of silver and copper jewelry hung from her ears and climbed up her bare arms. This was my good friend Talisa, transporting her freshly picked vegetables and looking as beautiful and luminescent as any film star. I'd bonded with her months before when she and her partner Billy had visited us at Greenleaf.

"Welcome, Carol," she said.

Bending at her waist, she placed her basket on the ground and gave me a hug that didn't last long enough. I clung to her.

"Clint's sleeping with another woman," I blurted out. "I couldn't take it, so here I am."

"So here you are," she said, taking a small glass pipe out of the pocket of her ragged cutoffs. "Who is she?"

"Georgia. A doctor from Texas. She can suture a wound, fly a plane, and she's from Texas."

Again, the image of Clint and Georgia's bodies writhing on the banks of Flores Creek sent me into insecure hell.

"And she's a total bitch," I continued, "who didn't take her do-no-harm oath seriously. The only thing she took seriously was Clint."

Talisa laughed at my little pain-filled joke. I loved her for that.

"Stay with us, Carol...for as long as you need."

How comforting it was to hear those kind words. About to cry, I was stopped by what I saw in the distance: another tanned, dark-haired woman scaling a huge alder tree. She climbed with the grace and speed of a lithe South Sea Islander harvesting coconuts.

"Who's that up in the branches?" I asked.

Talisa let go of me but didn't turn around to look behind her because she already knew the answer.

"That's Doli—she's my sister."

I watched as Doli drew an ax from her tool belt and, hugging the trunk with her thighs, hacked away at a branch.

"What's she doing?"

"Cutting off dead limbs for firewood. It's her job."

"Jesus."

Talisa handed me the pipe. "Everyone here has a job," she said. "Right now, mine is to help you feel better. Forget Doli and try this. It's only my end of season shake, but it'll put your problem in perspective."

"You think so?" I asked, greedy for anything that would take away the pain in my gut.

"Yes," she said as she lit the pipe, inhaled deeply and passed it. Talisa and Doli were Jewish on their mother's side and Italian on their father's: a stunning ethnic combo. Doli, a shy, nymph of seventeen, was unattached, while Talisa, at twenty-two, was with Billy, Highbridge's cogent, powerful, and difficult leader. Billy seduced women with a knowing glance and an energized slouch. Beneath his fine looks, was a mocking omniscience. If there ever was a leading man with bad boy vulnerability, it was Billy.

Talisa took my arm and walked me down a deer path bordered with giant bracken fern six feet across. She stopped and pointed out a berry bush that held a small brown bird fluttering between its leaves. I would have never noticed it on my own. She was, in that way, like Clint, seeing what my eyes missed. After another toke followed by that sweet burning rush, Talisa smiled ruefully and told me her sister Doli was also sleeping with Billy. They were sharing him. That brought me to attention. Doli was sleeping with Talisa's lover, her partner, her old man. It was radical, Mormon-esque or even incestuous. I wasn't sure which one, but I couldn't wait to hear more.

"Your sister? Do you compare notes ?"

If anyone ever had any personal boundaries, I never noticed them.

"Sometimes," Talisa said warily.

I'd met Billy only once before—at Greenleaf, where I'd accidentally handed him Moonlove's frozen placenta, thinking it was steak. When he took the butcher-wrapped package from my outstretched hand, I saw his eyes cloud over in judgment: "Jewish princess," they seemed to say as he turned away from me without a thank-you.

"What does he do differently with Doli, than he does with you?" I persisted. "Does he do it more with one of you and do you do it all together?"

"I can't tell you, Carol. It's private."

Private was not an option. This was a commune.

"Please give me details, Talisa. Just one...maybe two."

Compared to Talisa's, my woeful story seemed ordinary. Things were looking brighter. Curiosity cauterized my heartache. The cottony haze thinned, my hearing became unstuffed. Woman dumped by lover for another woman—prosaic, it happened all the time. But a woman sharing her lover with her younger sister—that was theater! Blessed be.

"We take turns. We've got it all worked out."

"A week for you? A week for her? Every other day? Who gets what, when?" I pictured the three in various combinations: lean legs, tanned backs pounding and undulating in the glow of kerosene lantern light.

Talisa answered none of my questions, she just smiled sheepishly, put down her basket and pulled me toward Highbridge's two-acre garden patch. It was bursting with color and surrounded by a barbed wire fence. Deer and goat skulls were attached to its ancient tin gate—old death adorning new life.

"Carol, leave your backpack here, we'll get it later," Talisa said. At the sound of her voice, my own private porno ended.

Talisa lifted another basket hanging off the fence and undid the simple knot that tied the gate to the frame. She motioned for me to step inside, and was not about to give me any further information. Putting her pipe in her back pocket, she removed a small tin canister and took out a perfectly rolled joint. "It's Indica flowers from last year, best we have," she said. "It'll get you through the rest of the day." I took it even though I was already high. Getting through the day seemed like a great idea.

Inside the garden, bushels of fruited tomatoes ran along wire trellises—red, golden, and plum: Heirloom, Beefsteak, Brandywine, Cherry, Early Girl, and Gold Dust. Alongside them, in perfect harmony, sat bridal bouquets of lettuce: green and bib, red and leaf, romaine and butter. Squash, peppers, purple and white cauliflower, kale, chard, broccoli, spinach—each had their own section, bordered by endless rows of roses, poppies, zinnias, and gladiolas. Inside a ring of giant sunflowers, Talisa's dazzling marijuana forest stood eight feet high, their buds dripping with dusty crystals of THC. This was the Garden of Eden of my dreams.

As I stood mesmerized, Talisa took my hand and steered me toward a sea of shiny green basil bushes.

"We need to pick for pesto," she said. "Just pinch off the lower leaves, but leave the tops on so the plant will keep growing."

I got on my knees and began. The sweet aroma of basil, transported me—but not far.

"How can you stand Billy and Doli being together? Aren't you jealous?"

"No, I'm happy about it."

I didn't believe her, not one bit.

"Why?"

"Doli being my sister makes it okay. Other people around here switch off, but I'm not comfortable with that. Besides, I know Billy and

Doli would stop if I asked them to, but I won't."

"Not ever?"

The copper arm cuff that Talisa wore flashed sunlight into my eyes.

"Maybe if we decided to have a baby, but right now Billy's way too much for me. He always wants us to be together, but I need time to hang with friends; so I told him it was okay for him to step outside our relationship because I couldn't give him everything he needed."

Talisa, I thought, was a hippie Wonder Woman able to scale convention in a single bound. She shared her man without resentment—no anger, no jealousy. Billy had her consent. Clint never asked for my approval. While Billy wanted more of Talisa, Clint wanted less of me. Clearly, Billy hadn't become Talisa's world as Clint had become mine. Even though she was from Baltimore and had grown up as part of the urban middle class, Talisa was much more self-reliant and capable in this new alternative, primitive world than I could ever hope to be. She could change a tire, chop fire wood, deliver a baby, cook for fifty, sew, knit, play the fiddle, and make something out of anything. After we'd gathered enough basil, she began weeding. I tried to keep up with her, but it was useless, her hands moved like lightening. She was hypnotizing as she danced between her vegetables, yanking crab grass and weeds from the soft, dark, well-worked earth.

Maybe, I thought to myself, my critics had a point. I was funny and engaging but no one could eat funny, and engaging kept no one warm or dry. Was it possible I'd become a burden to Clint and that he'd grown weary of caring for this New Yorker who, despite her best half-hearted efforts, would rather pay or trade for goods and services than provide them for herself? Maybe he needed someone who would not lean on him so heavily. Maybe this beautiful but taxing life style was all wrong for me and I'd made a terrible mistake. I hadn't tried to understand why he'd dumped me for Georgia and I'd never asked. Running away from the pain had been my solution. As I weighed my counter-culture self against both Talisa and Georgia, I felt sadly wanting. Once, I'd been surer footed. But not anymore.

As we closed the gate and walked from the garden, Talisa dumped the contents of her small basket into a bigger one and hoisted it onto her head. We were, she told me, on our way to the summer kitchen where she'd drop me off to help Billy prepare dinner (for 25).

At Highbridge, men and woman shared labor equally. Men cooked, women chopped wood and the reverse. Their summer kitchen, with its upright piano, its mound of musical instruments, and outdoor grill had a huge seating capacity—many times that of Flores Creek. They took their work seriously and it had a formal structure. Even though everything was given freely, including dope, you were expected to work and work hard.

Highbridge's Summer Kitchen was a post and beam structure open at both ends. It had a rough wooden floor and stone steps. On a big green chalk board, the words: "DINNER-FISH," then in parentheses (BILLY). I interpreted this to mean we'd be having a fish dinner, supervised by Billy. A fresh catch lay heaving and flapping in a huge bucket. This was great, I decided. I was good with fish. Scaling and gutting were one of my acquired skills and I knew exactly how to remove the bitter spleen and inedible gills.

"Hey Billy," Talisa called out. "You remember Carol from Flores Creek. She's living with us for a while and is here to help."

"Good," he said. And that was all.

Talisa wrapped her arms around me and gave me a bear hug. "See you at dinner," she called back as she disappeared into the trees. Despite being high, anxiety shot through me. Talisa, my friend, was gone.

I modulated my tone to what I considered warm and friendly; something mellow that would work well as a voice-over for a fabric softener commercial.

"Hello, Billy."

"Hello," he mumbled and plucked a fish that might have been a largemouth bass from the bucket. A bear claw necklace hung around his neck; the claws were black at the base and white at the tip, an inch or more in length, some reaching down to his clavicle.

"Um...Billy, do you mind if I ask you a question?"

"You just asked me a question."

"Right," I said, realizing there was no fooling around with this guy.

"It depends on the question," he continued, turning to face me. Broad-shouldered and slim-hipped, Billy was swarthy and shockingly handsome. His tattered shirt was ripped in just the right places, exposing his flat stomach and underlying muscles. A fringed leather pouch and buckhorn knife hung from his belt while a heavy braid of jet-black hair fell below his shoulders. His aura emitted a strong theatricality that immediately overwhelmed and took center stage. Billy had been establishing Highbridge's direction for three years and was its unacknowledged but apparent leader—a star. Compared to Highbridge, Flores Creek was a commune of novices. Together for three years, the Highbridge commune made or "liberated" their own clothes, spun their own wool, and only used hand tools. Unlike Flores Creek, they purposely refused to use any machine that ran on a battery, gas, or electricity. We loved anything that could lighten our load and looked forward to alternative energy sources. Highbridge looked backward to move forward—using only their hands and animals for needed work. Their horse, Che, and their mule, Jackson, plus pigs, chickens, goats, and ducks foraged and wandered, often finding refuge under the floor of their stilted main house.

Turning from the general to the particular man who stood next to me, I could not hold back.

"Billy, do you like being with Talisa and Doli, the same? I mean... equally...with them both?"

Billy slapped the bass into my hand. It was cold and slimy but in a nice way.

"You gut. I'll scale," he said, whipping his buckhorn knife from its sheath and handing it to me.

I ran my finger along the edge of the knife. It was razor sharp. Billy looked into my eyes as if searching for a reasonable mind.

"That's the first thing you say to me and you actually expect me to answer?"

"Yeah, I guess so," I said as I stabbed the fish's yellow underbelly. It parted like paper. "My preferred method for bass," I said as I continued to slice, "is to leave the head on and make an incision behind the gill cover and then cut along the backbone around the ribcage. Does that work for you?"

"Yup," he said as he half smiled at me.

"Separate but equal," he continued, "that's my policy. I appreciate both of them, although my ties to Talisa are stronger and older. Sleeping with two women is traditional. We're using the Native American model and going back to the Old Way."

It sure was the "Old Way," the really, really Old Way. Those guys in the Old Testament, like Abraham and David were into it, too. The custom was biblical, but so was stoning a woman to death.

"Not that we don't have our problems," he continued with no prodding from me. "Because they're sisters they have a close bond and sometimes I feel like they're ganging up on me...maybe that's traditional, too."

With that, he wiped the edge of his other scaling knife on his jeans. It didn't seem to bother him that a thin line of fish goo stuck to the denim. I grew giddy. My brain fog lifted. Billy was answering my questions as if he were relieved to finally let it all hang out. I loved being intrusive and intimate and I loved it even more when I got a response.

"What about the other guys at Highbridge, do they have two women, too?"

He barely took a breath before he continued. I'd hit the mother lode. Billy wanted to talk and needed someone to listen.

"No. A lot of guys don't have a woman at all. They don't like it and they have let the three of us know. They think it's wrong and that they should get a chance. My brother is really pissed. He wants Doli. That freaks me out. If he gets her and Talisa goes off, I could wind up with nothing; so I turn into kind of an asshole—territorial and protective."

Just after I'd removed the innards and tossed them into a compost pail, Billy placed his big hands on my head and pressed steadily down. As he increased the pressure, I suspected he had an evangelical Orville Roberts streak and waited for him to cry out: "Oh Lord, heal this bourgeois sinner, make her a worker among workers, help her to give her life and blood for The People! Heal! Heal!" I was wrong—instead he just asked, "What's your name, lady with the questions?"

"Carol, Billy, my name's Carol. We've met before. I used to live at Greenleaf. Don't you remember me?"

"No. Not really...the capitalist system will collapse. You know that don't you...Carol?" he continued on without missing a beat while pressing his thumbs even harder into my skull, as if to imprint the thought on my brain.

Of course I knew, I was on a Back-to-the-Land survivalist commune in the middle of the Oregon wilderness.

"We're preparing for it by creating a land-based alternative society. The United States is going to self-destruct and it won't be safe in the cities. Come Revolution and collapse, we want to be ready."

As he spoke, he lifted his hands from my head and held them high in the air, seemingly to summon a divine spirit. I was hit with a sudden longing to gut more fish.

"The only way is to build our own homes," Billy went on in the only voice I'd heard in Oregon louder than my own, "to grow our own foods and live as much as we can without petroleum or electricity. We don't even use that word any more. Around here, we say 'electrocity,' meaning off the grid. We use our only running car once a week. The rest of our transportation is horse or mule. We plant hay to feed them and use their manure to grow the hay. It's a perfect ecological circle, a 'circulization.' That's our word, too."

I picked up a walleye still alive and wiggling. Billy took it out of my hand, lay it down on a board and smashed it over the head with the blunt edge of his ax.

"I was once asked," he continued without a pause, "why political hippies were moving to the country and I answered that it was because Stalin said that you can't have a Revolution without a peasantry and since we don't have a peasantry in America, we had to create it. We had to become self-sufficient, but if that wasn't possible we'd at least become self-reliant and produce enough to get by."

"Right on, Billy!" I agreed.

If he heard me, he didn't acknowledge it. I stared at his fringed tobacco pouch. It was embroidered with a beaded red rose that was an exact replica of the one on Flaming Rainbow's loin cloth, and it made me realize who had been the object of Rainbow's unrequited love—Billy. He was now talking so much, I grew fearful he'd never stop.

"We are beginning to understand we have to have cash and having cash means being tied back in or breaking the law. It's a problem. But breaking laws that don't serve the people is an act of liberation. We never liberate from the little guys, the ones with small profit margins, just from big corporations—like Safeway."

"I hear ya brother, Safeway sucks."

I was lying. Safeway didn't bother me. They took food stamps and I loved their ketchup.

After we'd scaled and cleaned for what felt like hours, Billy took a huge wad of lard from a bucket under the sink and threw it into a frying pan the size of a manhole cover. The lump of fat had a grayish hue and smelled like rancid bacon. Billy was about to melt it down and toss in the delicate catch. The man knew his politics, had amazing survival skills and great influence but didn't know jack about cooking. I did.

He had to be stopped

"You doin' the fish in lard?" I asked him, deliberately dropping my "g" to sound folksy. It didn't work.

"You betcha, best way there is," he said, trouncing me.

"In a puddle of pig fat?" I asked, with what I considered a stinging emphasis on the words *pig* and *fat.*

"Nothin' wrong with that," Billy answered with a smile that said he might have me for dinner instead of the fish. With courage I didn't know I had, I continued on.

"Yes, there is. It'll ruin the flavor and it's unhealthy..."

Billy smelled like horses and hay. Sweat and mud.

"Scuse me lady but our pigs are good eatin'. They're our garbage disposal system and our rototiller. We tie three or four of them together, let 'em loose and they turn the earth for us. Can't beat it. We damn near love our pigs."

"Billy...I didn't mean the whole pig, just their fat...besides bass has a very delicate..."

"Tell you what," he said, his punitive grin moving toward a bite, "we'll cook 'em your way next time. Meanwhile, you take the slop bucket over there, the one with the fish guts, and haul it over to the pig pen. Mama Cass is our sow—you can't miss her; she's got six at her teats. They're all gonna love those fish guts."

"I don't want..."

"...First footpath on the right," he said, handing me the slops pail. I held it as far away from my body as I could. A shining pearl mountain of intestines and innards lay almost to the rim. To keep from gagging, I pulled my shirt up over my nose and my own pink stomach popped out. I hoped Billy didn't notice.

Mama Cass lay on her belly and stared at me with beady, dead eyes. Her piglets popped off of her slackened teats and stumbled over each other as they ran toward me. Before I had a chance to feed them, they'd nipped at my heels. It hurt. Even though they were still nursing, they had sharp little teeth and might have taken a small chunk out of my calves if I hadn't kicked them away. Once I dumped the contents of the slop bucket, they forgot all about me and sunk their piggy heads deep into the offal. Snorting with pleasure, they gobbled down everything but the mud. Pigs will eat anything. Back country folk joked about it: "All that was left of poor Jim-boy was his teeth. But he done what he wuz told: fed them damn pigs!"

For the rest of my stay at Highbridge, feeding the pigs became my permanent work assignment. As the days passed, I adjusted to the chore and appreciated the swine for what they were: piggy recycling machines. Whatever went in one end came out the other: the by-product of rapid pork and fat production—almost elegant in its dirty, smelly way. "Siouxeee! Hey, Sheyna Medele," I'd shout as they rooted and snorted at my feet. "Guess what I've got for you today? Moldy old potatoes; they're your favorite. Moshe, my sweetheart, don't look now but I saved the chicken heads just for you because I know how much you like them." As a pig caller and whisperer, I had a real talent. For a few moments, I thought they liked me, really, really liked me. But as soon as reality kicked in, I knew the little gluttons could have cared less. They just wanted what I had and couldn't wait to gobble it up—they were, after all, pigs.

After the feeding, I had nothing to do but explore. From the pig pen, I could see the Suislaw and returned to its bank to look for my backpack and sleeping bag. The dogs had disappeared and all I could hear was the slow flow of the river over rocks. On the near shore were my belongings—all that remained of my past life. Removing my jeans, I waded in to wash away the fishy-piggy stink of the day. With my flesh rejuvenated by the clear, cold water, I was beginning to feel myself again when a rustle in the grass made me think someone or something was watching. But all I could see was the shadow of a giant maple tree darkening the green pasture.

CHAPTER 24

Me Too

September 1972

After smoking the joint Talisa had given me, the rest of the day disappeared and dusk came on fast—much faster than I'd expected. I'd returned to the summer kitchen and dinner was over. The fish had tasted like bacon, and with others, all new to me, I sat on a bench flying with live banjo and guitar music. It was when thick night blanked the sky and the musicians stopped playing and left that I noticed I was alone. Neither Talisa, Doli, nor Billy were anywhere in sight. Talisa had asked earlier if I'd be okay for the night and without thinking, I'd told her "yes," and then she was gone. Weed had put me so deeply into the moment that it had stolen my thoughts for the future. It had not occurred to me to secure a safe place to sleep. No one had been watching out for me. Clint wasn't there to lead us to our nice warm bed. The fire would go out and I didn't have a flashlight. With nearby canisters filled with leftover food, I'd be forced to sleep in the open. There were cougar and bear in these woods...big two-hundred-pound cats and even bigger black bear. I had no lighter and had used up my matches. Gall rose in my throat—this was all Clint's fault. I hated him; hated him because I was terrified, because I could be torn to shreds, because he wasn't there.

A rumbling in the distance, a bush quivered. Branches cracked. I flicked open my knife, then grabbed a frying pan and held it like a shield in front of my chest so if worse came to worse, I'd use it to bash whatever came at me over its head.

A hundred yards away I saw a storm lantern light flicker. Someone was camped close by.

"Hello, anybody there?" I shouted, but got no response. I scooped up my sleeping bag, jumped from the kitchen platform and ran, my heart pounding, through the trees toward that light. Nothing attacked me. The quivering and cracking was the forest breathing. My eyes adjusted to the darkness. Through the leaves and branches of the trees, moonlight illuminated a footpath. It led to a small clearing where I could see a tent. A lantern glowed inside it, turning the canvass a bright lime green. "Hello?" I called out. No one answered. I tried again. "Anybody home?" Not a sound—so I brazenly opened the tent flap and looked inside. A lantern sat on the floor at the foot of a cot where a man lay drinking from a wine bottle. When he saw me, he bolted up as if to make sure I was really there and not a dream.

"Hey!" he said.

"Hi," I said.

"Wow. Cool. Come on in."

His tent reeked of stale beer and animal want.

"You're Talisa's friend, right?"

"Yeah, I am. It's my first night here."

He swayed, got up from his cot and walked unsteadily toward me. In the lamplight, I could see he was sinewy with deep acne scars pockmarking his face, making him look both rugged and pitiable.

"I saw you at dinner," he said, "and down by the creek."

"You were watching me?"

He gave me no explanation or apology. Finding his silence unsettling, I continued on. "Everybody disappeared. I saw your light and... I...I don't know where I am or where everyone went."

"They're around."

"If you don't mind," I asked, wary of the situation but preferring it to the alternative, "could I bed down here for the night?

"Course you can."

"...I'm not sure how to say this," I stammered, "but please don't try anything. I've had a rough day. No sex. No fooling around. No nothing. Please. I mean it."

His tent was piled high with books and that gave me a little confidence in him. I trusted people who read more than those who didn't.

"Hey, no problem," he said.

"You promise?"

"Sure I promise...you got enough bedding?"

"Yes, thank you. I brought my sleeping bag."

Even though his body told me he was hungry for what he didn't have, I trusted his word.

"The floor's cold," he continued. "I got a piece of foam so you'll be comfortable. Carol's your name, right?"

"Right."

"You got nothing to be afraid of, Carol. I know how to treat a guest."

He seemed like a nice enough guy whose adolescence must have been hell driven by pimples. Leaving my clothes on, I lay down on his thin piece of foam and placing it as far away from him as I could, I zipped myself up inside my sleeping bag. "Goodnight," I said. Again, just silence. As soon as he blew out his lantern, all went black. I soon fell into a deep sleep and was having a bad dream about being back at Yale, when I awoke unable to breathe. My bag had been opened and my jeans pulled down to my ankles. The man, who'd never told me his name, was lying on top of me, his hands pulling my legs apart and his penis forcing its way inside me. I tried to push him off but his body was too insistent. "Stop it! Stop!!" I screamed and raised my hand to hit him but he caught and pinned it to the floor. The rest of me couldn't move. He felt like he weighed a thousand pounds. To fight was not in me. I was too exhausted, too out of it and—I just let him. My mind drifted away and my body went limp. I felt nothing except a nasty tickle between my legs and then wetness on my thigh. He had had the insane decency to pull out. It was over as abruptly as it had begun. He tried to kiss me on the mouth, but I buried my head in the foam. Without a word, the man got up, lay down on his own bed and almost immediately began to snore.

Clutching my knife in one hand, I pulled up my jeans with the other and with my sleeping bag draped over my shoulders, stumbled out into the night. There was no way I'd spend another second in that tent. Outside, nothing was visible. A rustle—then a snort. With the courage that very few women who had ever sprayed Light and Bright in their hair to bring out their blond highlights ever summoned, I reached out and felt a wet cold nose...ears...a mane. It was Che—Footbridge's big black gelding. His skin felt like warm silk, it was as if he'd materialized from horse heaven to protect me. Together, we stayed close for the rest of the night. At first light, he left, leaving me to walk as fast as I could toward the summer kitchen.

As I made my way down a now visible path, I heard voices and wood being split. The others at Highbridge were moving into their work day. However, before I could face another human, I returned to the banks of the Suislaw, took off all my clothes, sat waist deep in the cold water and wept as it flowed through my legs and washed away the night's degradation.

At least ten people had beaten me to breakfast. Smoke was pouring out of the outdoor kitchen's stovepipe and the air was crisp and clean. Some, who I didn't know, were seated at the long tables, drinking coffee, talking and eating. I walked toward a huge pot of bubbling oatmeal and scooped it into a bowl. The bowl's heat felt wonderful to my cold hands. Adding raisins and goat's milk, I was about to sit on a bench, when there he was again, moving towards me—my rapist. I wanted to throw my steaming cereal in his face—but didn't.

"Get away!" I hissed.

He came closer. "Come on," he said. "It wasn't that bad."

This man was not of the world where women were people. He smiled at me as if I were a hissing kitten, both angry and cute.

"You raped me, you fucking asshole!" Birds flew from the trees and squawked with me.

Others turned and stared. Doli, Talisa, and three other women, Honey, Blue, and Chirpa, had arrived and heard the exchange. My big voice had reached them. It had reached the Cascades.

"You left your hairclip in my tent," the man said, nonplussed. "You wanna come back for it tonight?"

"Die and go to hell!!"

By this time most of Highbridge were seated. My new best women friends, whose vibrations were so attuned to each other that they got their periods on the same day, stopped eating. Without my having to tell them or say anything, Doli walked to the utensil box near the stove and grabbed a serving fork. Talisa got up, hocked up a glob of phlegm and spat it at the man's foot. I was touched. Both were powerful female fighters. They stood up for and protected each other and now I was one of them. When the man saw what was coming at him, he hunched over, lowered his head and shuffled away. It was beautiful.

Talisa put her strong arm around me and said, "He's outta here, sister. Consider him gone." These women would do battle for me. Never had I felt such solidity with my "sisters," not in New York, not at Flores Creek, and in the instant understood that when women put their bodies and voices on the line for each other, their strength was unlimited. The man would get the banishment he deserved. I was hoping for a little horsewhipping, too, when I overheard him trying to explain himself to Billy. It was pathetic.

"She came on to me," he whined. "The chick shows up at night at my tent...just askin' for it."

No way, I thought. He lied and raped and if karma had anything to do with it, he was in for a lifetime of misery.

The man took Billy's arm. Billy shook him off.

"That's not how I heard it," Billy said.

"I was horny, brother—you know how it is."

Billy didn't.

"You got till tomorrow morning to get your shit together and get the fuck out of here."

With that, Billy walked away from the man whose name I would never learn and came toward me. His handsome face looked kinder and sadder than I'd ever seen it.

"Really sorry about last night, Carol," he said. "We got a nice place for you to stay. Just an old chicken coop, but it's clean and has a door you can lock from the inside."

It was as if an angel had taken over Billy's body. As he walked me down a deer path towards my converted coop, I let loose. "Billy, that guy was a friend of somebody at Highbridge's."

"Yeah, I know."

"How could they have asked him here? A commune means people doing the right thing–shining on their brothers."

Billy gave no comforting touch, but said, "Carol, it's just the way it went down. Some things you can't figure."

A slug inched his way up my calf, leaving a line of gunk in his wake. I flung him off into the bushes.

What little wisdom I had, told me that my rapist didn't know better. He was a lost mongrel...clueless, mangy, and alone. If he had been a dog, I would have had him put down.

Billy, feeling he'd set the rapist issue to rest, moved onto the next thing requiring his attention:

"When you make night soil," he said, "be sure to hit the same spot away from the river and the well. A bunch of us got staph infections from bad water or getting feces on a cut. One guy almost died. The sores eat your skin away and leave big holes."

"That's horrible," I said, my mind moving along with Billy's. "Anywhere I should dig?"

Billy leaned up against a Maple tree and stood like a man whose body knew how to offer a great ride. I was not attracted to him, but it was easy to see why so many others were.

"Hey," he answered, unable to keep from grinning, "you have free will–use it." And without another word, he turned away from me and disappeared into the woods.

Once inside the tiny room, which contained only a bare mattress, I realized this morning at Highbridge was like no morning I'd experienced in Oregon. For the first time since leaving Manhattan, I was totally on my own–without money, without a flashlight, and without Clint.

CHAPTER 25

Bird On A Wire

Late September 1972

Most men act so tough and strong on the outside because on the inside, we are scared, weak and fragile. Men, not women, are the weaker sex.

JERRY RUBIN

My breasts gave me the first clue. They'd swelled beyond my usual 36C and could only tolerate the softest of pure cotton. My nipples could detect the faintest hint of polyester and if touched, the poor tender things went mad. I'd been at Highbridge for nearly a month and time had flown. Talisa, the master gardener, had taught me which plants needed alkaline and which needed acidic soil, the superiority of deep drip watering over intermittent hosing and the necessity of constant weeding so that the baby vegetables could breathe and stretch their roots. My skin had darkened with sunbathing and my soul had been fortified by weekly women's meetings. At Highbridge, the women had an agenda: to strengthen each other in spirit and solidify against male domination. With a leader like Billy, it was a necessity. At Flores Creek, our women were haphazard with their mutual support and content to let the men do the heavy lifting. If any man was too overwhelming or powerful, it was handled individually and case by case. We were similar to Highbridge, but essentially different.

Because our mountain climate was dryer in summer than their wet river basin, we rarely got infections and had better hygiene. Cuts were never left unwashed and human waste was never left untreated. While Flores Creek dreamed of wind and solar energy, Highbridge dreamed of horse logging and cattle grazing. We were better educated, but they knew and understood nature. More cohesive, daring, dark-haired, and dangerous than my women friends at Flores Creek, the women of Highbridge wielded chain saws, galloped horses, and often slept outside. They robbed when they had to, shared child-care, drank to excess, freely roamed the forest, rolled their own, and made each day more exciting than the last.

☾

Talisa, Doli, and I were on our way to civilization in a terrible junker whose floor boards were so rotted away that as we passed Triangle Lake and Low Pass, I could see highway 136 and 99 zip by below my feet. We were headed sixty miles east to Eugene to take from corporate robber barons and to give to ourselves. Talisa was driving. When she passed me her hash pipe, her copper arm bracelets jingled as did mine. Her style was now my own. I proudly wore the huarache sandals she'd cobbled. Their thick soles, crafted from old tire treads, were uncomfortable, but Talisa assured me that they'd grow less bumpy with wear. To hide their loot without detection, she and Talisa and Doli wore oversized Mexican ponchos. I didn't have one yet, but was promised I would.

Doli was making a list of needed items: garden hose, peroxide, Vaseline, turpentine, nails, rope, sirloin steak, and ace bandages. Then, as an afterthought, she asked if anyone needed Tampax. I wasn't sure. I hadn't gotten my period in...well, I didn't know in how long, but knew I was late. So, when we hit Mill Street, I begged off "shopping" and asked to be dropped off at the Whitebird Women's Clinic. Within minutes I stood in front of the white clapboard building with its peeling paint and splintered hand rails and trusted what was inside.

After my intake interview, during which I gave the name of Myrna Loy but truthfully answered I'd had no history of venereal disease, I sat down on the funky waiting room couch to wait, and watched an aged television that had a grainy picture and muffled sound. To my amazement, my former classmate from Yale Drama, Henry Winkler, appeared on the screen. I frantically turned the volume up as far as it could go to hear Merv Griffin, the talk show host say, "*Fonzie*" and then "break-out hit on the new sit-com *Happy Days.*" I slapped the console and the picture cleared. Henry was smiling his open, I've-got-this-covered-but-I'm-humble-anyway smile. I knew and liked that smile and had no way of knowing that in the future he'd receive recognition as a great character actor and an American icon, with his *jumping the shark* routine forever added to showbiz lingo.

Lying flat on my back, my legs splayed, I felt the ice-cold speculum go where no stainless steel had gone before. My "this-can't-be-happening" mind departed and flew back to New York, to the *Public Theater* where audiences were giving me a nightly standing ovation for my American Housewife section of the *American Pig review*. The laughter had been endless and I'd had to stop in midstream to let it roll over me. Nothing made me happier than that sound. I loved it so. Henry, also part of the show, stood in the wings grinning and holding his dry cleaning. He had liked my performance and was very complimentary. He also liked his clothes to be clean and pressed. Joseph Papp, our forward-thinking producer sat in the bleachers. He admired our radical directors but wasn't fond of the Yale Drama School dean. "You'll always have a home with us," he'd promised me at our wrap party. With my success assured, I was certain I'd always be able to say what I had to say and the world would listen.

"You're at the tail end of your first trimester."

The nurse practitioner's face was plain and her voice had a flat twang that spoke a simple truth."We have excellent pre-natal classes," she continued, "with a certified nutritionist you can sign up for."

It had been the wind in the trees, the long nights of lovemaking that had done this. From that first bolt of lightning in New Haven, I'd imagined what beautiful babies Clint and I could make together...but now...

"I...I don't know."

The nurse practitioner changed gears.

"We can assist in termination if that's what you want."

"Thanks, I have to think about it," I said. "Tell me...have you ever seen *Happy Days* on T.V.?"

"Hey," she said, lowering her voice and sticking her thumb up in the air to imitate Fonzie's signature salutation. "It's my favorite show."

I slid down from the examining table and pulled on my jeans. My legs went through easily but zipping and buttoning them was a struggle; not because of Talisa's delicious sour dough bread but because I had something...someone growing inside me. When I stepped out into the Indian summer, a very young college student, in her skimpy cut-offs and University of Oregon tee shirt peddled past on her bike. Although I was only twenty-five, I envied her carefree youth, her clean looks and straight direction. All options, it seemed, were still open to her. In the name of absolute freedom, mine were closing.

Regret and mid-day heat hit me hard. The city of Eugene no longer looked sweet and innocuous but vapid and baked: a nothing place dotted with nothing buildings, offering nothing. I'd changed, too: a baby, no, a zygote, had taken hold inside of me and I wasn't sure I wanted it to stay.

Talisa had a thing for New York steaks, so when she and the others drove up to the clinic, I was forced to sit in the back seat next to a mound of raw, packaged sirloin. On the floor below my feet was a purloined pick ax and a spool of bailing wire. How they were acquired required skill, practice, and luck. My extraordinary new girlfriends were rip-off revolutionaries; I just liked to take things and not pay for them.

"How'd it go at the clinic?" Talisa asked me as she unwrapped a cigar and put it to her lips without lighting it.

"I'm almost three months." Then, to prevent her from congratulating me, I quickly added, "Looks like you guys really scored."

Talisa took the bait. She was proud of what she, Doli, and Honey had accomplished.

"It was easy. The guy at the checkout took a whiff as we passed and said…'ahhh country' and let us through. He was totally into helping us—a brother in disguise."

She hesitated for a beat and then said, "It's good news, Carol… about the baby I mean. Unless it's bad news…then it sucks."

"Yeah," I said noncommittally and then asked her to drive me to the post office so I could send Clint a postcard.

The thin, blond card had a preprinted eight-cent stamp. On the back I drew a stick figure of a pregnant woman with a baby in her belly and signed it: "Guess who?" I hoped Clint would know the answer.

Then…I decided not to send it.

The baby, who had been conceived before I ran away from home, was, I was sure, his.

☾

After our return to Highbridge and before helping Talia shuck corn for dinner, my body felt heavy and in need of a nap. As I approached my chicken coop/bedroom, there she was, her downward dogging bunny-butt saluting the sky, her hands splayed on the ground—Georgia.

"Howdy Sister," she said, looking at me through her muscular legs.

"Fuck you, bitch." Was what I wanted to say, but instead said, "Hello Georgia. I never expected to see you here."

Sitting back on her haunches, she dropped into a child's pose. Symbolically, I liked that.

"Hey," she said, "I'm on my way to Vancouver and stopped in to say goodbye."

I was stunned. Friends say goodbye. Georgia was no friend. I wanted to rip her thick glasses off her button nose and stomp them into the rich, manure-enhanced earth. As she spoke, she touched my arm with her soon-to-be a surgeon's hand:

"Carol," she continued, "I want you to know that I think Clint's a really nice guy and a great fuck. You're lucky to have him."

"Have him, Georgia? You had him, now I have nothing."

"That's not true, Carol. All he could talk about was you."

"Bullshit, Georgia. I was there loving him and he left me. You wanted him; he wanted you and neither of you cared about me."

I expected an apology, but didn't get one. Georgia had no apology in her. All she said was, "Well...he's coming to get you."

Her teeth were bright white, just like Clint's. I imagined her toothless and old, unable to chew. Then said, "What are you, Georgia, his fucking emissary?"

The woman had taken a hippie pill I'd never swallowed. She tried to throw her arms around me to give me a hug, but I stepped away. Getting my message, she pouted like a child, turned and walked toward the Siuslaw and the trolley that would finally take her out of my life forever.

☾

The next morning, I saw him from a distance. It didn't matter how far away he was, I always recognized Clint. He and Billy were working together to remove rotten shingle siding from Highbridge's Main House. It was just like Clint to jump in and lend a hand. The Main House, with its vaulted roof and mismatched windows, was built on stilts and stood on a steep hillside. A small herd of goats sat under its floor, chomping on hay. When Clint saw me, he dropped the nails he held between his lips into his palm and smiled: big, wide, and open. In response, I rolled my eyes and shook my head "no."

He'd come, I was sure, because Georgia had left him. He was not the kind of man to sleep alone. I approached him slowly, careful not to come to close.

"Hey, baby," he cooed.

So wrong.

I fixed my gaze on a medicine wheel that hung from the porch wall. Its feathers were brown and gold and it served to protect.

"How've you been, Carol?"

"Fine."

Silence. I would not engage Clint in conversation. Instead of allowing me the pleasure of watching him struggle for words, his big feet in shabby sneakers, that pointed inwards, shuffled in my direction.

My Viking god was pigeon-toed.

"I missed you a lot," he said.

"Sure you did, Clint."

His shoulders drooped. His head hung low.

"I know I fucked up," he said, "but if you come back home with me to Flores Creek, I promise it will never happen again."

I didn't believe him and told him so, but he went right on talking. "The thing with Georgia didn't mean much, I just had to get it out of my system."

"What kind of a system was that?" I asked. "The I'll-do-whatever-I-want-and-to-hell-with-you system?"

"Kinda," he said, finally looking me in the eye. "I just got off track. We're a couple, Carol. We belong together. You know that."

How convenient, I thought, for him to now decide we were inseparable.

"Clint, you don't know what I sacrificed to be with a man like you. I gave up my career! I gave up the theater. Joe Papp loved me. You don't even know who Joseph Papp is! I gave up all my brilliant friends who understood what I was talking about. When I said *Dante*, they said *Inferno*! I'm not over it. No way!"

"Whadda ya mean a man like me?"

How had I ever loved this self-centered lummox?

"A Neanderthal," I answered. "The kind of thick-headed, testosterone-heavy ape who gets an A-plus for his fuck-fest with another woman. Congratulations, Clint. You graduate to being alone with your big frisky dick."

With that, I believed I'd covered the roadmap.

"It wasn't that way," he protested, "we only did it a few times."

"And you think a few times doesn't count? I thought you were my best friend, Clint."

He took my hand and pressed it to his chest. It was a schmaltzy gesture, but I felt his heart pounding fast.

"Ride back home with me, Carol, to Flores Creek. We'll talk and if we don't get things right between us, I'll bring you back here—all you got to do is ask."

I felt my own heart opening up to him even as I tried to slam it shut; but I managed to never mention my rape. The violation, I felt, had been mine, not his. It had sickened me but not broken my heart—he had.

Carol," he said, "Kokia asks for you all the time; he wants to know when you're comin' back."

"As soon as Georgia splits; did you tell him that?"

Clint put his big hand against the small of my back and drew me to him. I didn't object.

"Carol, I've always obeyed the rules and done what was right. I never knowingly hurt anybody. Oregon was my one chance to break free of all the football warrior shit Texas and the Navy pounded into me. What I learned is that there's Spirit Laws you can't break. If you do, your life falls apart. I broke one and now nothing feels right. Clarity moves you forward. What's amorphous holds you back."

"What's amorphous holds you back." The man could actually talk when he wanted to. Weakened, I wanted to burrow my way into the homey curve of his neck and forget everything.

Seconds later, the moment passed. I pulled away from his big body and knew, as God was my witness, I'd never let him fuck me over again.

☾

The inland heat quickly evaporated as Clint drove us past the city of Florence. We were soon on the 101 headed south toward Coos Bay, my favorite coastal town with its towering international harbor and mountains of wood chips. After an hour, the Bandon jetty came into view and as an empty Heinekens' bottle rolled out from under the driver's seat, I waited for Clint to say something, anything—but there was nothing but silence between us. Keeping my focus on his bashed-in odometer, I whispered,"You broke my heart, you bastard."

The blue veins in his hands surfaced as he gripped the wheel.

"I'd get down on my knees and beg you to forgive me, Carol. I'd swear I'd never be unfaithful again but I can't do that and drive straight."

"Then stop the truck."

It wasn't until twenty miles later, when we came to the hundred-year-old Myrtle tree marking the end of the Flores Creek country road that Clint finally pulled over, set the emergency brake, hit the ground, and said, "I love you, Carol. I always have and I always will."

"Keep going."

"It's cold on the gravel. My knee is starting to freeze up."

He tried to stand. My voice wouldn't let him.

"Clint..."

"...What I did was selfish and stupid," he continued. "If it takes my whole life, I'll make it up to you."

Clint was making the serious, unbreakable commitment to our relationship I'd assumed he'd made in the first place.

"Every man makes mistakes, Carol. It's what makes him a man."

"That's just macho bullshit," I said. "But I'll forgive you anyway... just this once and never again. And you owe me one—remember that."

"One what?"

"I'm not sure yet, but you'll find out. And Clint..."

"Yeah?"

"I'm pregnant."

CHAPTER 26

White Rabbit

October 1972

It's no use going back to yesterday,
because I was a different person then.
LOUIS CARROLL, *Alice in Wonderland*

My homecoming with Clint was sweet and for the first time in our relationship, he went down on me. For a Texan, that's about as apologetic as it gets. The next morning, my lower chakra still tingling, I stepped into the Main Cabin to find Katerina and Louise canning peaches, pears, plums, and tomatoes at full throttle. The fire box in our hundred-year old cook stove had been burning from morning till night and the porch was piled high with wood. With a pair of tongs, Louise carefully lifted the sterilized Mason jars from the boiling bath and spoon-fed them the fragrant and steaming fruit mixture. Katrina then put the filled jars back into the water to cook and when they were done, placed them on a wire rack.

This was serious business. No one who had endured our first winter would soon forget how delicious a canned peach, dripping in its own sweet juices, tasted when no fresh fruit was to be had. Both my old and very busy girlfriends hugged me, welcomed me home, and then put me to work. My job was to wipe each filled Mason jar clean with a steaming cloth before shelving it. When they were finished, the glass jars stood spotless in the sunlight sparkling like giant jewels—red and purple, yellow and green— dazzling. Once again, Louise, Katerina, and I were like indigenous women, working together to sustain our tribe. And like those women, we gossiped.

"Carol," Louise asked, "Did Clint tell you that Agung's come back to live with us?"

No, Clint hadn't told me. He was Clint.

Louise dribbled an inch of juice off the top of a jar of tomatoes and into a bowl to be saved for sauce. "He broke up with Skybird," she continued, her lips sinking towards her chin, "and now he's living down at the Creek near Two Turtles. The little shit got her pregnant!"

"That's awful Louise."

"Skybird's having my Eurasian baby!" she screeched. But instead of trying to console her with a hug or pat, I backed away. Something in Louise had changed. Her voice had become more strident and nasal, the pores on her sallow skin had enlarged, making her look less attractive and more downtrodden. Disappointment had taken over her face. I was trying to warm up to the Louise I once knew when Katerina screamed, "Stop! Stop it! Clint, what are you doing?!"

Clint had stomped into the cabin covered in mud and wiped his hands on a clean cloth draped over the back of a chair. His palms and fingers were covered in oil and grease—the gooey residue of engine repair. The cloth, a perfect square of white cotton, was destined to be a diaper. Katerina had scrubbed it hard and long enough to turn her knuckles red. Snatching it out of Clint's hands, she held it up in disbelief.

"You see nothing, Clint," she said. "It took very long to clean this, now it is useless. You think I, too, am useless? What I do is nothing?"

A doltish look sat on Clint's face, as if it had been smacked by a banana cream pie. He had never seen Katerina angry. No one had.

"Men," she continued, "you are all stoned. Puff Puff Puff—and your brains go up in smoke. Things must be clean for the babies. Babies are more important than your stupid machines!"

Katerina threw the ruined cloth on the floor and dashed out onto the back porch, her red hair waving behind her like a cape. She was just five feet; Clint was six-three but she'd knocked him silly.

"She'll get over it," Joey said as he spooned blackberry dregs into his mouth. "She's all different since she got pregnant. Not as nice."

Katerina was pregnant! It was the first I'd heard of it. A month apart, the two of us would take our great gestating ride together. My delight at hearing her news fizzled when Clint muttered, "Yup. Now she's having a baby, Katerina's gotten all uppity."

Uppity? Who says uppity? Hippie cowboys with vestigial 50s mindsets—that's who.

I was so fucked.

And fucked I was.

Open and wet Katerina and I had had our babies planted in us during the soft Oregon summer nights. The warm earth between our toes had set a fecundity that coddled our eggs into acceptance. My body knew why the earth was always called "Mother"—because what took root in her always grew. However, with motherhood, I knew I'd be more dependent on Clint than ever. That scared me. I'd never be good in the wild. Without Clint's help, I might drown like a turkey in the rain; a bird too stupid to close its mouth in a downpour. With my mouth open and my eyes shut, I knew I was too intrinsically urbane and clumsy to acquire real survival skills. And history had shown me Clint was a poor candidate for a monogamous family life. My past, the one in which I could depend on my own resources and talents, called to me.

I had to answer.

☾

Night—echoing off the hills of the neighboring one thousand-acre Morrill ranch; now the distant howl of coyotes felt like a familiar plaintive tune. Clint's eyes were closed; his big hands were folded across his chest like an entombed Gaelic king—so ancient and still. The gas flame in our kerosene lamp fluttered and died. We lay in total darkness. Not seeing made it easier to say what I had to say.

"Clint?"

"Yeah?"

"I'm going to Los Angeles."

"Whaaa?" he mumbled.

"I gotta go to L.A."

"Don't be crazy, Carol. You just got back."

His voice was filled with a sleepy irritation. I'd hijacked him from a better place.

"Clint, I have to go."

"Carol, you don't have to do anything. Please," he begged, "lemme sleep."

I rested my hand on his chest. It was covered by coils of curly man hair—a telltale sign of the opposite sex.

"Before I have a baby, Clint, I need a safety net, to know what I can accomplish without you. I can't survive here alone."

"You're not alone. You got me. You got us. All you gotta do is have a healthy baby."

"IF I have a baby."

"What do you mean IF?"

His voice, filled with fear, cut through the night. In a power move, I raised my head above his and looking down on him, said, "Before I give birth, Clint, I have to see what I can do on my own." His head popped up, trying to inch above mine, but it was too filled with sleep to make it.

"Carol, you got everythin' you need right here."

He hated it when I woke him up to talk. I could have spoken to him during the day but daylight was too rational and Clint was rational. Night time was my time.

"I don't have everything I need, Clint. Or want."

"What about us?"

"That's some question coming from you."

He sat up. Now fully awake, he found a box of matches and lit our kerosene lantern.

"You wanna go and be a movie star? Is that what you want? Jeeze Carol, get real."

"I have the skills, Clint. I have the connections."

"You look in the mirror lately?"

What did he mean by that? Then I remembered I was three months pregnant and hadn't bathed in weeks.

"Don't leave, Carol, it's just plain stupid. Where you gonna sleep? Where you gonna stay? Just take care of our baby. That's your job—that's all."

That did it. Growing a baby inside you, loving and caring for it wasn't a job—it was a calling, a devotion, a prayer. A job was a job. Being an X- ray technician was a job, washing windows was a job, managing an automotive plant was a job. Furious, I lashed out at the not-yet-father of our not-yet child: "Clint, that one time I met your mom in New Haven, we got into a big argument. Right in the middle she said, 'Honey, let's jes have a Harvey Wallbanger and forget all 'bout it.' Then she mixed herself three, one right after the other and drank them down. The woman had been a concert pianist, an artist, but she gave up what she loved, what she'd trained for her whole life, to raise three hell-raising, probably thankless little boys in Dipshit Texas. I'm so not her, Clint. I'm not squelching my spirit. I might not know exactly who I am, but I'm not like your Mom."

"No, you're not, Carol. My mother had some sense. Goodnight."

His response didn't touch me. I'd moved on.

Without another word, Clint blew out the lantern and lay back down. Soon he was breathing with the slow, steady rhythm of sleep. But not me. No way. My head was too busy planning.

CHAPTER 27

On the Bus

October-November 1972

In our every deliberation, we must consider the impact of our decisions on the next seven generations.

WINTU WOMAN, 19TH CENTURY

It had taken twenty-two hours to get from North Bend to the Santa Monica Greyhound terminal; then another hour by Metro bus to reach the end of Venice Boulevard with its Italianate pastel arches and rampant tattoo parlors. Minutes before I'd left, Clint had given me the sixty-five dollars he'd earned picking cedar and fir brush for Christmas wreaths so that I would have money for the trip. He hadn't wanted me to go, but gave what he could to keep me safe. With most of the cash I had left after paying bus fare, I rented a bed at the Venice Youth Hostel. Then unpacked my clothes, hurriedly washed at a shared sink and bolted. A block away, I discovered *Aardvark,* a fantastic vintage, second-hand clothing store where I purchased a nubby, green wool cardigan, and a pair of Rita Hayworth fuck-me platform heels.

Through Marty, my former New York agent, I had miraculously wangled an appointment with *Zimmerman, Toda, Cunningham and Foxe* in Beverly Hills. They represented Jack Nicholson and to my amazement, had said they'd be happy to meet me. As soon as I put those strappy, still glamourous shoes on my feet, the old showbiz thrill returned. In my soon-to-be-a-movie-star outfit, I fluffed my wild mane and stuck out my thumb on Abbot Kinney Drive, certain I'd catch a ride.

In the early 1970s, the freewheeling late 60s' embers of Southern California hippie era were still burning. Hitchhiking was not illegal and for the young and penniless, was a standard mode of transportation. *Charles Manson, Squeaky Fromme* and the Helter Skelterers had been in lockup since 1971. *Altamont* (the Rolling Stones concert, policed by the *Hells Angels* that ended in a riot and death) had dampened the exuberance of the alternative film, art, and music community. *Good Vibrations* was no longer on the charts. Ocean Front Walk, a block from my hostel, was filled with hawkers, fortune tellers, and street musicians. From where I stood, I could smell incense and coconut oil mixed with the sea. A battered Jeep Cherokee pulled up in front of me and faster than you can say *Ferry Cross the Mersey*, I was on my way. My chauffeur, the front man for the *Tadpoles*, a struggling rock band playing at the *Troubadour*, was going to his first Alcoholics Anonymous meeting. As we travelled East towards Wilshire Boulevard, he complained about bands that were making it big while his wasn't. When he dropped me off on Rodeo Drive, he refused the joint I offered him, crouched down in his seat to snort a line, and then sped off.

For the first time in almost two years, I pushed a button and rode up in an elevator. The door to the theatrical agency was massive and the carpet under my feet was soft and fine. However, the reception area was just functional and the front desk empty. I had no watch but the clock on the Tadpole guy's jeep had read twelve. Sandy Zimmerman, an agency partner, came out of his inner office, asked me to follow him back, and once inside, offered a low chair by his side. As he looked me over, he took my unmanicured hand and said he thought I had a bright future. I was "gorgeous, a real knock-out" and had come highly recommended. That sounded great. No one had told me I was beautiful in a long time and I knew at my age, it was a requirement. My nervousness settled. Did he mind, I asked, since I had no demo-reel with me, if I showed him something?

"Of course, Sweetheart," he said. "Show me anything you like. I'm here for you."

In moments, I transported myself to Scotland, put a dagger in my hand and became Lady Macbeth—filled with agony and female prowess.

"Come to my woman's breasts and take my milk for gall,

You murdering ministers wherever in your sightless substance...

"That's terrific kid," he interrupted, "Loved the knife part. Tell ya what. We'll rep you if you lose twenty pounds and sleep with me."

"Do you want me to lose twenty pounds and then sleep with you?" I asked, "Or sleep with you and then loose twenty pounds?" He smiled but there was no warmth between his thin lips.

"The choice is yours, Wendy."

The sad old Hollywood story was true. I could feel my cheeks redden and my stomach turn. After that great comeback, I had nothing left.

"But Mr. Zimmerman," I sputtered, wishing I hadn't worn such tight jeans and that he knew my name, "I'm a genius. I can write and act."

"Good for you, sweetheart."

"I'm a girl Woody Allan."

"Honey, I've had him, too. Look, here's a year's exclusive contract. Sign it, bring it back to us and as soon as you get that weight off, we can fuck and I'll launch you into the stratosphere. It's gonna take time, but you'll get there."

"Really?"

"You got something. If I see it, everyone else will. It's in the eyes."

"Thank you soooo much."

"It's gonna be hard work."

"I love hard work! The sex part...you were just kidding, right?"

"About money and sex, kid, I never kid."

I wanted to tell him that what he could fuck was himself, but didn't—I wasn't that brave. Instead, I tried to come back with something that would let him know I wasn't to be had, but ingratiating enough to make sure he still liked me. All I could come up with was a pathetic: "I have a very large boyfriend."

Forgetting my beautiful, new sweater on a swivel back chair, I stumbled out the door of his office. That sweater could go round and around without me. I couldn't go back to get it. Just as I stepped out of the elevator and back onto the street, the heel of my forty-year-old vintage shoe broke off. On the endless walk to the nearest bus stop, I was forced to limp past La Scala, a four star restaurant where beautifully svelte and manicured women dined on lambchops with mint jelly and no doubt discussed the difficulty of finding a good nanny or a three-picture deal.

The cliched show biz casting couch was still real. Powerless, with no money or famous relative behind me, I realized I'd be forced, in one way or another, to bend over. Thoughts of my rape flooded back to me and I understood that in Hollywood, in the most nepotistic, venal business in the world, Sandy was just the beginning.

The bus back to Venice rumbled past Fairfax delis that served New York bagels and Melrose boutiques with enormous crystal chandeliers dangling in their windows. Next to me sat an ancient diva in a musk-ratty fur jacket. With her blood red talons and thick, false eyelashes, she was the nightmarish, Norma Desmond end-of-the-movie-star-dream.

After a two-hour ride, I arrived at the youth hostel and headed for the beach. Distant surfers in their seal-black suits bobbed among the waves. I stripped down and dove in, in my panties and old bra. No one was looking and I didn't care anyway. The ocean overtook, rocked, and lulled me. Floating in her salty arms, I bucked the current of my miserable interview and fell in love with Southern California. Los Angeles, City of Angels, offered every fantasy imaginable wrapped in bougainvillea, swaying palms and the blue Pacific. A top agent wanted to represent me. I'd be in the movies and on TV. It was possible, I told myself, that he was only testing me. In showbiz, the big fish always went after the small ones—but some speedy, little swimmers did escape the death jaws. Sure—that was it. Sandy was just playing hardball. Well, I'd show him. I'd bat every audition out of the park. I'd create my own characters, write my own films, and would not let him reduce me to a rubber doll. Then, a sobering thought: I was a pregnant and penniless hippie. Just days ago, I was learning how to read bear scat. (A big blob with undigested berries in the mix means it's fresh.)

If I stayed and had my baby, I'd be all alone—with no car, no friends, no family and no Clint. I'd have given up on our future and abandoned our Utopian goals. Clint would never want to join me in another big, bad city where he didn't belong. If I miraculously did get steady acting work, I'd have to leave my baby with nannies—just as my own working mother had done. My child might grow up to be just as unmoored and unsteady as I'd been. With an abortion, I'd be free but barren. How could a person who hated the timber industry for decimating the forests, consider terminating the life growing inside her just because it was inconvenient. I couldn't. Could I?

That night I glided my hand along the tight skin of my growing belly. The bump felt loveable and alive. With my hard-won contract lying on my chest, I watched it move up and down with my breath until I fell asleep. In the morning, the unsigned paper lay on the floor. I looked out the window, saw nothing but the next door brick wall and knew I wanted to unruffle my feathers, nest in the woods...and to go home.

After tossing my clothes into my duffle bag, I rushed to the lobby phone and wrested it from the hands of a tall Norwegian tourist who was busy talking to all of Oslo. I dialed the phone number for the Langlois post office and when the postmaster picked up, I begged him to pass on the message to anyone from the Flores Creek commune that Carol would be dropped off at the Bandon bus stop late the next afternoon. He said okay, he'd do me the favor, but he wasn't sure it was legal.

The ride on the Greyhound that took me from one world to the next, felt so much shorter going back to Oregon than it had coming to Los Angeles. As I watched the barren hillsides of California become the great green forests of the Northwest, my hopes for the future grew wings.

☾

Clint had gotten my message and was waiting for me at the Bandon bus stop. I kissed him for as long as he would let me, then opened my duffle bag and handed him my broken Rita Hayworth shoe. Without questioning why I might need three-inch strappy heels in the wilderness, he slapped it back into place, assuring me he'd epoxy it later to make the fix permanent. He was that kind of guy. And I was that kind of a girl. Sitting inside his Chevy truck with its muddy floors and cracked windows felt almost as good as being in his arms. "I gotta big surprise for you, Carol," he said, as he turned the key in the ignition. No matter how hard I begged, he refused to give even a clue.

He asked nothing about my trip and I had nothing I wanted to tell him. Once again there was silence between us, but after the buzz of L.A., the quiet felt like a familiar, old friend.

The last six-mile stretch up Flores Creek road was equally as sweet and familiar. I knew every turn and tree by heart. Just before we reached the Main Cabin, Clint drove into the clearing where our tent had been. And there it was, flanked by a giant Maple—the beginnings of our own house. In the short time I'd been in L.A., he and Stu had framed it. The finished product, I knew, would be simple and perfect. Clint, the master builder, had considered everything...the direction of the wind and where evening shadows fell. From the picture windows, there would be a long view to the mountains and we'd even have a separate space for a kitchen. Uphill from the building site, a stream ended in a pond filled with tadpoles and frogs. It would feed our sink and tiny private vegetable patch—a dream about to materialize. Then there she was, like a fart in my rose garden: Anise, the perfect-titted nurse, walking down the path towards us. Clint scratched his head as if he were a chimp. Immediate gear switch: *Fuck the house, it could collapse for all I cared. He was at it again!* Picking up on my fury, Clint tried to tamp it down.

"Carol," he whispered, "I didn't sleep with her, Stu did. They had a thing going. She told me she admires you. She thinks you are an amazing woman."

"Really?" I said, "Did she mention that while you two were discussing the String Theory?"

"Hey! Quit it," Clint said, knowing I was making fun of him. "She came on to me, but I pushed her away. I don't go in for sloppy seconds."

He was talking like a frat boy, like a Beta Lambda total idiot. "Sloppy seconds?"—demeaning, sexist, repressive...

Before I could tell him how as a life partner he was an existential nightmare, Anise was upon us. She threw her unwelcomed arms around me.

"Carol! You're pregnant. Congratulations! That's so great!"

"Hi, Anise...it's not so great," I said, as I peeled her off. "I'm getting an abortion."

The words flew from my mouth with no thought behind them. All I knew was I'd have to depend on an undependable man who had promised not to hurt me again, but would.

Clint turned white. He stepped in front of Anise and pushing her aside said, "Whadda want from me, Carol? I didn't sleep with her or any of 'em who showed up while you were gone: Buttercup from Idaho and someone named Cindy or Mindy, I forget which."

Anise didn't belong there with us and she knew it. She'd been downsized to an "any of 'em." Saying a tepid goodbye, she walked back up the road and faded away. She didn't matter anymore. Anise didn't matter.

"Carol," Clint said, "you want our baby. I want our baby!"

"I'm sorry, Clint. I can't trust you with my future. Please just shut up and lend me your truck."

"What for?" he asked, his deep voice rising in fear and anger.

"I need to make a phone call."

"To who?"

"Just give me the damn keys, Clint."

"No. I won't!"

"Then I'll hitch."

"No, you won't. I'll drive you."

So like him, to try and maintain his control over me. It wasn't what I wanted in life. Not at all. But I let him drive, he was so much better at it than I was.

When we reached the phone booth in front of Stormy's Bar, I walked in, closed the door and left Clint staring at me through the glass. Since I had no change for the long-distance call, I had to open the door again and ask him for some—it was damned embarrassing. He gave me the money begrudgingly, but still gave it: three quarters and two dimes. Before he could stop me, I shut the door again and searched for the woman's clinic business card. I'd wisely saved it from my previous visit. The card was crumpled inside my jeans pocket but still readable. Each of the phone's little metallic squares, numbered from one to ten, made a ding when I pressed it. The number six was scratched out, but still worked. Ding-Ding-Ding-Ding.

"Hello, Eugene Women's Health Clinic? Hi...I was in to see you a while back...can you tell me if I'm four months, can I still schedule an abortion? A saline? Oh. What does that entail?"

I'd spoken to the receptionist in my best clear-headed, no-nonsense business woman voice. Outside the booth, Clint lit a cigarette, inhaled deeply and walked towards Stormy's Bar. He was about to go inside when he stopped, turned around and shuffled back to the booth. I hunched over the receiver and lowered my voice to make sure he couldn't hear.

"Yes...hello. Yes...I'm still here...Oh. Are you sure? Oh. That sounds terrible."

A saline abortion involved injecting a solution into the amniotic fluid through the uterus and forcing the mother's muscle tissue to push the baby out. What was flushed would be semi-formed. I couldn't bear to ask what semi-formed meant but envisioned something big-headed with fins and gills.

Clint was now banging the booth's glass door with the palm of his hand. The whole enclosure shook.

"100% success rate," the woman on the other end told me. "We have very few complications."

Clint pressed his body and face into the glass. It distorted his features and made him look like Quasimodo, a sad monster. Using both hands, he rattled the booth with such force it felt as if it might come off its foundation. I opened the door a crack, hoping to talk him down, but it was a mistake, he tried to force his way inside and I had to block him with my hip.

"Don't do it, Carol! I'm trying, you've gotta give me that!"

Beyond the phone booth there was only Highway 101.

"A forever life with you scares me, Clint. I'm afraid!"

"I'm scared, too, but don't take it out on our baby," he pleaded.

"We have no baby, Clint. Not yet."

It's funny how a man's face can change when he feels weak. Clint no longer looked like Clint, but a poor deflated replica of what he'd once been.

"Yes, we do and I'm his father!" he said with a voice that both begged and commanded. "But if you're so pissed you can't let him live, then go ahead, Carol; it's best he never comes into this world."

A tin voice came out of the phone. The long-distance operator announced I needed to insert fifty more cents to continue the call. I didn't have it and had to ask Clint for more quarters. He rummaged through his pockets even though he hated what I was doing, even though it was the last thing on earth he wanted.

"Nope," he said, "not even a nickel."

The clinic's receptionist returned to the line.

"Do you wish to schedule a date for your procedure? We'll need to do some blood tests first but..."

I didn't let her finish. "No thank you," I answered, "I've changed my..." And we were disconnected. Another quarter wouldn't have made a difference anyway.

☾

Hammering echoed through the autumn air. Everyone was building. Two months had passed since my return from Highbridge and Los Angeles. The heavy rains were due and no one wanted to sleep in the Main Cabin's crowded loft during the winter. Pavlo and Katerina's building site abutted ten thousand acres of Bureau of Land Management property which hadn't been logged for fifty years. The path to their house, bordered by enormous prehistoric Bracken Fern, covered a swath so well-proportioned it felt like the entrance to a great estate. Joey, the orphan, was trying to build a dome, but what he'd started looked like a wooden pancake. Stu's place had a long view of the mountains. Covered with used tar paper, it was shabby on the outside, but the inside was cozy and warm. Stu was like that, too. Unless he was drunk.

Agung, Two Turtles, and a newly arrived couple, Oscar and Barbara, were building houses a mile away down at the creek. Two Turtle's place was built around an enormous metal cone scavenged from a defunct lumber mill. The cone served as a huge fireplace, which Two Turtles used for both cooking and heating. Close by, in a small alder grove, was Agung's modest, covered lean-to. Despite its austerity, it sported a built-in throne made from a huge stump. All three homes were a short walk from the fast rushing waters of Flores Creek.

The question of who owned what never came up and I liked it that way. In the back of my mind, I thought one day it might surface, but knew I'd be grateful if it didn't.

The unclear always worked in my favor.

Louise was building a house, too. Being without a partner didn't stop her. No way. Agung having broken up with Skybird, the mother of his child, had returned to living with us. But Oscar, Barbara, and Two Turtles were his companions at the creek and those of us situated on the mountaintop rarely saw him. As a result, he and Louise developed a testy truce. Two Turtles and Oscar were both "relating" to Barbara, a plain and deceptively quiet woman. She claimed to love both men and I was told the feeling was mutual. Louise was spending her nights with Stu with whom she had an on-again off-again relationship. On when he was sober. Off when he was not. I was delighted. It made her an almost relative.

That afternoon, Agung, Clint, Stu, and Joey were helping Louise clear her building site. I joined in, sawing the smaller limbs off the downed alder trees. Louise and I worked well in tandem. The misery whip moving smoothly between us. Thrilled to be building her own home, she couldn't stop thanking all involved. As she was describing the layout to Stu, the roar of a nearby chainsaw came to an abrupt stop, followed by a horrible animal howl.

The toothy machine lay on the ground, buzzing like an angry fly. It had jumped from Agung's hand to slice through his arm, exposing fat and bone. His blood gushed onto the ground. From below his elbow, his arm now held together only by sinew and skin, dangled like a hammock. My knees buckled at the sight and the ground came up to meet my face. Everything went black. Seconds later, I opened my eyes and saw Clint staunch the flow of Agung's blood with a tourniquet improvised from a bungee. All color had drained from Agung's face and, with his eyes rolling back in his head, he went in and out of consciousness. Clint and Stu gently loaded him into Clint's Chevy to drive him to the hospital in North Bend. Agung didn't object. He said nothing about "the man" or corrupt capitalist institutions and gave himself over to be cared for. His "no doctors, no hospitals," policy gone.

Louise sat on a log and hung her head between her legs. Her long, wavy blond hair touched the ground. I grabbed an alder branch to help me stand. Louise, not even noticing that I'd fainted, asked if I remembered the day she married Agung in New Haven. "Of course," I said as I steadied myself, "it rained and there was no food." She lifted her head and brushed her hair from her face. Her mouth was twisted and cheeks wet with tears.

"There was fruit salad," she corrected.

"Yeah, Louise. I forgot."

"I pray Agung will be all right, Carol. It was so terrible to see him like that. I'm scared for him. I...I...he turned my safe world upside down and I loved him for it; but not now, not anymore, now...I don't..."

"What. Louise?"

"...now he can go to hell and stay there."

CHAPTER 28

Meat is Murder?

December 1972-March 1973

It is difficult to argue with the belly since it has no ears.
CATO THE ELDER

As fall turned to winter, the sun went down around 4 o'clock and stayed down. Being always stoned made it easy to adjust to the long dark days. They went by me like a shadow dance—moving slowly. Christmas had been wet and New Year's soaked us. The warm glow of the wood stove, the company of my tribe, and my beginning-to-kick belly, lifted me above the gloom. Time dribbled away. Contemplating a simple maple leaf could take an hour; its five-pronged, veined surface a roadmap to serenity. Not for a moment did it occur to me that my constant smoking would have any negative affect on my baby. I considered ganja to be a nutritional supplement, much like vitamin B. However, my continuous intake made me perpetually hungry, and I'd eat anything I could get my hands on as fast as I could.

One morning, even before I'd had my first toke, I awoke with a growling stomach. Our goat had stopped milking and our meat supply was gone. What I had to have was earmarked for the group's morning pancakes—our one and only egg. The few scrawny hens we had left had been traumatized by marauding coyotes and, as of the day before, had stopped laying. The tricky, four-legged critters had dug beneath the chicken coop's barbed wire fence and dragged off our rooster.

"Egg, Egg, Egg, Egg," my reptilian brain screamed as I dashed through the rain toward Main Cabin. When I push open the heavy front door and saw no one else, I rejoiced, because there it was, sitting on the counter, brown, perfectly elliptical, and all mine. Holding the egg up to the light, I searched for imperfections—a half-formed chick, a blood spot—none appeared. The shell was much harder than a store-bought egg; I had to bang it three times against the wood to crack it open. Someone kind and considerate had, the night before, already loaded the stove's firebox with kindling. All I had to do was light a match for the flames to heat the front burners, and then slide my gooey delight into a pan. Just as the dark yolk hit the cast iron, Katerina pushed open the cabin door and stood at the threshold...her eyes glued to my movements. Nine months pregnant, just weeks ahead of me, her big belly and petite frame stood firm in the pale morning light.

"Carol," she said, "I would very much like that egg."

"Sorry, Katerina, It's mine."

My baby needed the protein. The egg and I had bonded.

"Carol," Katerina said, "we live on a commune. Everybody who lives here shares. I think perhaps you are aware of that."

Sure I was, but not when my empty belly rumbled. Not when I wanted that egg so bad. So, pretending Katerina wasn't even there, I flipped the sunny side down.

"Carol, it is our only and last one, you must..."

To drown her out I sang the chorus of my favorite Band song, *The Night They Drove Old Dixie Down*. It came off their first album, the one with them standing around in shades of sepia and gray.

"Carol!" Katerina's voice rang out.

My volume went up a notch on the chorus.

"Carol, I must insist!"

I repeated the chorus.

"We will split it, Carol. That is the appropriation thing to do. That is what I think."

It was useless. I had to respond...or just slip the it whole into my mouth.

"Katerina, you had chocolate yesterday, Kokia told me."

"No, I did not. I gave it all to him. He is a child."

And then it hit me: I was a former upper middle-class woman fighting over an egg. Well, I wasn't upper middle class any more, I was of "the people." Besides, I loved Katerina. Whatever protein I needed, she needed. We'd share the damn egg. I divided it with spatula and handed her the smaller half. After all, she was shorter than I was.

Later that morning, the rest of Flores Creek had lumpy oatmeal for breakfast. They didn't seem to mind.

☾

It was almost dusk when the shot rang out. Pavlo, Katerina's husband, a man with a five-year-old child and another on the way killed the deer on his first try; but then begged off butchering it and handed the job over to Clint and Stu. Stu cut off the deer's head and tail and then hung the body from its tendons over the porch. Its hooves dangled over the blood-soaked earth. Clint slit the belly with a hunting knife, let the entrails spill onto the ground and then dug into the cavity to pull out the liver, gizzard and heart. Steam rose from the warm, dark maroon, meat. "It's a good thing it's cold outside," he said, as I watched, both horrified and appreciative, "If it wasn't, flies could have gotten into the flesh and laid their larvae. He then nonchalantly handed me the bloody catch: "Tell ya what Carol," he said, "you go flour and fry these up for dinner. You're gonna love 'em once you try 'em."

A live animal had been hunted and killed to serve Katerina and my nutritional needs and I had to respect that. So instead of protesting, I stoically walked into the kitchen, and as an amuse bouche, before our usual beans and rice, served the organ meat up with wild onions and mushrooms. They were impossible to chew and tasted like rusty nails.

The next week Joey made a kerosene lamp stand out of the dried deer hooves and legs. The stand was hideous in a very beautiful way.

CHAPTER 29

Evolution Mama

April 1973

The moment a child is born, a mother is also born
She never existed before.
The woman existed, but the mother, never.
A mother is something new.
BHAGWAN SHREE RAJNEESH

The seasons in Western Oregon are not as varied as there are on the East Coast. Summer is hot, but in autumn, although leaves fall, the drama of plentiful, fiery foliage is missing. Snow in winter is not usual and seldom lasts for long, but there is always the endless, freezing rain. Spring is another story. In spring, the air warms, the rain lightens, and babies appear. Flowers sprout; dark pine needles elongate and form lime green tips. Peeps and chirps come from overhead nests while white cotton lambs bound over the hillsides.

In the spring of 1973, *Two Gentlemen of Verona* opened in London, all 110 stories of the World Trade Center opened in New York, and the first cell phone call ever was made. At Flores Creek, the sun was peeking in on us once a week and I'd gained fifty-three pounds. The scale at the North Bend County Hospital read two hundred and twenty. I had only one maternity outfit, a dark blue burlap skirt with an elastic waist band worn every day despite its being scratchy.

Clint and I had been practicing our Lamaze; driving six hours to and from Eugene for classes. I'd promised myself never to give birth in a hospital, but a trained mid-wife couldn't be found in all of Curry County. My only other choice was to leave Flores Creek and stay in Eugene near the Birthing Center but I wasn't up for sleeping on someone's cold floor or bumpy couch. If I didn't trust conventional medicine, I trusted the universe even less and, unhippie-like, was terrified to give birth without expert supervision. What if my baby were a breach or needed post-natal care? What if I did? The possibility of squatting under the Birthing Tree over a dugout while clinging to a rope, faded into the low hanging mist. My baby, unlike Crazy Rachael's, would not naturally fall from my body via gravity and the Great Spirit. He would be guided out and caught by knowing human hands. The logical choice was the North Bend hospital: an hour and a half hour drive from Flores Creek along rough, wet roads. Dr. Moskowitz, the only obstetrician in North Bend, seemed like a nice, smart guy who knew what he was doing. His face felt familiar, similar to all the Larry's and David's, Saul's, Paul's and Robert's I'd known in my past life. It brought back the world I'd left behind—a world filled with Jewish doctors, dentists, and lawyers, where everyone had a secure future and a home with dual shower heads. But I was afraid that if I gave birth to a boy, the hospital would record his arrival and give his records to the United States government. A future draft would then know he was alive, find him, and force him to kill or be killed. My boy could be buried, maimed, or driven insane by their need for power and money. No, I couldn't allow that to happen. I was his mother.

And there was an even more immediate problem: Clint and I didn't have money for a doctor or a hospital, unless...

"Hello, Mom."

My belly was so big it pushed up against the glass door of the phone booth outside Stormy's. Through the misted windows of the bar I could see another game of pool in progress. "Did you get the tuna fish cans I sent you, Carol?" my mother asked, "and the coat hangers?"

"Yes, Mom. They are very nice."

"They're the good wood ones, not cheap plastic. I hope you use them."

"Mom...I don't know any other way to tell you this..."

Her gravelly voice rose.

"Are you sick, Carol? Are you hurt? What?!"

My father, as usual, was listening on the kitchen extension and shouted, "I told you something terrible would happen, Minnie!"

"Mom. Dad. I'm fine. I'm nine months pregnant."

"Are you messugeneh!?" My father screamed hysterically.

I ignored him as best I could: "And I could use your help. We need money if I am going to have my baby in a hospital. Otherwise, I'll have to have a home birth."

"In the forest? With those crazies?" my mother questioned. "You'll die a horrible death! Carol. Don't worry. We'll pay for everything. We're happy to. You were right to call us."

"What's right about it, Minnie?" my father asked. But before my mother could answer, he ranted on: "Carol, you listen to me, I'm your father. You marry that no good Goy right now or so help me God, I'll jump off our balcony—15 floors down. A dead father! Flat as a pancake. Get married! You hear me!?"

"Carol," my mother interrupted, ignoring my father, "hospitals are wonderful when you need them. The women in our family have a history of difficult births. Grandma Schneiderman couldn't get your Aunt Ruthie out so they had to pull at her little head with forceps. That's why Ruthie had those funny, crooked ears. When I had you, the placenta detached and I bled like a stuck pig. I would have died without a transfusion. And don't you worry, Daddy won't jump. Your father is a big faker."

"I'll jump if I want to, Minnie," my father shouted. "Tell her to marry the stupid Goy right now or I swear to God, I will!"

Again, my mother tuned my father out.

"How much do you need, Carol?" she asked with real tenderness.

"I think five hundred will do it, Mom," I answered.

"Don't give her the money, Minnie," my father demanded, "not till she marries that deadbeat!"

"Shut up Mike, she's due any second. I'm sending it out right now."

My father had grown hard of hearing: "What, Minnie? What did you say? Who's sending what..."

And they were gone.

The pool game at Stormy's was still in progress. As Clint helped me step onto the running board of his truck, a wistful look slid across his face. He was good at pool and wanted to play.

His face was a lot happier when, three days later, I received a check for a thousand dollars, five hundred more than I'd asked for. It had been sent Special Delivery, RUSH from Hallandale, Florida.

Most back-to-the-land hippie women in my place would never have considered a conventional birth and even if they did, were unlikely to have my financial support. I could have tried harder, but my dark secret was: I wanted to go to the hospital. Katerina's experience had convinced me. She'd delivered in March, a month before I was due; in the same North Bend hospital, and unlike me, hadn't considered anything even remotely alternative. She knew she wanted clean sheets, nursing care, and her meals served. When Katerina returned, she looked rested and happy.

"They gave me a new toothbrush with napkins and chocolate milk on a tray…it was magnificent. Is that the right word, Carol…magnificent?"

"Yes, Katerina, it is."

Her baby girl, Lena, was a perfect beauty.

"Carol," she continued, "the nurses, they were so very kind. They allowed for Lena to sleep in my arms. It was like a vacation and I am sorry to say, I didn't want to come back here."

"Look, Katerina," I interrupted, "Lena is smiling."

"No, Carol. She is not smiling; she is making a poop."

Alicia Bay Laurel in her popular 70s picture book, *Living on Earth* told us to "discover the serenity of living within the rhythms of the planet." Labor however, was less of a rhythm and more of an earthquake. Even using the method that Alicia suggested, with Clint rubbing my back and belly in slow concentric circles and joining me in the deep pants of the Breath of Fire—labor still sucked. It sucked even more when my contractions came six minutes apart (finally, a watch) and, with Clint guiding me, I slid into the metal bed of his truck. The rain was coming down in relentless sheets and our terrible road was melting away beneath his wheels. Rivulets of water turning what had been solid into mud and exposing pointed rocks. I was jostled along, wrapped in my engagement sleeping bag and lying belly up in the camper-covered flatbed. Clint had laid a thick piece of foam on that bed to absorb the jolts caused by his worn-out shocks. It helped, but not a lot. Every endless bump and road fissure caused me searing pain.

The night was impenetrable and the low headlights illuminated the heavy shower. Water poured down the small glass window above my head. The hard rain had turned the truck's metal shell into a kettle drum and pelleted it with the sound of exploding raindrops. Just before my next contraction, Clint's left rear tire hit a jagged rock. The explosion drowned out the rain and the jolt to my body felt like the blazing hammer of Thor. We were in a pitch-black, rain-soaked night on a backwoods country road and I was in hard labor—very, hard. When I caught my breath and looked up, I found Clint leaning over me, his high beam flashlight sending a ray of light through the darkness.

"Don't worry sweetheart," he said, "it'll just take a few minutes; I've got a good spare. We'll be ready to roll in no time."

My life and the life of our baby were totally in his hands. Is this, I had to ask myself, where my bottomless need to be taken care of had taken me: giving birth alone in the wilderness with no help, no nothing? I thought of all I had ever been and all I had ever hoped to become, and instead of despair I felt the familiar tickle of absurdity. This was what I thought I'd always wanted—a natural childbirth. No hospitals, no modern medicine. God was laughing at me and in his infinite wisdom, forced me to laugh along. If it hadn't been in excruciating pain, my belly would have hurt from laughing. Clint yelled up from under the undercarriage. "Carol, what's so funny?"

"Bloomingdales!"

What?"

I wasn't in Oregon anymore but in the elegant and glittering department store of my youth. Up...up...the silver steps of the escalator to the third-floor designer dress collection, where lovely models sprayed Channel #5 in my direction. As I decided whether to get the one-ounce or two-ounce bottle, Clint opened the camper door. Damp, cold air smacked me in the face and I stopped dreaming.

"You okay in there, babe? We're good to go."

"Go! Go!"

Behind him, through the back window and rain, I saw two yellow eyes gleaming in the darkness—a cougar.

"Clint!" I screamed.

He didn't hear me. He'd slammed the driver's door shut and was safely inside. The cat's golden eyes were gone but I couldn't help wondering what if...then the contractions started again and I stopped thinking.

When we arrived at the small North Bend hospital, Clint was covered with mud. His boots puddled tracks across the shiny, waxed floor. There was a twig stuck in his beard. The patch on my burlap maternity skirt had come off and left a gaping hole. The attending nurse slipped what was left of my tattered outfit into a plastic bag. While Clint scrubbed up, I was wheeled into my room and given a sitz bath.

Thirty-five hours passed. They did not pass quickly. Clint reminded me to pant during contractions and placed ice cubs on my tongue to relieve the thirst. His efforts did nothing. The pain was so intense that jumping out of the second story of my room seemed like a great solution.

A sudden flurry—nurses and doctors were rushing in and out of my room. An aide wheeled in a fetal heart monitor and put it beside me. The monitor registered distress and the subsequent sonogram showed my son's umbilical cord was wrapped around his neck. With each contraction, the cord squeezed tighter and was cutting off his air supply. I needed, they assured me, an immediate Cesarean section.

I felt nothing as Dr. Andrew Moskowitz cut me open from pelvis bone to pelvis bone. The most endearing thing about him was his steel-rimmed eye glasses. They made him look like Goethe—whatever Goethe looked like. Perched over the delivery table, a large mirror allowed me to see what was going on above. My mind floated over my body and left it behind. The woman I saw below looked exactly like me but had a dark, red hole in her belly. A white latex-gloved hand hovered above and then dipped down deep inside the bloody cavern. I felt a strong tug and looked helplessly at Clint, who was standing to the side of the doctor. His eyes did not say, "What a miracle." They said, "Get me the hell out of here!" This man, who could blithely decapitate a deer, was not prepared to see the mother of his child filleted.

Another tug and where there had once been only pain and blood, was my boy: almond-eyed and covered from neck to torso with black, fuzzy down. He looked like a cross between a Sasquatch and my Bessarabian Grandpa: a big, hairy Cossack. He hadn't taken the momentous journey down my birth canal, he missed that ride entirely, but he'd never be like Aunt Ruthie with her lopsided ears squished by forceps and fate. My son emerged gorgeous.

Elated and so high I couldn't stop talking, I was wheeled to my room. Clint ran alongside me, holding my hand and kissing my cheek.

"He's really big isn't he, Clint?"

"Yeah. He's big, really big. Thank you for my son, sweetheart, thank you."

The nurse placed all eight pounds four ounces of our son in my arms. He took to my engorged breasts like a sweet leech. Thanks to Alicia Bay and her "how to" book, my nipples had been treated like cracked cow udders and hardened with constant applications of gooey *Bag Balm*. My boy never seemed to want to let go of my tits and that was fine with me. I'd fallen utterly and madly in love. Here was someone to both live and die for.

My next plan of action failed miserably. For my hospital stay, I'd packed a rope, a wool poncho and a six-foot madras Indian scarf in a dark blue peacock pattern. It had matched my blue burlap maternity skirt which, mistaken for a potato sack, had been incinerated. As soon as I'd had a night to recuperate and the nurses left me alone in my room, I planned to sneak out of the hospital, either through the front door or an open window with my day-old baby wrapped tightly to my chest. Clint would be waiting outside with his truck to drive us far, far away, and our son's existence would be kept a secret. He'd receive no social security number (or driver's license or passport). He would not have to live in an upside-down world where what was valued should not have been, and what was priceless was destroyed. However, I had not considered that my stomach would be stapled together, that I'd be hooked up to an I.V., unable to walk without excruciating pain, or that I'd be running a 103 temperature. Instead of escaping, I lay on my back on my soft, clean bed thanking The Universe for hot running water, fruit cup, and most of all, an indoor toilet.

The moment I had dreaded came and went without protest—I signed our son's birth certificate. There were his little feet, stamped in ink and there was my signature: Huckleberry Schlanger Helvey—Mother: Carol Schlanger, Father: Clinton E. Helvey. Born: April 29th, 1973. All I could do was hope for a saner future for an America where our able-bodied young men would not have to fight another senseless war.

Fat chance.

"L'Chiam," Dr. Moskowitz said as the three of us clinked wine glasses after Huckleberry's impromptu bris. His Episcopalian-born father, at my request, had travelled fifty miles to Florence to find a kosher brand.

"Like ham," Clint said.

CHAPTER 30

In Stitches

May 1973

One Earth. One Mother.
CRAZY HORSE

Clint brought us home, helped me lower my newly sliced body onto our mattress, tucked us in, lit the fire and disappeared. What if, I wondered, I had to go to the bathroom. I couldn't walk without pain, much less squat. My stomach was stapled together, my incision encrusted with blood and I had no hot water. There were winged termites crawling in and out between the wall slats above my bed. What, I wondered, if I'd married someone like Dr. Moskowitz...someone conservative and Jewish. We'd take ocean cruises...we'd have elegant dinner parties with smart people we didn't have to live with all day and every night and best of all, a "girl" would come in to wash and iron. I had to admit to myself that what I'd rebelled against so unequivocally now seemed attractive. Curling my altered body close to my son's milky warmth, I stopped thinking and fell into a deep sleep.

I awoke to post-partum euphoria—my depression gone. There he was, my baby boy with his lips like raspberries and cheeks like fresh peaches. I couldn't get enough of his perfect hands, his adorable feet, and his lashes so long and dark they looked like they'd been brushed with mascara. The glow spread. I loved my partner, my home, and my sister/brother/friends who had gathered around me after our return. When I looked out the window and saw the mountains in the distance and the trees shimmying in the wind, I gave thanks. It was as if I'd been chosen for a life and purpose that would, because it was so right and humane, eventually resonate with an accepting world.

Katerina was my baby guru. She was brimming with old-world child-care knowledge, passed down to her by her Greek mother and grandmother. Without her, I'd have been lost. She helped me make diapers out of old sheets and taught me how to fold and pin them. She assured me it was okay to sleep with my son and feed him on demand. My body would, she said, instinctively keep me from rolling over and smothering him. But she advised me not to stay stoned.

"Are you sure Katerina?" I asked plaintively.

"I cannot say suffocation never happens. I don't know that, Carol. But it would be best for you to be sober, no?"

"Sober? I don't drink."

"The marijuana. It's best to stop smoking it."

"Really?" I said. She might as well have told me it would be good to stop breathing.

"Do as you wish," she said, staring at the cradle Clint had made out of twigs and Myrtle wood. "Bundle him tight and rock him when he cries instead of picking him up—he'll adjust. But remember Carol, whatever you smoke goes straight into your milk."

Was that good or bad? I didn't know.

☾

Kangaroos had nothing on me. After two weeks, I walked without pain and binding Hucky to my chest, I took him everywhere. But despite my best efforts to join in, the parameters of what I could and couldn't do were closing in and my universe grew smaller. The more I was left out of communal activities, the more marginalized I became. I was no longer Carol, I was Carol and baby. Long, late night group conversations were out of the question, hopping aboard the truck for a wood run, logistically impossible. My company, when driving to town, was more burdensome to others than helpful. No one really wanted me along for the ride. With the exception of Louise, who was always considerate, any man whose conscience got the better of them: Clint, Stu, Joey, Two Turtles, or Pavlo, would shout back at me as they burned rubber on their way to someplace exciting, like the gas station or post office, "You or Hucky need anything, Carol?"

"Yeah! A driver."

Steering with my baby on board was close to impossible and dangerous. Without a car seat, I was forced to hug him like a mommy vise between my legs as I tried to downshift. So, like Katerina who never learned to drive, I became a permanent passenger. An offer to hold him while I drove never came. My driving scared them off. No longer able to accomplish what the others did with ease, I remembered

Moonlove and baby Heaven. How quickly I'd judged her, how annoyed I'd become when she sapped group energy. Now I understood. Before motherhood, when I'd done just as I pleased, I'd considered Katerina a goody-goody, a killjoy who demanded quiet, structure, and organization: "Carol, when do you think we might make dinner?" she'd ask with a dignity that refused to plead, "Kokia is hungry."

"Whenever."

What a self-involved jerk I'd been. Not anymore. Now I was a mother.

CHAPTER 31

Apartment 15 E

June - November 1973

All I know is, if you listen to society, you'll never get anywhere.
JERRY GARCIA

Time kept on slipping into the future. The soft spot at the top of Huckleberry's head hardened. The lambs on the hillsides were growing into sheep and Katerina and I, to give each other freedom had become each other's wet nurse—a fantastic form of cooperative childcare if you can get it. Neither Hucky nor baby Lena seemed to notice the difference. For them, one mother's breast was as good as the other. The love I felt for Lena while nursing her was the same as I felt for my boy and her sweet face was just as dear. Katerina, I was certain, felt the same. For both of us it was a tiny but welcomed step toward independence.

☾

All by myself! Hucky was with Katerina and I was free to drive Clint's truck to the Post Office to pick up the group mail from our Star Route 73 box—alone. As a chicken hawk swooped through the sky, I heard Clint's voice in my head: "Don't ride the brakes, don't pop the clutch, keep 'er in third going down and in first coming back up." It wasn't easy for him to trust but he finally knew how frustrating it was for me to always be at the mercy of the driver.

He knew because I mentioned it daily.

I'd been to our little Langlois post office often, but never alone. On previous visits the wary postmaster had never so much as spoken to me. This time was different.

"Got a telegram for one of you hippies. You know a Carol Schwanginger?"

"I'm Carol."

"Got any proof a' that miss?"

"No, I'm sorry, I don't. Is the telegram from Florida?"

"You guessed it," he said as he handed me the yellow piece of paper. I tore it open and read: "Visit us now. STOP. Dad and I have to see Hucky before we drop dead. STOP. Will pay airfare and expenses. Mom."

☾

My parents were big on the number 15. They lived at 1515 Golden Isles Drive, Apartment 15 E. In the Manhattan of my childhood, we lived in apartment number 15 F. Their not-elegant Florida lobby was rife with mausoleum and funeral announcements: "Eternity is forever, make the most of it. All credit cards accepted." Death hovered over the lobby's Ionic columns, gold-flecked mirrors, and dribbling water feature. Approaching the elevator, while Hucky beat him over the head with his tiny fists, Clint made way for aging tenants, who, in varied shades of pastel—pink and beige, baby blue and yellow, looked like little Pez candies fresh from their dispensers. A large woman, carrying a beach chair, stood next to me. Her fire-truck red toenails perched on her sequined flip-flops.

"Are you Minnie Schlanger's daughter?" she asked.

"Yes, I am."

"So, you're the one who lives so far away in Oregon."

I'd known her a half minute, but it didn't matter. I prayed she lived on a lower floor so our ride together would be short.

"Yes, I am."

"And that must be your little boy with the meshuggeneh name."

"You mean Huckleberry?"

"I knew it was some kind of fruit! You have your mother's face, but yours is much prettier and your baby is adorable. What's his real name?"

"Huckleberry."

The elevator lurched to a stop. The floor bounced beneath our feet.

"Be careful," she said. "He's gonna need a sun hat when you take him outside or he'll get a stroke and be damaged for life."

"Thank you," I said. "I'll remember that."

"See you soon, sweetie," she said as she got off on the 12th floor—there was no 13th. The numbers skipped. The one thing a new building full of old New York Jews and an occasional Italian didn't want was bad luck.

My mother answered the doorbell in a flowing, floor-length, silver dressing gown. If the beautiful and glamourous Loretta Young had been fat and Jewish with a big nose, they might have been twins. "Come in, come in," she said in her familiar gravelly voice. My parent's large apartment was bathed in sunlight and filled with almost real plants. The floors were white marble and the furniture, blond. My mother had given me a big hug, hugged Clint and was holding her arms straight out to signal she wanted Hucky to be placed in them when her phone rang.

"It's Ida Fimmelman," my mother said. "She always calls at the worst time. She has an ear to our wall. That woman is one big pain in my ass," and she let it continue to ring. Then in a voice as piercing as my own, she called out: "Mike! Mike! Your daughter Carol is here, wake up!" Moments later, my father, a little rumpled in his lavender checkered pants and a matching shirt walked into the living room. He had a remarkable ability to fall asleep anywhere even standing up and was just rising from his afternoon nap on the terrace. His full head of once red, now pink, hair was wind-mussed but otherwise he looked Florida dapper. As he hugged me, I could feel his heart beating against my chest. After I'd kissed the paper-thin skin on his smooth cheek, he moved on to Clint and enthusiastically shook his hand. "Welcome, Cliff. Delighted you could come."

"Glad to be here, Mike."

Not five minutes had passed when the phone rang again. This time my mother rushed across the length of her shiny, slippery floor, and answered it: "Hello, Ida. Yes. I know my daughter is here. She's standing in front of me in my living room, right now. Thank you, Ida. I'll tell her you said so. Goodbye."

She crossed back to us.

"Ida Fimmelman says you are beautiful and Clint is the most handsome man she has ever seen in her life and if you go down to the pool, don't forget the sunhat."

As we all sat down on their gold brocade-covered couch, Clint handed Hucky to my father who stuck out his tongue and made silly faces for his grandson. When Hucky landed on my father's lap, his little smile lit the already bright room.

"I'm Grandpa," my father chirped. "Say Grandpa, sonny."

"Daddy, we call him Hucky. He doesn't talk yet."

"Say Grandpa, Hucky," my father said again. "Say Grandpa."

"Who wants tuna on rye with pickles and mayonnaise?" my mother said.

My father's tone became anxious.

"Why can't he talk, is there something wrong with him, Carol? Say, Grandpa, sonny."

"He's only three months old, Daddy. He doesn't talk yet."

My mother came in from the kitchen, and when she turned her back, I saw her dressing gown had a brown stain that spanned the whole of her buttocks. It made me think that perhaps she'd wet herself or sat in something awful.

"You and Clint can have the guest room, Carol. But I'm sorry to tell you, you've gained weight."

"I just had a baby, Mom."

"Can he drink chocolate milk?"

"No. He's still nursing."

"Still? Oy Vei."

My mother knew nothing about nursing. She'd never tried.

Our time with my parents in Fort Lauderdale was filled with sunshine and delicatessen. Each day we swam in their pool, used their towels, applied sun block and got to know them again. I read the *Miami Herald* after my father finished it and had fallen asleep. Historically, he had first dibs on the paper. In the news: Vice President ("that schumck") Spiro Agnew pled no contest to tax evasion and resigned. The Yom Kippur war began ("a shonda") as Syria and Egypt attacked Israel, and Phil Everly stormed off stage declaring an end to the famed Everly Brothers. Clint repaired my parents' overactive toilet, their underactive air conditioner, rewired all their lamps, changed the hinges on their closet doors, and reset the idle on their Oldsmobile Cutlass. My mother took all three of us shopping for new, unwanted clothes, bought Hucky a high-end baby carrier and insisted that I accompany her to a play revival of *Peanuts.* "Whadda ya mean you don't want to go? You love the theater." She introduced us to every friend and relative she had in the building and beyond: "Carol, you remember your great Aunt Rosalind? She's your second cousin Marsha's mother. Marsha never married because she was so tall...things were different then."

My father slept through most of it.

One afternoon as we set the table for lunch my mother said, "Carol, I think Clint's a very good man. He's kind, he's helpful, and I like him very much but he has no ambition. You'll be poor for the rest of your life."

"What's poor, Mom?" I had to ask her.

"What's poor? Poor is never having any money. It's having to live off your in-laws. It's not being able to do what you want when you want to, and don't forget the placemats. I don't want any scratches on the table."

"I love him, Mom. And I love Hucky. We have a beautiful piece of land. That's not poor."

"It's not rich, either. Not what Dad and I wanted for you."

"But it's what I wanted, Mom. Should I use the good China?"

"Yes. The Limoges with the rose pattern. Okay. If that's the way you feel, I'll love them, too."

"Thanks, Mom."

I pecked her on the cheek. She beamed and continued: "And forget the salad plates, they just make more work."

The four of us were about to sit down for a feast of herring and sour cream, bagels, lox, and prune danish when my mother noticed a typewritten notice had been slipped under the door. While my father continued eating, bits of pumpernickel falling out the side of his mouth, she got up from the table, grabbed the note and read it. "A five-hundred-dollar fine," she shouted. "That's ridiculous! They have their goddamn nerve. I'm not gonna pay it Mike and neither are you!"

"Here, Carol, read this," she said and handed the slip of paper to me.

Dear Mr. and Mrs. Schlanger:

"We regret to inform you that your guests have continually used the pool facilities without wearing a bathing cap. As the by-laws of the Golden Isles condominium stipulate, and because we have received numerous complaints from Apartment 14E regarding banging noises past reasonable hours and shower overuse, we require you to pay the above fines or we will be forced to take legal action.

Complaints have also been lodged regarding indecent exposure and lewd behavior, but since our regulations do not address these types of occurrences, we will overlook them. We sincerely hope that your visitors will honor our requirements. They are good-looking people.

Sincerely yours, Moe Fimmelman, Co-op Board Chairman."

Ida Fimmelman had been spying on us.

My mother's short hair style, feathered and stiff with lacquer, shifted sideways, making her look like a freaked-out cockatiel.

"How many times did I tell you to wear a bathing cap in the pool, Carol? Now, look."

"I wore a cap, Mom."

Apartment 15 E, which had appeared spacious and bright on our arrival, now felt oppressive. The jeweled coral tree had a thick layer of dust and the cactus on the terrace was turning brown.

"You never pay attention to the rules, Carol," my mother continued. "Sometimes even you have to do what you don't want to."

"I didn't wear a cap, either," Clint confessed. "It's partly my fault, Minnie."

"Men don't wear bathing caps," my father said. "The Fimmelmans are crazy. Moe Fimmelman got hit in the head at the golf course. His wife is a whore."

"Carol, what did you do that was indecent," my mother asked. "Tell me...Clint what did you do?"

She loved sordid details. It ran in the family.

"I don't know, Mom," I answered. "We let Hucky go naked and I nursed him behind a towel."

"Enough already," my father said. "What our daughter did was not lewd."

"You should have won the election instead of Moe Fimmelman, Mike," my mother said. "I think someone tampered with the vote count. No one would have made a better condo board President than you."

"Moe Fimmelman can go to hell!" my father shouted. "He thinks a naked baby is obscene. I'll show him obscene! With my fist!"

It was the last straw. We'd been sleeping on the lumpy convertible in the guest room for over a month. It had seemed like a year. The thin walls of 15E were closing in on us. Clint didn't want to wear a cap in the swimming pool, so he didn't get back in—not once. Although he and my father had bonded over boxing and my father had given Clint a pair of, "there's more coming to you when you get married," gold cufflinks, Clint couldn't wait to return to our naturally air-conditioned life in the Northwest.

Aside from swimming in the Atlantic, the best part of our visit to Hallandale had been watching my parents get to know and love their grandson. Listening to my father snore as Hucky lay sleeping in his lap, was beautiful music. But we'd all had enough of each other. Clint and I couldn't wait to leave. My parents weren't sorry to see us go.

CHAPTER 32

Bad Moon on the Rise

January 1974

Distribution is the process whereby the total social product is divided up among the population. Exchange is the practice of trading of different products of equal value, between different individuals or organizations.

A MARXIST DEFINITION

Past Pauline Sullivan's thousand acres of green rolling hills, past Woody's swimming hole and orchards and past the landmark Myrtle tree, the last two miles of Flores Creek road were evenly lined with hundred-year-old second-growth fir trees. We followed them all the way home. Clint and I were bursting with new ideas: The others could get money from their own parents to buy the general store. We could start a food co-op for income and collect Foxglove to sell for digitalis. Florida sand trickled out of my nursing bra as I wiggled out of it, balled it up and threw it into the glove compartment. The evening air was alive with the fragrance of wet earth and leaves. Smoke curled out of the Main Cabin's chimney. When we stepped inside, that cabin's rugged mayhem looked more beautiful to us than all of Florida's marble flooring and faux gold faucets. A fire was crackling in the wood stove and the room was comfortable and warm, but not welcoming. Something was off—rotten. The only faces looking up at us belonged to Pavlo and Katerina. Kokia lay blissfully between them, examining a bird's nest. His head lay his father's lap and his feet on his mother's. As soon as he saw us, the little boy untangled himself and all three stood to shower us with bear hugs. They couldn't get their arms all the way around me because Huckleberry sat asleep on my back carrier, but the feel of their familiar bodies against my sunburned shoulders felt like an extension of my own flesh and blood.

While we were still embracing each other, Stu suddenly slammed down his beer bottle on the dining table. The noise caused Clint and Pavlo to jump apart. As soon as they did, Stu stepped in and hugged his older brother.

Over their heads, I saw Louise. "Welcome back," she said with a restrained smile on her not pretty face. Agung, whose arm had healed well in the months Clint and I had been in Florida, and Two Turtles were seated at the dinner table, sharing a joint. All they gave us were tepid nods. "Hey guys," I said and almost added, "What the hell?"

Clint's right eye was twitching. I'd never seen that before.

Hucky's little legs hung from the baby carrier his grandma had bought him at the Aventura shopping mall. I'd planned on carrying him on a papoose board made with deer hide but had succumbed to nylon and chrome.

"It is wonderful that you are both back," Pavlo said. "We very much need you here."

"Did you bring me anything?" Kokia asked.

I had—a miniature toy logging truck I'd ripped off from a souvenir shop in the Eugene airport. When I put it in his hands, he threw his little arms around my waist and hugged tight.

Stu put his arm over Clint's shoulder.

"Care to step outside a minute brother?" he said softly.

"Sure thing, Stu," Clint answered. "What's up?"

Peeling off Kokia, I followed Clint and Stu out onto the porch and in the light drizzle reached into my vest pocket to hand Clint Hucky's little woolen cap.

"Brother," I heard Stu say, "'fraid you and Carol got some trouble comin' your way."

Clint placed the cap on Hucky's sleeping head. Whenever he touched our boy, it was with the gentleness a big man's hand brings to the small and vulnerable.

Stu held a joint between his thumb and middle finger, cupping it with his palm. In the way of seasoned smokers, he passed it to Clint.

"They've been bad mouthin' both of you," Stu continued, "Saying... how yer cheatin' them. Saying how nothing's fair or right here. Since you've been gone, this place has been theirs and they want to keep it that way. Gotta say, it feels grabby to me."

While I'd been perfecting my backstroke in sunny Hallandale, a Revolution, aimed in my direction, had been brewing. I'd been labeled a robber baron, feasting on the life blood of the people.

What the group wanted, we were to learn, was ownership of the prime forty acres that bordered both sides of Flores Creek. That creek acreage was golden. It contained the rich bottom land and if it were separated and sold off, the remaining hundred and twenty acres, which I would still own, would be greatly devalued and could be used only for logging and never built on or legally developed. When it came to real estate, legality meant a lot to me.

Given the room's nasty vibe, Clint and I only stayed long enough in the Main Cabin to grab a bowl of Katerina's lentil stew and then drive down to our little house.

"What do you think, Clint?" I asked as his truck bounced along the washed-out road.

"I hate to say this, Carol," he answered, "but you gotta admit they have a point."

Fury rose from my belly, but I said nothing.

"Well...if they're gonna make their lives with us..." he continued and then stopped mid-sentence, not knowing what to say next, but knowing he had to say something, "They need to feel it's worth their while. For that to happen, they need to own."

"Who's stopping them from owning anything?" I screamed,"They can own whatever they want, Clint, but not my land, not our land!"

"My name's not on the deed either, Carol," was his unsettling reply. The truth hit me hard. When it came to land ownership, we were not equals and never had been.

Clint parked the Chevy, turned on his massive flashlight, opened the heavy truck door and walked out into the night, purposely leaving me alone in the passenger seat with Hucky asleep in my arms. Minutes passed. Wind whistled. Lantern light glowed through the window of our house and I heard the familiar chop of Clint's ax. Balancing Hucky on my chest, I slid out of the truck on my back and walked toward the light. His father had not come to help us.

Inside, a fire was going but the room was still freezing. Warmth always took a while. The afghan my grandmother had knitted for me was folded at the foot of our bed and our raingear hung from wooden pegs. The place was as clean and dry as when we'd left it. Someone who cared had helped keep it that way. Turning toward me, Clint said, "You'd feel the same as they do, Carol, if the tables were turned."

"If the tables were turned," I thought to myself, "what if everyone else owned the land and I didn't...what if I was building my future on their good will?" Shit, yes, I'd want insurance for the future. A guilty part of me felt Agung and the others were right. I had been taking advantage of their good nature and naiveté. It was true; they had helped develop land that did not belong to them. They'd tilled the soil, built homes, shared food, clothing, and their lives. We were, we all assumed, building a community based on mutual good faith. What did I owe them and what did they owe me? I wasn't sure and we'd never hammered it out. But aside from hunting, gathering, and growing dope no one had come up with a legal way we could earn enough to stay together and survive. Would that evolve? Maybe. Maybe not.

The reality of wilderness living, the danger and pain of living alone in isolation was something else I'd never considered. Now, I considered it. Life alone with Clint, without the others for protection and companionship, would not be enough. Alone, I'd be more dependent on him than ever. Alone—just the two of us: the concept was terrifying. Alone, how could we have dealt with a serious accident like Agung's, or survived the elephant Rock invasion? How could I have lived without Louise and Katerina for care and guidance?

I couldn't have.

Without the women at Highbridge, I might not have healed from Clint's abandonment and my rape. Group unity and support was everything in the wilderness. Once, I'd had a Tarzan and Jane dream of living alone with Clint in nature; now no more and no way.

Hucky's little hands formed a fist, as if he were about to wake, but then relaxed. Our son mattered more than anything.

"I'm afraid, Clint," I said. "What if I say no and they all leave?"

Clint ran his fingers through my hair:

"Don't be afraid babe, there's nothin' to be afraid of."

The fire blazed. Shadows danced on the walls, the room warmed, and while Hucky continued to sleep, Clint and I made love. Lost in the assurance that a perfectly attuned man's body can bring to a woman in need, I believed him—there was nothing to fear.

The next morning, I was half-asleep and lazily nursing when there was a timid knock on our door. Leaving me exposed to the morning chill, Clint kicked off our covers and stumbled out of our bed.

"Who is it?" he asked, his voice still heavy with sleep.

"It's me, Joey."

Standing in our doorway, Joey was hunched over and looked ashamed of himself...like a little boy who had peed his pants and was covering the wet spot.

Having had a baby made it easier for me to see the child in everyone.

"Come on in," Clint offered.

"No thanks, I'll get your place all muddy," Joey said looking down at his puddling rain boots. "Agung asked me to tell you we're meeting in the Main Cabin first thing after breakfast and both of youse are invited."

"Sure," Clint said. "We'll be there. Thanks."

Clint had spoken for us both. I wished he hadn't.

"What's this meeting about?" I asked Joey, already knowing the answer but wanting to make him squirm.

"Just stuff...land an' all," he mumbled. "See ya then."

And he was gone, dashing up the path toward the cabin like a spooked deer.

Usually, Clint made a fire to warm up the room before I got out of bed, but not this time. This time, in the morning damp and cold, I hurried into my too tight jeans. I could not get them to zip over my belly and kept them up with a row of oversized safety pins. While I carefully bent over to lace up my work boots, Clint's lightening hands changed Hucky's diaper and dressed our little boy in a frayed but functional onesie. Hucky lay still and looked up at Clint with wide-eyed awe.

Later, as Clint and I walked the gravel path toward the Main Cabin, Hucky slept protected from the rain inside my poncho. In the downpour, his parents' footsteps were slow and heavy—the puddles and mud helping us delay what lay ahead.

A milky skin covered the leftover oatmeal on the cabin cook stove. I spooned it in thick, warm hunks into our wooden bowls. Clint placed them on the dining table side by side. Agung, Louise, Joey, Two Turtles, Stu, Katerina, Pavlo, and Kokia were already seated, their bowls scraped clean, their coffee mugs emptied. Once again, Pavlo alone greeted us with a welcoming grin. Agung, absently picking at his nonexistent eyebrows, greeted us with a wan "good morning." "Good morning," I whispered back and focused on Huckleberry who was rooting at my sweatshirt; when I rolled it up, he latched onto my swollen nipple, his tiny hands resting on my blue-veined, engorged breast. I loved nursing him, the feeling satisfied me almost as much as it did him. But not that morning. That morning Hucky's tug and the warm rush of my milk into his mouth, was a distraction—an imposition.

While the steel Oregon sky beat the sun into submission, Agung skewered me with Harvard MBA assurance. "Carol, I hope you understand we cannot continue to live and build our future at Flores Creek without a real stake in that future."

"Yeah," Joey parroted, "we want to own the land just like you guys.

It's only fair."

Agung hadn't created this nasty rift, but was directing it. Subtle influence and manipulation was who he was. He had not killed the corporate honcho that lived inside him. No one else spoke. Agung stared at me and waited. As far as I was concerned, he could wait forever. No matter how strong the argument, no matter how painful the consequences, I knew I'd never give in and share ownership of my land. I'd left New York and come to Oregon to find it. My parents had trusted my instincts enough to invest with me in its future. Clint and I were married to its trees and soil, water and air. It bound us more than a wedding. And Flores Creek was our son's inheritance—all of it. A realization flowed towards me like lava: slowly then picking up speed. Despite living a communal lifestyle, despite reducing to basics and embracing self-induced poverty, I was still a capitalist. No matter how much I gave to the group, I still wanted what was my due, what I believed was mine.

I turned toward Louise, hoping for a compassionate word or glance. She knew better than anyone how hurtful and damaging Agung could be. My old and best friend would surly see my side. Instead, Louise turned away from me to face the others. Her voice, that high-pitched nasal toot, filled with rancor, "Carol, we are not the proletariat and you are not the ruling class." Her dogma was a perfect complement to Agung's. Despite their forever split, he finished her thought, "We all deserve common ownership of production; otherwise, Carol, we're indentured servants."

"What production, Aggie?" I asked. "Dope doesn't count."

Slapping his hand on the table for emphasis, he answered without hesitation.

"We've produced a community, Carol. To own is our right. Two Turtles has put in thousands."

"Yeah," Joey parroted, "Two Turtles put in big bucks."

"Five thousand," Two Turtles confirmed. "I put five thousand into this place. Hell, that's a lot of money for a poor dude not from swanky New York City."

I barely knew Two Turtles. He was a friend of a friend and lived down at the creek. Now Two Turtles was my partner for a lifetime? I couldn't believe Clint had taken the money from him. I grabbed Clint's hand and asked him to move with me out of earshot. At first, he looked dumbfounded, then followed me towards the cookstove.

"Clint," I hissed into his ear, "what the hell, you took five thousand!?"

Clint folded in on himself, his chin collapsing into his chest.

"You were busy with the baby n' all, so I handled it. I figured that's what you wanted."

Half asleep, Hucky gummed down hard on my nipple. It stung. I was being attacked from all sides. No woman, I realized, could win a battle while breast feeding. Even a tigress could not defend herself and give suck. I unlatched Huckleberry, his fat lips dripping milk and handed him over to his father. Clint received his son perfunctorily but with open arms.

"Why'd you take the money from Two Turtles, Clint?! The land's paid for."

"Timber rights, Carol," Clint said in a barely audible voice, "Two Turtles bought the timber rights. I tried to talk to you 'bout it, but you acted like you couldn't be bothered and then it slipped my mind. Sorry."

I'd always run from the details of financial responsibility. The legal was colorless and I found it impossible to follow—my mind froze trying to read its small print. I'd only skimmed the purchase contract, trusted Clint to interpret it for me and knew nothing about timber rights. Painfully slow reader that he was, Clint understood and respected the clear but tedious.

As we sat back down, Clint with Hucky cradled in his arm held out his other hand to help me. It was a gallant move—physically helpful, but belied a deeper truth: he could not protect me from myself.

Agung was now picking at his hairline. While speaking, he examined the thin, dark strands he held between his thumb and forefinger.

"Carol," he said, "we all have to have equal share in the land."

He then let the strands float to the floor and picked at his scalp again. As I listened, I calculated how long it would take to pick himself bald. A month, tops.

"I bought this land with my inheritance, Agung. It's all I get."

"Stop obfuscating, Carol," Louise broke in, now siding with a man who had treated her like roadkill.

"What the hell does that word even mean, Louise?"

Obfuscate. It was one of Agung's two big words. The other one was dialectic. Although no longer inside Louise's body, Agung was still inside her head.

"It means beating around the bush, Carol," she said. "You're a master at that."

"Fuck you, Louise."

"Fuck you back, Carol."

Clint looked close to tears. Caught in the middle, he took out his pocket knife and with great purpose walked back to the wood stove to scrape ash residue from its sides. Louise, however, lashed out at me—her fury rattling like a sidewinder. "This is my family, Carol! This is my home. I have nothing else and you want to take that away, too!"

I scoured her face. She had a little mustache made of tiny golden hairs. I used to like that silky line, now it creeped me out.

"I'm sorry you are all alone, Louise. But..."

Before I could continue, Joey interrupted, his tone urgent, "I didn't want to tell you this, Carol. But I think I have to."

"What, Joey?" I asked, forgetting about Louise.

"No, I better not say."

Not to be forgotten, Louise spewed, "It's you and Clint who are going to be all alone here, not me!"

"They talked about killing you," Joey blurted.

Kill me? Kill me!!

"Who?! Who did?! Tell me, Joey!"

"Don't tell her anything, Joey," Two Turtles warned.

Joey tried but could not hold back.

"Barbara and Otto," he whispered.

Who the fuck were Barbara and Otto? I knew they lived down at the creek with Two Turtles and Agung, but I'd only met them a few times and barely knew anything about either one.

"Barbara and Otto would never hurt you," Agung promised. "They are good, gentle, people. It's just foolish talk, foolishly repeated."

Charles Manson seemed good and gentle at first. He didn't appear insane. Intelligent and artistic folks invited him into their homes and to their parties. They laughed at his jokes. They slapped him on the back and passed him their joints...beautiful Sharon Tate. Stabbed endlessly in the belly. Both she and her unborn baby—dead.

"Your friends hate me, Agung! Who knows what they'll do!"

This was my reward for judging no one and accepting all? Death threats?

It was so cosmically wrong.

Maybe Otto and Barbara took drugs. Maybe they'd gone psycho. The devil was in the blood and enzyme.

"Now," Agung continued, totally ignoring the possibility of my being murdered, "we'll pay you fair market value minus Two Turtle's five thousand."

"Do you want me dead, too, Agung! Is that what you want?"

Agung was right there with a righteous answer. Again, it felt like he was a moral notch above me. My shoulders lowered and moved toward one another for protection.

"Of course not, Carol," he said, his voice turning warm, "I care for you. Everyone here does. We only want what's fair."

Louise, damn her, was still on Agung's wavelength. That I might be snuffed by two possible lunatics didn't faze her either. "Carol," she said, "we're not here to become serfs on the master's fiefdom, that's not the life any of us want."

Even though I was standing in the same Main Cabin with close companions I'd lived with for years, I entered a new universe in which I floated in space like an untethered astronaut—totally alone. My words clawed their way up my throat. It hurt to say them.

"Louise I've given you a free place to live. A place where you can stay free, forever."

A row of Daddy longlegs had made their way from under the sink, marched across the floor and up the table leg toward me. They were my new best friends. Maybe my only ones.

"We do all the work around here and don't need you to 'give' us anything," Louise spat. "Our hearts and minds are our assets and they are priceless."

If her saliva had touched me, I was sure it would have burned a hole in my skin. Rage fired up my belly.

"Louise, I own 160 acres of hard assets. So, you can shove your minds and your hearts up your ass!"

Goodbye Oglala Sioux, hello White Woman.

The Native American belief that no human could own the land, now seemed like a half truth. A human could either protect or abuse the land...as they could a child.

Great Spirit forgive me. I'm a closet capitalist. I've reached the end of the hippie line. I could share my clothes, my food and my life, but not my real estate. Hucky woke and whimpered. The sound caused my breasts to refill. Two wet spots appeared on my sweatshirt. I was leaking. Pavlo, who had been uncharacteristically quiet, looked at me and shook his head as if to say, "I'm so sorry, I can't help you." He took Kokia by the hand and led him out the door. Katerina followed. Cold air rushed in from the outside. I felt numb. Agung continued but with less verve, knowing he was getting nowhere but still determined.

"Carol, we've all lived together as brothers and sisters," he said. "How can you forget that?"

"Clint...Clint," I asked, "can you help me out on this, help me explain?"

It was like trying to lean on a wave. Clint was silent. He was incapable of saying what needed to be said.

"For the last time, Carol," Agung threatened, his voice cutting through the unnatural quiet, "we've laid out fair terms. What's your answer?"

That was it; the moment when everything would change. All I wanted was for things to be like they had been; to go back in time to a place where I didn't have to make this terrible choice. My ancestors, my grandfather Schneiderman, the high Cohan, who'd employed forty workers even though he couldn't read or write, my mother, the only woman in her class of five hundred men to graduate Fordham Law School, my Grandma Schneiderman who loved me best of all, and my ethereal cousin Freddy; they were all calling out to me, giving me the permission I needed: *"Don't be a schmuck, you bought the land—it's yours."*

I could say no to a powerful Muslim prince, because I was, after all, a Jewish princess.

"Aggie, I can't do it. I want to but I can't."

As soon as I'd spoken I wanted to take the words back. "Here, take my shoes, my frying pan, and my autographed copy of *Be Here Now*, take my son and raise him as your own, just don't do this. Don't go. Don't leave!"

"Then that ends that," Agung said.

He took a pack of imported Indonesian cigarettes from the back pocket of his jeans, lit one and then held the rest out to Two Turtles to share. A sweet clove scent filled the room.

"It sure does," Two Turtles said after he inhaled. "It sure does."

Benches moved, bodies stood, the door opened and in the silence that holds finality, everyone left the Main Cabin. Clint and I watched them go. Then I remembered—my life had been threatened. I turned to Clint.

"What about Barbara and Otto?"

"They won't hurt you, Carol," he said. "They were riled up, that's all. Joey's an idiot."

I believed him. He knew Barbara and Otto better than I did. But he'd lost my trust when it came to Two Turtles. He'd hidden their cash transaction from me—let it slide because he knew I'd object. Tricked me.

"Clint, why did you let Two Turtles buy the timber rights? How could you?"

Clint looked at me with steely eyes that were strong and unwavering

"I let him do it because he wanted to, Carol. It was as simple as that."

☾

The breakup began. There were no goodbye parties, just a steady, slow departure. A multiple divorce with all involved still speaking to each other but not forgiving. I would miss them, their censure made it hard for me to forgive myself, but I stood by my choice.

Louise left to find work in San Francisco, righteously giving her ax, blankets, bedding, books, and the antique sewing machine she knew I coveted, to the Goodwill. It hurt, even though I didn't sew. Like Cassy Jane and Pete before her, she left without saying goodbye. Katarina, feeling the necessity to raise Kokia and baby Lena in a more child-centered world, returned to her supportive family in Athens. The conflict between the Greeks and Turks was ending and although Pavlo lingered on, he planned to soon follow his wife and children. My always indulgent parents bellied up the five thousand and repaid Two Turtles for the timber rights. He immediately went into negotiations to purchase nearby acreage and invited no one else to buy in with him. Agung reunited with Skybird, the mother of his daughter, and moved with them to a cottage in the nearby town of Coquille. Joey fell in love with a woman he'd met at the Bandon food Co-op and left to live with her. Stu, wanting to continue his relationship with Louise, sobered up and a few weeks later followed her to San Francisco to find himself a "real" job. Each of their departures was a painful extraction leaving a hole that could not be refilled. The hurt was fleeting, but the emptiness remained.

From Vermont to Taos, communes were falling apart, hippies dispersing and returning to the world they'd rejected. Free love was poised to die in the arms of AIDS, never again to return with the same wanton innocence. In 1974 NASA'S Mariner 10 became the first space probe to fly by Mercury; U.S troops were a year out of Vietnam; Nixon was disgraced by the Watergate scandal and LBJ was dead. Newspaper heiress Patty Hearst would soon be captured by the FBI and her kidnappers, the Symbionese Liberation Army, in a violent stand down, would burn up in flames, providing the last dying embers of the radical fringe. In 1975, The Manson Family's Squeaky Fromm would fail in her attempt to assassinate a clumsy, but not terrifying, President Ford.

The great economic boom of the late 60s and early 70s was over. Interest rates skyrocketed as did unemployment and inflation. A deep recession hit the entire country. Affluence could no longer be taken for granted. The great cushion our middle-class parents had provided was disintegrating. Economic downturn fueled a scramble for professional positions, the same scramble that hippies had fled for years. Life in the margins had lost its glamour. Highly commercial Barry Manilow's *I Write the Songs* became the most popular recording in America. The era of endless possibilities and an economy based on faith and freedom had ended.

Jerry Garcia of *The Grateful Dead* had said, "There was a moment when there was a vision; there was a very wonderful vision. See, it had to do with everybody acting in good faith, it had to do with everyone behaving right." For all of us who lived at Flores Creek that moment was over. The great collective unconscious and dream that had connected hippies everywhere, were lost.

CHAPTER 33

On Heaven's Door

March 1974

I had never thought the liberty of man consists in doing what he wishes, but rather in not doing what he does not wish.
JEAN-JACQUES ROUSSEAU, Reveries

There were three things in life I swore I'd never do: travel in a Winnebago, drink Coca Cola, and become a housewife, but there was little for me to do but care for Huckleberry, feed Clint, and clean house. I tried to come up with less horrific names for my new station: domestic minimalist, mammary dispenser, but couldn't kid myself; I was housebound and being supported by a man.

My only form of entertainment was KCOOS, the local country western radio station. Not excluding the news that the Grand Jury finally concluded that president Nixon was involved in the Watergate cover-up, it also gave hog, cattle, and feed updates and showered me with unusable recipes. The desserts often involved marshmallows. *Spam* was a prime entree, paired with pineapple but sometimes with peaches. Everyone who listened to KCOOS was hungry or lonely or both. The folks out on those air waves collected buttons, stamps, cigar boxes, and dress patterns; they'd lost their dogs, had too many kittens, needed bear traps, and wanted used shovels. I might have called in, too, but had no phone. If I'd had one, I would have told Mattie from Gold Beach that I'd love to buy one of her hand-made pot holders that also doubled as a scrubbing brush. The call-ins aired only at night; during the day the station played the music their listeners loved. I loved it along with them. Their wailing guitars and twangy voices sang of family, drink, love, loss, and revenge. Roy Orbison, Crystal Gayle, George Jones, Merle Haggard, Patsy Kline, Tom T Hall, Kitty Wells, Hank Williams, Tammy Wynette, Johnny Cash, Loretta Lynne, and so many other country music greats I'd never heard of in New York, became a part of me. Everything they sang I understood. Deep country had gone straight to my Jewish city-girl heart.

To earn money, Clint, like the hard-working husbands of other rural housewives, disappeared for most of the day. In the rain, he mended fences and took on small construction jobs for neighboring ranchers. At home, my karma was spanking me. I'd refused to share, so now I had no one to share with. The hand-built houses each person had left behind stood like counterculture ghosts, whispering memories. I could see their faces, hear their voices, and I missed them all... even CassyJane.

Clint knew I was unhappy (I mentioned it a lot) so he traded in his best chain saw for an eight-inch portable television. Since we had no electricity, he ran it off his truck battery. I could only watch for a few hours a week before it had to be recharged. If I watched for too long the battery would die and, he warned me, we could be stranded.

One night, there he was again—my old classmate Henry Winkler as Arthur Fonzarelli—Fonzie on *Happy Days*. It was as if Henry had followed me across the airwaves, dogging my soul. What, I asked myself, were the chances of catching him twice? It was a sign. Even on the tiny screen I could see Henry was on fire. The live studio audience loved his every move and he loved them back. It was right there in front of me—that thrilling exchange when the audience both leads and follows the actor like a lover. I missed it the way a mother misses her lost child and longed for that magic zap when the player ignites the played and the energy boomerangs back: "Thank-you, thank you so very much. I love you, too." And then the tiny television screen went dark. The battery was dead and Clint was home.

Seeing me staring at the empty screen and before kissing me hello, Clint began his search.

"Where's my socket wrench?" he asked. "I gotta unscrew the terminal and recharge the battery."

"Clint, I've been thinking about my mission on earth. Why God put me on the planet."

"Forget it, Carol. I'll use the pliers."

I followed him to his toolbox.

"Clint, remember Henry Winkler from Yale? I just saw him on T.V."

"Yeah. I remember him...you're gonna have to cut down on your TV. I can only recharge so much...What's for dinner?"

I had nothing. Dinner had never crossed my mind.

"I was just as good as he was, Clint."

"There's nothing to eat?" Was all he said and then looked at me as if I'd stolen his wallet.

"How can I live off the land," I asked, ignoring his question, "raise our child in nature and still fulfill my destiny, Clint? How can I do that?"

"I dunno babe, but you'll figure it out."

"Clint, I miss acting."

"Shit," Clint said, his head emerging from behind the uneven curtain I'd strung across our food storage shelving, "I found some peanut butter but there's no bread."

☾

Bang! Clint was working on our house and the noise was overwhelming. I couldn't stay inside and our Hucky, our baby boy, couldn't sleep so I decided to visit Pavlo in his quiet and cozy cabin. He missed his wife and son and I was certain he'd be glad for my company. After a wet tromp through the woods and the high grass, I stood outside his well-built tiny house and removed my boots. It wasn't easy pulling them off, but nothing was easy while carrying a baby. Pavlo must have heard my groans because his door flew open before I had a chance to knock. As soon as he saw me, his face lit up.

"Carolita," he said, "I am so glad you've come, I've been thinking about you."

"What were you thinking, Pavlo?" I asked as I stepped inside the high- ceilinged, warm room, always happy for a Carol-centric conversation.

"I was thinking how much I've loved living here and that I have you to thank for it."

Finally, someone at Flores Creek appreciated what I'd done. Gratitude surged through me as I opened up to this kind and sensitive Greek.

"Pavlo, have you ever heard of Henry Winkler?"

"No, Carolita, who is this man?"

"A friend from Yale. I saw him on TV and it made me want to act again."

"What we want gives us direction, Carolita...no? Is this not true?"

Pavlo was a head shorter than I was and I outweighed him by twenty pounds but his dark eyes held depth, wisdom, and sorrow. *Fuck. He was cute.*

"You have forgotten who you are, Carolita my friend—an artist. An artist does what she must. An artist knows no boundaries."

I centered my baby carrier: still fast asleep Hucky was listing to the side and throwing me off balance.

"Pavlo, when Henry and I worked together the audience loved us."

"That is because you are so funny and so very beautiful," he said as he ran his fingers across my cheek and down my neck. His fingertips were smooth and without the hard calluses I was accustomed to. My insides did summersaults. Pavlo! Pavlo, who'd read Kafka and Proust; Pavlo who I knew would take his time with me as he did with everything. His wife was a dear friend, whom I chose, at this moment, to forget existed. Riding Pavlo would not be a gallop to the finish but a slow climb to the top. Pavlo who understood who I was. Pavlo was who I needed.

"Carolita, Carolita," he whispered as together we sild a sleeping Huckleberry onto Pavlo's bed platform. As we brushed against each other, he corkscrewed his tongue deep into my ear. My body quaked. Oh God ! Oh, the Greeks! Pavlo and all of Athens inside me—the Acropolis, the Parthenon, the Temple of Hephaetus, that was all I wanted. Oh yes, yes, yes!

No. As if shot, Pavlo suddenly crouched over and drew away from me. My desire went with him. Gone. Just like that. I didn't want him anymore. He looked too sad and too small. Clutching his belly, he explained his ulcer was acting up and the sudden pain was "very, very bad." And to make matters worse, he was all out of Maalox, his medication. Without hesitation, he asked: "You will go into town soon, no Carolita?"

"Yes, soon," I said, wiping his spittle off my ear.

"Please, you will bring me back a bottle from the drug store. I would not ask you, but I am in need."

"Of course, Pavlo," I cooed, knowing that I'd give him anything he wanted for at least the next five minutes.

"And if you don't mind," he said as eased down onto his bed, "a cup of mint tea with honey would be very nice."

As he lay there, with his knees curled up under him, I tore down a handful of dried peppermint leaves that hung from his ceiling. As I brewed them, I looked over at his contorted body and saw he was just a man who needed a woman to soften his world. After serving him, smoothing his covers and making certain still sleeping Hucky was tightly wrapped and protected in his carrier, I said goodbye to Pavlo and stepped outside into the downpour. Tromping through the dripping woods, I forgot the thrill he'd given me, but could not forget what he'd said: "*An artist does what she must, an artist knows no boundaries.*" The man had reminded me of who I was, and I loved him for it.

But then there was Clint. Along the forest path toward our house, as if to punish me for my trespasses, overhanging branches stung my face and slapped my torso. When I reached our home, I opened to door to find the fire out and our living room dark and cold. Clint lay in our bed under a pile of blankets and sleeping bags.

"Carol, where were you?" he asked weakly.

"At Pavlo's," I said, and opened the door to our woodstove to hopefully find a few live embers. There were none. The firebox was empty.

"I think I have a temperature," Clint said. His voice rose. It was almost shrill–a decimal above his usual. "And what were you doing at Pavlo's?"

"Just talking."

"Please don't lie to me Carol, you have that look."

"What look?" I asked as I walked toward him to touch his forehead. It was clammy and warm.

"You had sex," he said–almost crying.

"I did not," I answered. "But the thought did cross my mind. So, tell me, do I have the look of a woman thinking about having sex?"

For three years Clint had pushed free experimentation. Now he'd turned into a conservative Billy Graham son of a preacher man.

"I don't want you spending time alone with Pavlo, Carol. Promise me."

Even though I thought him a terrible hypocrite with serious control issues, I felt sorry for Clint as he struggled to sit up–his physical prowess all but gone. Still, I would not let up.

"You can't be serious, Clint. What about Anise, what about 'come on baby, try it for me?' What about Georgia?"

"Everything's different now that we have a son. Hucky changes everything, Carol."

Dry hacking sounds came up through his chest.

"You're really sick," I said and gently lowered our still sleeping baby into the cradle his daddy had made for him.

"Swear to me, Carol."

"Jesus, Clint. What's got into you?"

"I'm a father. I want to protect my family and give them the best life I can. Anything that threatens that, threatens me."

Another round of coughing overtook him. He turned toward the wall as not to infect us. I wanted to both cover him with kisses and slap him silly.

"I won't swear Clint. You can't have say over where I go or who with, but I promise I'll never lie to you...not ever."

"I guess that's okay," he said, too unwell to argue, "but can you please...?"

"What sweetheart?"

"Some tea—mint...with lots of honey."

Men. One was more than enough.

☾

A week later, Pavlo took a plane out of Eugene and headed for Athens. Clint began work at the Sullivan ranch, building a gate and fixing their barn roof. Days, even weeks passed with only Hucky as my daylight companion. The solitude had a lopsided beauty and gave me the hidden luxury of spending days on end with my boy. I learned his every move and expression. His laugher was music to my ears. A crow that pecked for seed in my garden became my sidekick. He followed me along paths and swooped in every morning to squawk, "Hello." I named him Freddy after my dead cousin. "Hi, Freddy!" I'd call to him as he flew over my head. Freddy was a slick, black bird with a two-foot wingspan and ancient eyes who liked to perch on the outcroppings of our roof and peer down at us. One day he disappeared and never returned. Spring was coming again and I missed Freddy.

On a Saturday night Clint and I caught the *Last Picture Show* at the tiny Majestic Theatre in Port Orford, twenty miles Southwest of Flores Creek. The final scene took place in a desolate, dead-end Texas town where there was only wind and tumble weed. We stepped out of the theatre into the same backdrop—without the tumbleweed but with just as strong a wind. Driving back up Flores Creek Road, not one car passed us. There was nothing ahead and nothing behind, nothing except the dark night and the scattering of gravel. Even though my window was half open, I was suffocating in the cold night air. The silence beyond the engine was dense and smothering. Hucky had been asleep in my lap, but was just beginning to stir. I could feel milk rushing in as he rooted for my breasts.

CHAPTER 34

Light Comes Shining

September - November 1974

If you belong to the land, you'll stay there; but if the land belongs to you, you'll lose it for sure.

RAYMOND MUNGO, TOTAL LOSS FARM

Morning. Smoke everywhere. Unpleasant to inhale but not dense enough to choke on. The Langlois ranchers were burning their fields, destroying the inedible tansy and thistle weed that threatened their livestock while enriching their depleted topsoil.

Those red-necked, tractor and pitchfork guys sure knew their stuff—and controlled their fires. Naked under my quilt, I wanted to stay warm in bed but a gurgle cut the silence. Huckleberry was awake. He had rolled against the bars of the cubby Clint had carved out for him in a wall and was nuzzling the rabbit fur that lined its floor. The wind from the Pacific pushed the branches of the old Maple tree against our cedar shake roof and was not threatening but musical. The day was special. A bushel of fresh-picked plums were ready for canning. To boil them down would be a day's work requiring constant wood for the fire. Clint had dumped a half cord on our porch, split five rounds and taken off down the road to work.

I chopped cedar kindling, savoring the smooth cuts that snapped across the straight grain, then piled them wigwam-like in the firebox, lit a match and soon had a crackling fire. Hucky played quietly with a wood block at the center of his bed. In a wrought iron kettle, I began cooking the plums, stirring and adding sugar until a lavender foam appeared. As the brew thickened, ten feet above my head, the metal stove pipe that cut through the shake roof grew red hot. I'd foolishly overloaded the fire box. The wood surrounding the pipe smoldered and the ceiling glowed with a widening circle of embers. Near panic, I filled another tin bucket and without thinking, threw the water into the firebox. Thick, black smoke filled the room. The glowing hole above my head expanded.

The forest surrounding us was bone dry. I was six miles from a phone without transportation or a fire extinguisher. Clint had taken our only ladder with him. I desperately cranked the pump, refilled the bucket, climbed onto a chair and threw the water into the air, praying it might hit the ceiling—it didn't. I'd doused myself instead. Tearing the sheet from our bed, I soaked it in more water and wearing it like a tent, scampered with Hucky down our path. Over my shoulder, I saw a thick cloud float toward the old maple tree. A new gust of wind fanned the roof flames higher. Not watching where I was going, I tripped and fell to my knees, still managing to hold onto Hucky. The little fellow laughed. The fall had been his fun ride. Pebbles had ground into my elbows but the bleeding was slight and nothing was broken. Sitting stunned, I was filled with recrimination: Alone in the woods, facing a possible inferno of my own making, I was a pot-head, a New York City provincial who knew nothing of the real danger surrounding her. I'd put my son's life and my own at risk out of trust in a benevolent universe that couldn't turn on me. I pushed myself to my feet and ran with Hucky toward the steep road that would take us to the blacktop. Then, from out of nowhere, two Elephant Rock men and Crazy Rachael appeared. Seeing them, I screamed uncontrollably. They'd again walked the ten miles over the mountainous terrain to Flores Creek. With only a word or two between us, they dashed to our house, grabbed all our pails and pots, filled them with water and standing on each other's shoulders hoisted themselves onto the roof. They were so agile and quick I was convinced that in their past lives, they'd been acrobats. Their timing was a miracle beyond understanding and I stood awestruck as Smoke, Orca, and Rachael doused the flames. "Why had they come?" I asked when all that remained of the fire was a charcoal smell and a plume of smoke. Because, Rachael explained, she'd heard I'd had a baby and brought him a present: a smooth, round stone with a smiley face etched on it. Astounded and touched, I gave them everything I had to give: A screwdriver, a bucket of plums, my best cast iron frying pan and a blanket with a picture of Elvis in the weave. They refused everything except Elvis and after Rachael said a prayer in Hebrew over Huckleberry, continued down the road toward the highway. They were planning to camp at the Ocean—with only one sleeping bag between them. And Elvis.

The fire had burned a hole through the shingled roof and charred the rest. All would have to be replaced, but I knew it was a job Clint would take on without complaint—thankful that what was of most value to him had been spared. The incident, like the fire, was searing in its intensity. It branded me with a new realization—immediate, certain, and immutable. My time at Flores Creek had ended. I was too vulnerable and too alone. My dream of living with the man I loved in nature had come true, but the reality was not the dream. In the year Clint and I had spent alone together, my spirit had been dampened by living in isolation in the woods with a man who didn't talk. I loved to talk. The trees listened but had nothing to say. No. That's not true. They had plenty to say, but only if I listened. Each was a friend whose majesty told me of our connection to the whole. Their roots spoke what could not be said—that we were one. I was no longer the same woman I'd been three years before. I'd learned to be a steward of the earth, feeling in my own heart the heartbeat of nature.

"Henry Winkler's office," the female voice chirped. A white-tailed deer and two fauns ran across the road in front of the phone booth. Its glass doors quivered at the rumble of an approaching big rig. I looked down at my hands, the nails were jagged and dirty but I was wearing my Grandma Schneiderman's diamond engagement ring. She'd given it to me for my eighteenth birthday and I never took it off.

"Hello. This is Carol Schlanger, is Henry available?"

Years out of the game but I hadn't forgotten my show-biz phone etiquette. A receptionist chirped back at me, "Does Mr. Winkler know what this call is in regard to?"

Slightly annoyed that I had to explain myself, I spoke with an assured but ticked-off calm, "No, he does not. I'm a very good friend from Yale. Please tell him I'm on the line."

I waited. The deer was long gone. The truck had passed. The cold Oregon air chilled my windpipe. My boots were covered in mud and the ragged lining hung out from my wool jacket. Thankfully, Henry could not see me through the phone. He was a very discerning dresser with high standards. But I forgot all about that when I heard his familiar voice on the other end. It was filled with delight.

"Carol! I can't believe it! How the hell are you?"

"Wonderful, Henry. I just had a baby."

"You're kidding! Congratulations!"

I couldn't resist. Henry was always so conservative: "His name is Huckleberry."

"Jezze, Carol. You're still a hippie!"

I looked down at the rivulets of water sliding down the glass doors of the phone booth and to the pastures and mountains behind them, felt the damp penetrate a widening hole in my sleeve.

"I am. But Henry, I saw you on *Happy Days*. You were soooo great."

"Yes, I was."

Henry was having the time of his life and what amazed me was that I wasn't jealous, just happy for him. I really liked the guy.

"Henry...I'm thinking of coming to L.A...you think...you think you could help me out? Introduce me to your agent?"

"Whatever I can do for you, Carol, I will. You know that."

I was choking up. Henry was being sooo nice.

"Henry. You're a real friend."

"Hello? I'm a great friend! Is Clint still doing construction? I bought a new house and could use him."

"You bet, Henry."

"Call me when you get here, Carol. Gotta run-through, gotta go. Great to hear from you."

"Thanks again Henry, you can't imagine how much this..."

"Bye, sweetie."

And he was gone. He'd help me. He'd help us.

☾

"You can't take my son away from me," Clint said.

We were in bed and his knees were poking into my back. I didn't want to take his son away; I just wanted to keep my son with me. Clint's body felt like it was part of my own. I never wanted to give that up. Whenever he touched me, all was right with the world.

"We're a family, Carol, and that means everything to me."

"I know Clint, but I can't stay."

"Then I'll go with you."

His voice was filled with death row loss and resignation, but I would not allow myself to feel sorry for him. We were about to experience a karmic reversal. Clint would have to follow me into unknown territory where he would be inept. But California was of the West and so was he. Even in the glitz and glamour, he could find his place—the West loved cowboys. Huckleberry needed his father and so did I. For me, single motherhood did not have an upside; and I loved Clint despite his daily marijuana habit and need to control, despite his unwillingness to share his deeper feelings and his crippling fear of the urban unknown.

I'd never wanted a husband but now it seemed, I had one.

"Clint, if you come, you'll resent me."

"I resent you already."

"You can stay right here in Oregon, Clint. Take care of things. We'll be fine."

I didn't mean it. Without Clint, the going would be rough, but if Clint felt pushed he'd push back. Hope moved me forward. Yes, I promised myself, I'd get cast in a successful sit-com. Yes, my talent would rise again. I'd buy a car and learn to drive the freeways...or wind up on the streets selling oranges.

"I'm coming because I want to."

"No, you don't, Clint."

"Don't tell me what I want, Carol. I know what I want."

"In L.A., Clint, they judge you by what you have and who you know and you won't know anyone and you'll have nothing."

"I'll have you and Hucky and that's enough for me."

There he was again, with one of his syrupy Christian platitudes. I melted.

"Clint, it won't be so bad. Los Angeles has all kinds of trees and birds and even wild animals. I heard of a place called Topanga Canyon that has folks like us and there're no subways anywhere. Everybody drives. You'd like that, wouldn't you?

"I'm adaptable, Carol. Much more than you think."

He was being so impossibly generous—so saint-like, I was moved to confess, "Everybody left because of me, Clint. I know it hurt you."

"Hey," he said, throwing his arm around me. "It was just the way it turned out. It was Woodstock that blew my mind. I couldn't get it out of my head, so many people in one place, getting along, getting free. I thought we could do it, too."

"We did do it, Clint."

"Yeah. We had a great run—sharing with everybody, everybody the same, getting the same...but I'm no Communist."

No. We weren't Communists but had lived on what I had thought was an anarchist commune; but in reality, it was a disparate group of people who landed together without a plan except to stay alive and live the way nature intended. We were folks who had tried to live for the common good, but had a stronger vision of their own individuality; tried to cooperate, to realize the best of ourselves, but not when compelled to do so. Most of us were middle and upper middle class...able to give up luxury because we'd always had it and without the understanding that it might leave us and never return. No one could force me to give away what I wanted to keep—my land. I'd stood my ground and accepted the consequences of my actions. At twenty-seven I looked adulthood in the face and said, *Okay, I'm here, take me, I'm yours.*

In just a week's time, Clint and I were loading up the back of his old Chevy. It had brought us to Flores Creek and now was taking us away. Hucky sat on the ground, protected from the damp by Clint's Pendleton blanket and a waterproof tarp. Our little boy picked up a stone the size of a robin's egg, and put it in his mouth. With the speed that only a mother knows, I stuck my fingers between his cheeks and pulled it out; then wiped the sand and mud from his tongue and lips with the sleeve of my sweater. A few feet away, Clint was pushing my steamer trunk filled with old costumes towards us. I'd had it shipped from New York and had dragged it everywhere with me. Inside were my greatest treasures: a silk Chinese warlord's kimono and a 1920s beaded evening purse.

"Clint, leave the trunk."

"But you love this shit."

"I know, but we gotta travel light."

With that, as Clint dragged my trunk back toward our home, I stepped inside to carry out our butane heater. Filled, it held ten gallons and weighed almost more than I could handle. But by hugging the heavy metal body close to my belly, I managed. My time in the woods had given me the strength of a Russian weight lifter.

"We might need this, Clint. The nights can get chilly and what if we have to live in the truck?"

As if it were weightless, Clint took the heater and strapped it with a bungee cord to the truck's inside panel. Together, we carried my trunk the rest of the way back inside our house, careful not to scratch its aging bottom. Inside, before I locked it, I dug inside to find the beaded purse and let it dangle from the crook in my arm. The purse's insides were mildewed, its rose-colored satin lining in shreds. No matter, I told myself, I'd clean it up and the lining wouldn't show when I carried it with me to the Academy Awards. Meanwhile, I could use it to hold spare change and Hucky's diaper pins. It had a mother-of-pearl clasp and an amber-colored Bakelite handle and would be right at home in Hollywood.

"I'll keep this up front with me," I told Clint.

"It's real pretty—like you, Honeybee..."

Honeybee. I liked that.

"...Pass me my chain saw, would ya?"

The chainsaw, which I would have struggled to lift a year before, felt light.

A slapping sound; Hucky was bounding toward us. I'd never seen him move so fast. Then plop, his tush hit the wet and the mud. A look of astonishment crossed his face. Clint knelt down, favoring his good knee, and lifted his son into his arms. Watching them, I saw the two most gorgeous males on the planet. "You really wanna take this guy with us?" Clint joked. "He weighs a ton."

"Yeah," I said, "I do."

The Coastal route 101 from Oregon south towards L.A. is beautiful and long. It spirals along the Pacific through Gold Beach and then flattens out only to become steeper as it nears Eureka. Big rigs would pass us, blasting their horns like locomotives and blowing wind and smoke in our direction. After they passed, the road ahead was clear again.

The End

Postscript

This country and this people seem to have been made for each other, and it appears as if it was the design of Providence that an inheritance so proper and convenient for a band of brethren, united to each other by the strongest of ties, should never be split into a number of unsocial, jealous, and alien sovereignties.

JOHN JAY THE FEDERALIST PAPERS FEDERALIST NO. 2
DATE: OCTOBER 31, 1787

Epilogue

Clint and Carol: Have been married for forty-five years. They live in both West Los Angeles and rural Oregon, but wherever they are, they call each other home. Clint maintains a sustainable forest and apple orchard in Oregon and has built and designed for Hollywood luminaries such as for Jane Fonda, Jeff Bridges, Beau Bridges, Ned Tannen, Jill Eikenberry, Michael Tucker, and Henry Winkler. A master carpenter, he became a first time grandpa at 80. Carol has appeared in such films as *The China Syndome* and *You Don't Mess With The Zohan*, and is a working actress, appearing on television shows such as *Brooklyn 99*, *Mike and Molly*, *Rizzoli and Isles*, and in Independent Films. An ex-television writer and Humanitas nominee, her plays have been produced in both L.A. and N.Y. She is in great demand as a storyteller; but has yet been nominated for an academy award. Their adult children **Huckleberry** and **Sierra** (born in 1980 in L.A.) share the family farm when not pursuing their own careers in architecture, theatre, music, and real estate.

Agung: Returning to Jakarta, Agung's future caught up with him and he travelled the world as a highly successful, high-level executive. He remarried in Indonesia and he and his wife of 35 years had a son who, like his dad, attended Harvard. Their extended family lives on their Jakarta family compound where Agung loves watching his grandchildren thrive and grow. Over the years, our family and his have remained good friends, our lifelong friendship cemented by our joint experience. **Skybird** and Agung's daughter and American grandchildren live in western Oregon.

Louise: Had two daughters with Clint's brother **Stu.** After twelve years of sobriety, Stu died at sixty-eight of early onset Alzheimer's. Louise owns and heads one of the most progressive, sought-after highly regarded pre-schools in Los Angeles. A successful author and psychotherapist, Louise continues to be a practical, whirling dervish of a woman.

Pavlo and Katerina: After returning to Athens, Pavlo worked as an architect, while Katerina became a senior cultural affairs specialist at the United States Embassy. Kokia and his Turkish wife live in Athens, and Istanbul. Baby **Lena**, an architect like her father, lives in Athens with her American husband and their son. Clint and Carol keep in touch with them via Facebook and Facetime and look forward to the time when all four can get together again in either Oregon or Greece.

Sky and Lila parted ways after living together for several years. Sky maintains a green construction architectural practice. Lila became a nurse.

Moonlove raised her daughter **Heaven** as a single mother in Texas.

Pete and Cassy Jane broke up but stayed close. Cassy Jane met an early death from cancer but was supported and loved by Pete and his family until the end.

Joey stayed single and worked as a salesman throughout the Northwest and California. He looks back on his time at Flores Creek as the best years of his life.

Froggy spent years in Indonesia translating and studying Balinese dancing and puppetry and then moved to L.A. to become an actor.

Two Turtles stayed on the Oregon coast where he bought his own creek front acreage and had a son with **Barbara.** Whenever Agung visits Oregon, he and Two Turtles play a gentleman's game of golf in nearby Bandon.

Talisa and Billy, now grandparents, raised both their adult children in deeply rural Oregon. Along with their extended family, they have lived off the land for almost fifty ears and serve their community as dedicated and respected leaders. Talisa, a jewelry designer and master gardener, grows enough organic vegetables to feed not only her own family, but the tens, if not hundreds of guests that visit them each year to learn from their cooperative, land-based lifestyle. Billy, a rancher, an author, a foundation head and a natural resources consultant has travelled from Russia to New Zealand to Africa, teaching conservation methods and bridging cultural gaps. Over the years, his cooking has vastly improved.

Of my long-ago, New York women's group: **Ellen** worked as a socially conscious, progressive architect in London and is a highly respected author and expert on the topic of women's health and breast cancer. **Claudia** became a ground-breaking television and film director. **Stockard** remains a star of film and Broadway. **Faith,** is a world-renowned poet, teacher, and author.

Henry Winkler, while working steadily as a highly successful and respected actor and producer in television and film, became the best-selling author (with Lyn Oliver) of the *Hank Zipzer: The World's Greatest Underachiever* children's book series. In 2018, fifty years after creating the iconic role of Fonzie in the TV series *Happy Days*, he won an Emmy for his role as Gene Cousineau in the HBO series *Barry*.

Acknowledgements

Without the support of my friends, family and fellows I'd be lying on my couch watching Seinfeld reruns and trying not to eat a frozen spinach lasagna. Luckily for all involved this has not happened, and I have these people to thank:

First in line, my lifelong and brilliant friend and author Barbara Bottner who, along with our Writer's Block encouraged and supported me all the way. Barbara, I love you. As for the others, the beyond talented and generous, Susan Cuscuna, Arlene Schindler, Roberto Loederman, Kathleen Garrett, Stephanie Satie, Rick Friesen, Melonie Charnoff, and our founder, Susan Merson. Thank you to the stars and back.

For my friends and fellow writers, all of whom gave me their invaluable time and attention: Gene Stein, Elida Stein, Arlene Sarner, Dolores DeLuce, Jordon Tabat, Ellen Leopold, Monica Piper, Ami Levy, Paola Pargman-Levy, Rae Allen, Maria Laghi, Yardenna Hurwitz, Blue-Cloud Garcia and Charles and Chelly Siegel

To my book group, who kept me reading and eating: Arlene Sarner, Christine La Monte, Paula Silver, Sarah Pillsbury, Susan (amazing notes) Wolf, Nita Tucker, Barbara Bottner, Lynzee Klingman, Rosie Schuster, Bonnie Arnold, and Cathleen Summers

For the editors along the way who helped me clarify and structure my vision: Susan Dalsimer, Holly Devon, Jan Cherub, Diana Faust, Erin Clermont, Elana Golden, Elaine Silver, Leslie Lehr, and multigenerational Tina Rogers and Felicia Rogers, as well as Karen Kibler and Cindy Muntwyler.

To the spoken word and theatre producers who gave me a platform for my work and let me see where the laughs came from: Wendy Hammers and Tasty Words, Jessica Tuck, Alicia Sedwick and SPARC, Cedering Fox and Word Theatre, Patricia Willson and Story Time at the Group Rep, Dani Moisette, Teri Mintz and Word, Amy Friedman, Pablo Marz and Tell It, Isabel Storey and Shine, Ann Buxie and Tales by the Sea, Lauri Singer and I Love A Good Story, Eve Brandstein and Poetry in Motion, Susan Merson, Literary Manager and Shellen Lubin, Artistic Director of the Untold Tales of Jewish Women Festival, Women in the Arts Media Coalition, and finally The Jewish Women's Theatre and artistic director Rhonda Spinack who gave me a home.

To producer/screenwriter Will Reiser for his insight and belief, and to Margaret Grundstein for her competitive spirit.

To the great, kind, and generous Henry Winkler for his long friendship and insightful foreword.

To Tchanan Ross, Johnny Sundstrum, Shiloh Sundstrum, Danelle Sundstrum, Michelle Holman, Richie Gross, Leonora Kent, Michael Zuchai and all those in rural Oregon who have lived the authentic life and given their all to keep what is natural, true and real, natural, true and real.

To my son, David Huckleberry Helvey, for his invaluable input, his direction, and unwavering love and encouragement.

To my daughter, Sierra Helvey, whose visual ability goes unmatched and can always see and hear the truth.

To my wise, tough, and tender agent Diane Nine, who always returns my calls and to author/playwright, comedian Steve Bluestein who opened that pipeline.

To my inclusive, outstanding, and delightful publisher, Nancy Cleary at Wyatt-MacKenzie who gave my work tangible form, my spirit strength, and my career a new future.

And lastly: To my beloved husband of close to fifty years, Clint Helvey, who gave me everything.

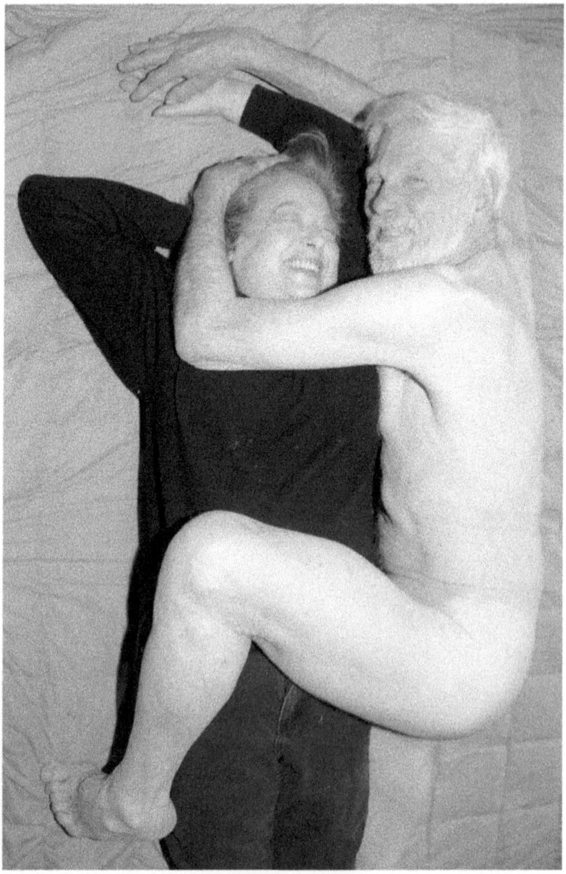

Kateharnedyphotograpy@yahoo.com

Aho Mitakuye Oyasin

LAKOTA FOR

We are all related,
All things need each other to survive.

CPSIA information can be obtained
at www.ICGtesting.com
Printed in the USA
LVHW030238240222
711814LV00008B/601

9 781948 018463